D1807374

Immigration Policy and Crisis in the Regional Context

Chin-Peng Chu · Sang-Chul Park

Editors

Immigration Policy and Crisis in the Regional Context

Asian and European Experiences

 Springer

Editors
Chin-Peng Chu
European Union Research Centre
National Dong Hwa University
Hualien County, Taiwan

Sang-Chul Park
Knowledge based Technology and Energy
Korea Polytechnic University
Gyeonggi-do, Korea (Republic of)

ISBN 978-981-33-6822-4   ISBN 978-981-33-6823-1   (eBook)
https://doi.org/10.1007/978-981-33-6823-1

© The Editor(s) (if applicable) and The Author(s), under exclusive license to Springer Nature Singapore Pte Ltd. 2021
This work is subject to copyright. All rights are solely and exclusively licensed by the Publisher, whether the whole or part of the material is concerned, specifically the rights of translation, reprinting, reuse of illustrations, recitation, broadcasting, reproduction on microfilms or in any other physical way, and transmission or information storage and retrieval, electronic adaptation, computer software, or by similar or dissimilar methodology now known or hereafter developed.
The use of general descriptive names, registered names, trademarks, service marks, etc. in this publication does not imply, even in the absence of a specific statement, that such names are exempt from the relevant protective laws and regulations and therefore free for general use.
The publisher, the authors and the editors are safe to assume that the advice and information in this book are believed to be true and accurate at the date of publication. Neither the publisher nor the authors or the editors give a warranty, expressed or implied, with respect to the material contained herein or for any errors or omissions that may have been made. The publisher remains neutral with regard to jurisdictional claims in published maps and institutional affiliations.

This Springer imprint is published by the registered company Springer Nature Singapore Pte Ltd.
The registered company address is: 152 Beach Road, #21-01/04 Gateway East, Singapore 189721, Singapore

Preface

The project originated from the "International Conference on International Immigration Policy: Public Management and Experience" held on November 4 2019 at National Dong Hwa University (NDHU), Hualien County, Taiwan. In the conference, scholars around the world including those from Germany, Poland, Estonia, Korea, Vietnam, Thailand and Taiwan had fruitful discussion on sharing their knowledge of different immigration policies of various countries in Asia and in Europe. After the conference, we found that the discussion should be heard by more people to contribute to the academic societies in Asia and in Europe. In order to share our results, we decided to refine our works and publish the book entitled: *Immigration Policy and Crisis in the Regional Context: Asia and European Experiences.*

We hope the inter-continental cooperation between Asia and Europe could make the academic societies of different cultures closer, build up linkage, and provide opportunities for both sides to learn from each other. In this difficult time for international travel, we found the bridge we had built especially valuable. Even though the travel ban makes some barriers for physical communication, the cooperation would definitely continue as long as we have the determination. The successful publication of the work across the two continents in this difficult time demonstrates that the cooperation, communication and interaction of humans would not be stopped no matter how difficult the situation is. And this may be an important hint for governments while initiating immigration policies in the future.

In addition, we would like to show our greatest gratitude to the sponsors of the international conference. We would like to thank Magistrate Ms. Hsu Chen-Wei of Hualien County, Taiwan, who provided both financial and administration supports. Also, we got funds from various ministries and public organizations, including Ministry of Technology, R.O.C., Ministry of Internal Affairs R.O.C., Mainland China Affairs Council R.O.C., Taiwan Foundation for Democracy, EU Erasmus+ projects and Department of Public Administration (NDHU). It is not possible to have the conference be successful without their strong assistances.

Again, in this tough time for the whole world, we strongly hope the successful publishing of the inter-continental cooperation could comfort those who feel frustrated in the suspension of international interaction.

Hualien County, Taiwan   Chin-Peng Chu

Contents

Part I
Immigration Policy in Asia

Introduction

Chin-Peng Chu and Sang-Chul Park

This book deals with human migration in the world in general and in Asia and Europe in particular. The migration has a long historical background that stretches back to the earliest periods of human history. In line with that path, migration continues in the modern era in order to provide states, societies and migrants various opportunities such as increasing population, labor force, and economic benefits respectively. At the same time, migration has emerged in the last few years as a critical political challenge in matters of integration, displacement, safety, border management, social exclusion etc. In 2019, the total numbers of international migrants were estimated 272 million globally that accounted for 3.5 percent of the world population. In 1990, it was estimated 153 million that was 2.9 percent of the global population. In 29 years, the total number of the migrants increased around 119 million in the world (Department of Economic and Social Affairs of the United Nations 2019).

United Nations Department of Economic and Social Affairs (UN DESA) estimates the number of international migrants globally based on data provided member nations. UN DESA defines an international migrant as any person who has changed his or her country of usual residence distinguishing between short term migrants with less than one year and long- term migrants with longer than a year. However, not all countries use this definition in practice that makes difficult to estimate the exact number of international migrants (UN DESA 2015).

In 2019, Europe hosted the largest number of international migrants with 82 million followed by Northern America with 59 million and Northern Africa and Western Asia with 49 million respectively. At the same time, the regional distribution of international migration was also changing rapidly. The migrant populations in

C.-P. Chu (✉)
National Dong Hwa University, Hualien County, Taiwan
e-mail: cpchu@gms.ndhu.edu.tw

S.-C. Park
Korea Polytechnic University, Siheung, South Korea
e-mail: scpark@kpu.ac.kr

© The Author(s), under exclusive license to Springer Nature Singapore Pte Ltd. 2021
C.-P. Chu and S.-C. Park (eds.), *Immigration Policy and Crisis in the Regional Context*,
https://doi.org/10.1007/978-981-33-6823-1_1

Northern Africa, Western Asia, and sub-Saharan Africa grew faster than in other regions. Most of the world's migrants lived in a relatively small number of countries. Two thirds of all international migrants resided only in 20 countries. The largest number of international migrants resides in the USA that accounted for 51 million and 19 percent of the world total international migrants. Germany and Saudi Arabia hosted the second and third largest numbers of international migrants with about 13 million each. The Russian Federation and the U.K. followed with 12 million and 10 million respectively.

At the same time, one third of all international migrants were originated from only ten countries in 2019. India was the leading country of origin of international migrants with 17.5 million. Mexico followed as the second largest origin country with 11.8 million. China, the Russian Federation, and Syrian Arab Republic ranked as the third, fourth, and fifth origin countries with 10.7 million, 10.5 million, and 8.2 million respectively. There is also a new global trend of international migrants in terms of gender. Globally the share of female in the total number of international migrants declined from 49.3 percent in 2000 to 47.9 percent in 2019, while the share of male increased from 50.7 percent to 52.1 percent during the same period. 74 percent of all international migrants were of working age between 20 and 64 years old. North America and Europe were the highest destination of the female migrants with 51.8 percent and 51.4 percent respectively, while the female migrants chose their final destinations lowest in sub-Saharan Africa, and Northern Africa and Western Asia with 47.5 percent and 35.5 percent respectively. The international migration has a significant impact on population size in the regions of destination. However, its impact in the origin regions is much less significant due to the large number of population (Department of Economic and Social Affairs of the United Nations 2019).

During the period between 2013 and 2017, the number of migrant workers fell slightly in high income countries, while it increased in upper middle income countries. In the high income countries, it declined from 112.3 million to 111.2 million during the same period. However, it increased from 17.5 million to 30.5 million in upper middle income countries that were the highest increase in the world. International remittances increased to USD 689 billion in 2018. India was the highest recipient nation with USD 78.6 billion and followed by China and Mexico with USD 67.4 billion and USD 35.7 billion respectively. The USA was the top remittance sending country with USD 68 billion. The United Arab Emirates and Saudi Arabia ranked the second and the third with USD 44.4 billion and USD 36.1 billion respectively. Remittances are currently standing as the highest inflow of capital to the developing countries, which has surpassed the foreign direct investment (FDI) and official aids. As a result, the remittance inflow has contributed to a reduction in the level of poverty particularly in the developing countries substantially and played significant roles in the economic growth (IOM 2020; Akobeng 2016; Masron and Subramaniam 2018; World Bank 2020).

In 2019, legal instruments related to international migration were ratified that varied in degrees by member states of the United Nations. Instruments designed to protect refugees and fight against migrant smuggling and human trafficking were ratified by more than 75 percent of the member states. Additionally, instruments protecting the rights of migrant workers were ratified by less than 30 percent of the member states. Therefore, migrant workers are the most vulnerable group in terms of international legal protection. In fact, two global compacts concerning international migrants and refugees were endorsed by a large majority of member states in Dec. 2018. One is the Global Compact for Safe, Orderly and Regular Migration, and the other is the Global Compact on Refugees. The former hosted around 181 million international migrants in 2019 covering 67 percent of the world total migrants, while the latter covered around 25 million refugees representing 89 percent of the global refugee population (Department of Economic and Social Affairs of the United Nations 2019; IOM 2020).

Migration patterns are diverse and vary from region to region. Most of international migrants born in Africa, Asia, and Europe reside within their regions of birth, while the majority of migrants from Latin America, the Caribbean, and North America live outside their regions of birth. However, the number of international migrants and those residing outside their region in Oceania remained about equal in 2019. Among the total number of international migrants, more than a half resided in Europe and North America. International migrants have made significant socio-cultural, political and economic contributions in origin and destination countries. They tend to have higher entrepreneurial activity compare to natives particularly in the USA. It is true that migrants have significantly contributed to innovation in Silicon Valley in the USA. The substantial change in the global governance of migration had been made in the formation of the United Nations Network on Migration and the two global compacts on refugees and migration in last two years. It is important that the two global compacts represent a near universal consensus on the issues of sustained international cooperation and commitment although they are not legally binding and limitations still exist in the world (IOM 2020) (see Table 1).

This book is composed of the two parts. The part one focuses on migration policies in Asia, while the part two deals with European migration policies. It approaches to the study of comparison in the two regions how they implement their migration policies and what we can learn from these each other. In the first part, six Asian cases such as China, Japan, Korea, Taiwan, Thailand, and Vietnam are explored. In the second part, four cases such as Estonia, Germany, Hungary, and Poland are analyzed. Additionally, as a comprehensive approach, the EU's immigration governance and political reaction to African migration are explained.

In the Asian migration policies, Sang-Chul Park wrote the migration policy in Japan and explained it from the cultural, economic, historical, legal and social perspectives. The author argued that Japan has launched a new immigration system aimed to bring in foreign workers into specific domestic industrial sectors as a whole. He also focused on examining how the Japanese migration policy has changed since the 1960s and analyzing what are reasons for the Japanese government to revise the immigration policies and what are roles of migrant workers in the Japanese economy and society. Finally, the author tried to estimate whether or not Japan could build a multicultural society as other advanced countries. He concluded that Japanese migration policy is a part of Japanese history and the government has maintained an efficient policy. However, at the same time, limitations such as a dualistic migration policy between highly skilled workers and blue color worker exist strongly.

Table 1 Key facts and figures of international migration from 1999 to 2019

	2000 report	2020 report
Estimated number of international migrants	150 million	272 million
Estimated proportion of world population who are migrants	2.8%	3.5%
Estimated proportion of female international migrants	47.5%	47.9%
Estimated proportion of international migrants who are children	16.0%	13.9%
Region with the highest proportion of international migrants	Oceania	Oceania
Country with the highest proportion of international migrants	United Arab Emirates	United Arab Emirates
Number of migrant workers	–	164 million
Global international remittances (USD)	126 billion	689 billion
Number of refugees	14 million	25.9 million
Number of internally displaced persons	21 million	14.3 million
Number of stateless persons	–	3.9 million
Number of IOM Member States	76	173
Number of IOM field offices	120	436+

Source IOM (2020)

Min Jeoung Kim dealt with political rights of immigrants in Korea. The author explained that the migration is common and has become a global phenomenon in the twenty-first century. She focused on long term foreigners living in a foreign country, but keeping their nationality affecting their political rights that are the part of the basic rights. Her finding is that political rights of foreigners are still limited although foreign migrants aged 19 or older with three years after having the permanent residency are registered on the foreign registration list of the local community and have the voting right in the local election. In fact, it is the first case in Asia to grant the foreign residents the local voting right. Additionally, the author concludes that such a local voting right for migrants in Korea has positive effects on the social integration of immigrants.

Wen-Chih Huang dealt with the nexus between foreign labor policy and human trafficking in Taiwan. The author described that the Migration Law was generally used to explain the flux of immigration in 1986. Taiwan began to import guest workers in 1989 to alleviate a labor shortage. Whereas, the Taiwan government was generally reluctant to publicly recognize her dependency on unskilled migrant laborers. Therefore, the foreign labor policy was set for the purpose of fulfilling the economic and social needs of the country. His study focuses on providing the background information about foreign labor policy and human trafficking in Taiwan and concluded that an excessive government intervention would only confuse local employers and cause needless displacement into human trafficking.

Ya-Chi Lin, Chan-hui Lin and Kuo-Chun Yeh wrote about China's soft power that could lure Taiwan's youth for overseas employment. They argued that Taiwan's brain drain has been a main concern for the government because of China's strong economic gravity, and the situation might have been worsened over the past decade. They tried to explore the determinants for Taiwan's youth overseas employment using the questionnaire administered in 2015 for residents between 20 and 45 years old. Their finding, however, is that the empirics do not show clear evidence to support Taiwan's brain drain by 2016. By contrast, they concluded that personal considerations, such as broadening international vision and encountering career bottlenecks are more important influences for Taiwan's youth to be employed in China.

Prateep Chaylee wrote about the immigrant policy in Thailand. The author focused on challenges and opportunities of the immigrant policy particularly in the context of the ASEAN processes. The author argued that immigrant workers and related issues have always challenged the economic development and the social policy since late 1980s in Thailand. Particularly, the political uprising in neighboring country in Burma/Myanmar generated the external factors. Consequently, the influx of Burmese migrants and later become the largest migrant workers in Thailand. He concluded that the immigrant Policy should be redefined based on the integrated immigrant policy frameworks among various stakeholders in the current and future contexts. Furthermore, the ASEAN 2025 strategy would be the new platform of rethinking on the policy implementation with the current and future contexts simultaneously.

Ngoc Tram Dang and Tuan Duong Nguyen explained the labor immigration policy in Vietnam. The authors explained that over 30 years of reform and opening up the economy in the era of globalization, Vietnam becomes now a nation of both sending and destination for migrant workers. They focused on the Vietnam's immigration policy based on the labor shortage model providing temporary work visas. Their findings are such a short sight immigration policy has generated instability in the labor market in practice. Therefore, they concluded that decentralization of policy-makers and management's agencies, high level of sub-state authorities' power, as well as more substantial role of foreign investors and contractors within the foreign-capital dependent approach of development, are main factors, which cause the ineffective of immigration.

In the European migration policies, Dieter Eissel discussed European political reactions to the African mass migration. The authors argued that refugees were warmly welcomed by thousands of people willing to help in the first stage, without whom the German administration could not have managed the so-called refugee crisis. However, this attitude has changed. In view of a growing number of migrants, more and more people turned against the refugee tide. In addition, the increasing criminality of the mostly young men from North-Africa contributed to changing the welcome-culture to rising xenophobia. They concluded that the German constitution guarantees the right of asylum and is therefore obliged to help refugees. However, the problem is a lack of solidarity in the European Union when it wants other member states to accept a certain quota of refugees. Eastern European member nations still deny it.

Yun-Chen Lai dealt with the EU's immigration governance focused on the development of immigration policy. In particular, the author examined the EU's refugee policy after the refugee crisis in 2015 in order to find out the consistency of normative power in the EU. She concluded that the EU has yet to accede to the European Convention for the Protection of Human Rights and Fundamental Freedoms, even though it is required under the Article 6 of TEU. Furthermore, the participation of EU Member States in protecting migrants' rights is rare in the reality.

Eike Christian Hornig wrote about European refugee crisis in 2015 particularly the German political parties' reactions. The author explained that migration quickly became the most dominant political issue in the country, reaching its peak in the second half of 2015 when in some polls, almost 90 percent of respondents identified migration as the most important political problem. He analyzed concepts on party positioning that help provide an understanding of the conditions under which parties are guided by policy or responsiveness. Finally he concluded that a further decrease of the saliency of the migration issue in Germany can be realized in the coming years accompanied by a change of the major parties toward more immigration-friendly position.

Ewa Rockica dealt with the migration policy in Eastern Europe particularly in Poland and Hungary. The author pointed out that the migration policies in Poland and Hungary are in conflict with those of Western Europe particularly towards refugees, Muslims, and asylum seekers. Her findings are that Poland and Hungary are emigration and immigration countries. There are attacks and dismantling of public institutions, undermine judicial independence, public slandering of the opposition and its supporters, as well as populist and xenophobic government rhetoric practiced by the media increasingly controlled by the executive. She concluded that Poland and Hungary have formed a hard line axis within the Visegrad group which is an informal caucus of four central and eastern European countries against the EU's interference in immigration policy and constitutional issues.

Mariliis Trei wrote about the formation of immigration policy in Estonia. The author explained that Central and Eastern European countries, which acceded to the EU in 2004, share several similarities deriving from their Soviet past. Compared to older Western European member states, this created a different basis on which to establish their immigration policy. As the 2015 European refugee crisis revealed, stark differences in values, interests and attitudes towards immigrants still exists between new and older EU member states. The author follows the development of immigration policy in Estonia during 1991–2019. Her findings show that immigration policy in Estonia continues to be guided by its historical experience with Soviet-era immigration and the desire to protect the preservation of Estonian population and culture. Immigration is framed from a security perspective and mainly characterized as being conservative. However, due to improved socio-economic development, Estonia is transforming from an emigration state to an immigration state. Such changes have created a somewhat schizophrenic situation where high-skilled immigrants are needed, but immigration is often perceived to pose a threat to internal security and the preservation of Estonian language and culture.

Overall, migrants and refugees' issues have become very serious in Asia and Europe since the 1990s in line with increasing international migrants and refugees. Each nation in the two regions faces different conditions and situations that are dependent on individual national migration policies. At the same time, however, all nations having migrants and refugees have approached to their migration policies based on the humanitarian, economic, political, and social reasons. Although these issues have caused economic, political, and social instability in some individual nations, these are our common assignments how to cope with various instabilities wisely and utilize our resources to the productive and peaceful direction.

References

Akobeng, E. (2016). Out of inequality and poverty: Evidence for the effectiveness of remittances in Sub-Saharan Africa. *The Quarterly Review of Economics and Finance, 60*(3), 207–223.

Department of Economics and Social Affairs of the United Nations. (2019). *International migration 2019, report*. New York: The United Nations.

International Organization for Migration (IOM). (2020). *World migration report 2020*. Geneva: IOM.

Masron, T. A., & Subramaniam, Y. (2018). Remittance and poverty in developing countries. *International Journal of Development Issues, 17*(1), 305–325.

UN DESA. (2015). *Trends international migrant stock: The 2015 revision*. https://www.un.org/en/development/desa/population/migration/data/estimates2/docs/MigrationStockDocumentation_2015.pdf. Accessed on 7 July 2020.

World Bank. (2020). *World development indicators*. http://data.worldbank.org/indicator. Accessed on 18 July 2020.

A Study on Migration Policy in Japan

Sang-Chul Park

Abstract Human migration has a long historical background that stretches back to the earliest periods of human history. In line with that path, migration continues in the modern era in order to provide states, societies and migrants various opportunities. Overall, the estimated number of international migrants had increased over the past four decades from around 85 million in 1970 to 244 million in 2015. Historically, Japan has a migration since it opened in the end of nineteenth century. Many Japanese migrated to the USA and Latin America till 1950s. During the two world wars period, many people from other Asian countries, mainly from Korea and Taiwan moved to the mainland of Japan. After the Second World War, the Koreans and Taiwanese were declared as foreigner in Japan particularly since April 1952 although they were called as old comers after Japan regained independence from the U.S. occupation on 28 April 1952. Therefore, the majority of foreign work forces were colonial immigrants and their descendants till the 1980s. Additionally, the recruitment of Nikkeijin, descendants of Japanese emigrants mainly to Brazil and Peru were given access to residential status with no restrictions on employment after the 1980s. They were regarded as new comers. Japan's latest revised ICA has come into force from April 1, 2019 amidst severe labor shortages resulting from the ageing population and falling birth rates. The new revised law allows around 345,000 blue color foreign workers in Japan over the next five years in 14 industrial sectors facing domestic work force shortages. As a whole, Japan has launched a new immigration system aimed to bring in foreign workers into specific domestic industrial sectors. The goals of paper examine how the Japanese migration policy has changed since the 1960s. It also analyzes what are reasons for the Japanese government to revise the immigration policies and what are roles of migrant workers in the Japanese economy and society. Last, but not least, it is also important to estimate whether or not Japan could build a multicultural society as other advanced countries.

Keywords Migration policy · Foreign labor force · Training program · Skilled worker · Aging society

S.-C. Park (✉)
Korea Polytechnic University, Siheung, South Korea
e-mail: scpark@kpu.ac.kr

© The Author(s), under exclusive license to Springer Nature Singapore Pte Ltd. 2021   11
C.-P. Chu and S.-C. Park (eds.), *Immigration Policy and Crisis in the Regional Context*,
https://doi.org/10.1007/978-981-33-6823-1_2

1 Introduction

Human migration has a long historical background that stretches back to the earliest periods of human history. In line with that path, migration continues in the modern era in order to provide states, societies and migrants various opportunities. At the same time, migration has emerged in the last few years as a critical political challenge in matters of integration, displacement, safety, border management etc. In 2015, the total numbers of international migrants were estimated 244 million globally that accounted for 3.3 percent of the world population. In 2000, it was estimated 173 million that was 2.8 percent of the global population. In 15 years, the total number of the migrants increased around 71 million in the world (IOM 2017).

United Nations Department of Economic and Social Affairs (UN DESA) estimates the number of international migrants globally based on data provided member nations. UN DESA defines an international migrant as any person who has changed his or her country of usual residence distinguishing between short term migrants with less than one year and long-term migrants with longer than a year. However, not all countries use this definition in practice that makes difficult to estimate the exact number of international migrants (UN DESA 2015).

Overall, the estimated number of international migrants had increased over the past four decades from around 85 million in 1970 to 244 million in 2015. During the same period, the proportion of international migrants in the world population increased from 2.3 percent to 3.3 percent. However, this trend remained relatively stable as a proportion of the world population since 1990 although international migrant population increased in size. Additionally, the proportion of international migrants varies significant around the world and around 72 percent of international migrants are of working age between 20 and 64 years who are composed of 52 percent of male and 48 percent of female (IOM 2017) (see Table 1, Fig. 1).

Table 1 Numbers of international migrants and proportion of the world population (As of 1970~2015)	Year	Number of migrants	Migrants as a % of world's population
	1970	84,460,125	2.3
	1975	90,368,010	2.2
	1980	101,983,149	2.3
	1985	113,206,691	2.3
	1990	152,563,212	2.9
	1995	160,801,752	2.8
	2000	172,703,309	2.8
	2005	191,269,100	2.9
	2010	221,714,243	3.2
	2015	243,700,236	3.3

Source IOM (2017)

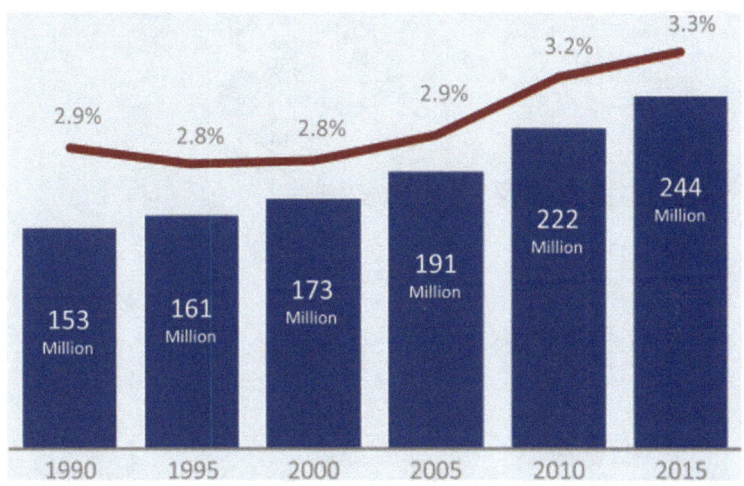

Fig. 1 Trend of international migration between 1990 and 2015 (*Source* IOM 2017)

Asia and Europe hosted 62 percent of the total international migrants that accounted for 75 million in 2015. These regions were followed by North America, with 54 million international migrants in the same year accounting for 22 percent of the global migrant stock, Africa at 9 percent, Latin America and the Caribbean at four percent, and Oceania at three percent. However, shares of the international migrants based on the size of the population in each region ranked Oceania, North America, and Europe at 21 percent, 15 percent, and 10 percent of the total population respectively. In comparison, the shares of international migrants in Asia and Africa were relatively small with 1.7 percent each in 2015.

In the recent trend, the international migrants have increased overall to Group 20 (G 20) countries since 2015, which generate over 80 percent of the global output. Large increase in migration flows among G 20 countries were registered in Korea and Spain with 25 percent each in 2018. To a less extent, it increased nine percent in Japan in the same year. In these three countries, immigration flows in 2018 were almost double compared to the early 2010s. In Japan, the total number of migrants was 287,000 in 2010 and increased to 520,000 in 2018 (OECD 2019) (see Table 2).

There are various reasons why the number of migrants to Japan has increased since the 2010s. First of all, Japanese society has been an aging society declining the total number of labor force since 2000 so that Japan needs to bring foreign work forces in order to maintain its economic growth. Secondly, the Japanese government revised its Immigration Control and Refugee Recognition Act so called Immigration Control Act (ICA), and the Japanese Diet amended it since 1989 continuously (Hamaguchi 2019).

Table 2 Migration flows in G 20 countries (As of 2010~2018)

	2010	2011	2012	2013	2014	2015	2016	2017	2018
EU	2473	2177	2097	2356	2326	2622	3019	3133	
United States	1897	1971	1976	2031	2163	2292	2315	2212	2178
Saudi Arabia	1640	1412	1922	1840	1962	2213	1823	1843	
Germany	684	842	966	1108	1343	2016	1720	1412	1416
Australia	580	608	698	768	773	765	756	770	752
Canada	482	458	488	494	487	490	549	539	573
Spain	330	336	272	248	264	290	352	454	562
Korea	293	307	300	360	407	373	402	453	556
United Kingdom	498	488	418	449	551	548	515	563	542
Japan	287	267	304	307	337	391	428	475	520
Russian Federation	192	206	283	346	439	421	384	391	375
Italy	424	354	321	279	248	250	263	301	
France	197	193	193	205	211	218	230	247	256
Argentina	178	259	292	279	206	269	223	221	
Turkey	50	74	96	95	199	164	177		
Brazil	96	117	133	148	133	137	108		
Mexico	92	91	79	118	109	103	101	102	103
South Africa		118	145	111	83	75			
Indonesia	65	77	72	69					
Total	8442	8141	8884	9322	9694	10,384	10,429	10,567	
% change to previous year		−3.6%	9.1%	4.9%	4.0%	7.1%	0.4%	1.3%	

Source OECD (2019)

Japan's revised ICA has come into force from April 1, 2019 amidst severe labor shortages resulting from the ageing population and falling birth rates. The new revised law allows around 345,000 blue color foreign workers in Japan over the next five years in 14 industrial sectors facing domestic work force shortages. Additionally, for the first time, the Ministry of Justice (MOJ) will start to accept online visa renewals for work sponsored visas including current technical trainee visa. As a whole, Japan has launched a new immigration system aimed to bring in foreign workers into specific domestic industrial sectors such as nursing care, building cleaning services, casting, industrial machinery manufacturing etc. (PWC 2019).

The goals of paper examine how the Japanese migration policy has changed since the 1960s. It also analyzes what are reasons for the Japanese government to revise the policies and what are roles of migrant workers in the Japanese economy and society. Last, but not least, it is also important to estimate whether or not Japan could build a multicultural society as other advanced countries.

2 Japanese Immigration Policy

2.1 Background

Historically, Japan has a migration since it opened in the end of nineteenth century. Many Japanese migrated to the USA and Latin America till 1950s. During the two world wars period, many people from other Asian countries, mainly from Korea and Taiwan moved to the mainland of Japan. After the Second World War, the Koreans and Taiwanese were declared as foreigner in Japan particularly since April 1952 although they were called as old comers after Japan regained independence from the U.S. occupation on 28 April 1952.

Although the Japanese economy faced labor shortages during the high economic growth period in the 1960, the government and private companies were not dependent on foreign labor forces, but tried to develop mechanical automation in their production. Therefore, the majority of foreign work forces were colonial immigrants and their descendants till the 1980s. Additionally, the recruitment of Nikkeijin, descendants of Japanese emigrants mainly to Brazil and Peru were given access to residential status with no restrictions on employment after the 1980s. They were regarded as new comers (Tsuneyoshi et al. 2011).

Japan, long known to be immigration averse, has formally opened its doors to blue color foreign workers for the first time in the post war period by amending the Immigration Control Act (ICA) in Dec. 2018. In the past, Japan has only granted work visas to professionals with high levels of skills and knowledge. However, the comprehensive condition in Japan particularly in terms of labor market has drastically changed due to the aging society based on a radically changed demographic configuration. As a result, the new positive policy allowing blue color foreign workers is regarded as a welcome move to make easy acute labor shortages in the Japanese industry. In spite of securing the necessary manpower required for their businesses, employers must be mindful to comply with the Japanese authorities' new guidelines for the new visa categories. As such, Japanese immigration policies on accepting foreign workers have varied by the periods and the necessity of labor markets (PWC 2019; Hamaguchi 2019).

2.2   From the Amendment to the ICA in 1989 to the Highly Skilled Foreign Professionals

In the 1960s and 1970s, the Japanese cabinet repeatedly approved the anti-immigration policies for foreign workers. However, debate on pursuing new policy challenges for accepting foreign workers legally began in the late 1980s along with the economic peak generating the so called bubble economy.

In 1988, the Ministry of Labor (MOL) currently changed as the Ministry of Health Labor, Welfare: (MHLW) proposed an employment permit system. It means that employers hiring foreign workers were obliged to obtain an employment permit before hiring. However, the Ministry of Justice (MOJ) holing jurisdiction over immigration administration objected the employment permit system. A year later after the debate in the government, the MOJ amended the ICA in order to provide Nikkeijin descendants in Brazil, Peru, and other South American countries their permanent resident ship with no restrictions on their right to work. It created a better possibility for Japanese companies to employ foreign workers. The amendment included the status of residence entitled trainee as well who is not a worker in name, but employers could engage foreign nationals as workers in practice (Hamaguchi 2019).

In 1993, the Technical Intern Training Program (TITP) was established. It was a program combining a period spent as a trainee being not classified as a worker and a period as a technical intern recognized as a worker. Such a complicated program was a product of compromise between the MOJ and the MOL. Given the program, the total period of trainee covered two years. The first third was the non-worker trainee, and the remaining two-third was the technical internship worker. Later, this program extended to three years with the same proportion of the period. In reality, however, there was practically no difference between the works conducted by the trainee period and the technical internship period. Owing to the discrepancy in the reality of the program, Japanese court judged that trainees were recognized as workers and called amendments to the ICA.

As a result, the Council on Economic and Fiscal Policy (CEFP) and the MHLW with the Council for Regulatory Reform called for revision to the program, and the Amendment to the ICA in 2009 established technical intern as a status of residence applying throughout the three-year internship period. It ensured that all activities except class room based learning are regarded as labor under an employment relationship based on a full application of labor law. At the same time, legislation was also introduced the system of supervising organizations acting as brokers matching labor demand with supply. They were business cooperatives, commerce and industrial associations seeking no business profits that accepted technical interns and assign them to technical internship at their affiliated companies and other entities (https://www.jitco.or.jp/en/, 2019).

Although the Amendment to the ICA in 2009 established a new status of technical interns, the TITP caused continuously legal violations and fraudulent activities in the reality. Such a trend prompted a strong call for improvement of the ICA. At the same time, employers also demanded an extension to the length for technical interns. Therefore, the MOJ and the MHLW formed a study group for experts. The study group completed a report and recommended to create a legal enforcement. As a result, the Technical Internship Act (TIA) was established in 2016 that concerned a proper implementation of the technical internship of foreigners and protection of technical interns. It enabled foreign technical interns completing three-year internship and returning to their home countries to come back to Japan for a further two years' technical internship. As a result, the total period of the foreign technical internship extended to five years.

Additionally, many problems involving supervising organization were reported by requiring such organizations to obtain license and allowing revoked licenses. The TITP was strictly regulated by obliging companies, farms, and other entities implementing the foreign technical internships to be registered and accredited for each technical internship program. Despite the TIA in 2016, foreign technical interns had limited permissions to work at specific companies and farms. As a result, they are still not allowed to switch to another working place. These cases have taken place particularly in companies and farms that provides low wages. Therefore, foreign technical interns leave their employers and work illegally for higher-paid companies in the urban areas. In addition to the illegal work of the foreign technical internship, sexual harassment and violation of human rights against the foreign technical interns take place in several occasions that raises social alert in the Japanese society (Hamaguchi 2019).

Compared to the foreign technical interns, there has always been a proactive approach to welcome highly skilled foreign professionals in Japan. Particularly from the beginning of the twenty-first century the global competition for advance human resources has been intensified. Japan is not an exception to attract to foreign workers in advanced professionals or technical roles. Accordingly, Japan has adopted the US Green Card system aiming at welcoming highly skilled human resources that allows the permanent residence. In 2012, Japan introduced a point based system for highly skilled foreign professionals that allowed preferential status of residence to the people exceeding a certain number of points for academic background, professional experience and other factors. Moreover, the Japanese government shortened the period of stay required for application for permanent residence to three years with 70 points or more and one year with 80 points in 2017. It is a selective immigration policy for the highly skilled foreign professionals granted by permanent residence from the start (Immigration Bureau, MOJ 2017).

2.3 The Amendment to the ICA in 2018

Despite the three amendments to the ICA including the TIA, the labor shortage has continuously increased particularly for the small and medium-sized enterprises (SMEs) causing severe problems in the national economy. Therefore, Prime Minister Abe proposed a policy for fundamental changes to measures accepting foreign workers at the CEFP in Feb. 2018. The new migration policy aims at accepting foreign workers as semi-skilled workers in a range of industries with upper limitations on status of residence and a general ban on their family members residing to Japan. A cabinet task force proposed a general framework for the system as a part of the Basic Policy on Economic and Fiscal Management and Reform in June 2018, and the MOJ reviewed a bill for amendment to the ICA. The bill was submitted to the Japanese Diet in Nov. and enacted in Dec. 2018 (Hamaguchi 2019).

Given the new amendment to the ICA in 2018, the newly established Type 1 is for people with a level of skills that allows them to work without receiving special training. The competency of technical interns is checked through industry specific examinations prescribed by the ministry with jurisdiction over the industry in question. Foreign workers with the status of Type 1 are permitted to stay up to five years, but not allowed to bring their family members to Japan. Combined with the technical internship period, they can work up to 10 years in total without being able to bring their families to Japan.

By contrast, the Type 2 for highly skilled foreign workers enables them to pursue advanced professional or technical tasks by their own judgment. Foreign workers with the Type 2 do not have any limitation to renew their period of residence and are allowed to bring their family members to Japan without any limitation Therefore, these two types of foreign workers are focused on the quality oriented immigration policy.

In pursuing the new immigration policy, it is also needed to concern that foreign workers may cause negative impacts on the labor market for Japanese workers. In order to prevent such a problem, the amendment applies only to industrial fields with labor shortages. These industrial sectors are specified by the MOJ upon discussion with the ministry with jurisdiction over the relevant industry. In line with such a guideline, the CEFP listed five industrial sectors in Feb. 2018. However, the Cabinet approved 14 industrial sectors because the various industrial circles complained about the labor shortages.

The revised Immigration Control and Refugee Recognition Act has come into force on 1 April 2019 that was enacted in Dec. 2018 and will allow around 345,000 blue color foreign workers in the labor market over the next five years in the 14 industrial sectors causing labor shortages. These are nursing care, building cleaning services, casting, industrial machinery manufacturing, electrical and electronic information, construction, shipbuilding and marine equipment, car maintenance, aviation, lodging, agriculture, fishery, food and beverage manufacturing, and restaurant business (PWC 2019).

By implementing the new law, Japanese workers fear their wages in the labor markets of sectors where SMEs are not capable to pay high wages for foreign workers at a minimum wage. According to the ministerial ordinance prohibits discriminatory treatment after the employment. It means that employers are expected to pay the foreign workers the same wages that at least equal to those of Japanese workers. However, in reality, the 14 industrial sectors cannot attract Japanese workers in the first place due to low wages so that these sectors may be dependent on foreign workers.

Additionally, the new amendment has been enacted that a large difference in wages between urban and rural areas in minimum wages having a gap of 30 percent between Tokyo (USD8.76) and Kagoshima Prefecture (USD6.77) could impact shifts of working places for foreign workers. Given the new law, there is no restriction on specified skilled working visas transferring to another employer within the same sector although these sectors are recognized as labor shortage sectors. In response to this problem, the government has proposed to a nationwide uniform minimum wage system. However, this proposal has not been approved yet (Hamaguchi 2019).

3 Immigrants in Japan

3.1 Background

The total population of Japan declined from its peak of 128.1 million in 2008 to 126.6 million in 2017. The average age also increased up to 46.8 years and the portion of aged population with over 65 years old accounted for around 28 percent in 2017 representing the most aging society in the world. Meanwhile, the foreign population also increased. In 2000, the total numbers of registered foreigner were 1.3 million that accounted for 1.02 percent of the total population in Japan. This number and proportion increased 1.5 million (1.17%) in 2005, 1.6 million (1.25%) in 2010, 1.7 million (1.34%) in 2010, and 2.47 million (1.95%) in 2017 (Statistics Bureau, Ministry of Internal Affairs and Communication 2015; Maruyama 2018) (Table 3).

3.2 Foreign Technical Trainees and International Students for Labor Shortage

During the high economic growth period in the 1950s and 1960s, a migration took place mainly from rural to urban areas in Japan. However, the economic boom continued till the end of the 1980s and a labor shortage in various industrial sectors appeared and short-term labor including illegal immigrants was accepted nationwide. It was rather positive trend that foreign labor forces were properly utilized during the economic boom period and the growing economy attracted to foreign workers to the nation.

Table 3 Registered foreigner in Japan by regions (As of 2017)

Regions	Numbers	Percent (%)
Asia	2,050,909	82.98
Latin America	247,938	10.03
Europe	73,151	2.96
North America	69,875	2.83
Africa	15,143	0.61
Oceania	13,854	0.56
No Nationality	588	0.02
Total	2,471,458	100

Source Ministry of Justice (2017), Statistics Bureau, Ministry of Internal Affairs and Communication (2015)

In order to keep legal labor with the estimation of rapid decline of Japanese population, the government has set up education and training programs for foreigners being able to work in SMEs in Japan for a short period and use their knowledge and skill after returning to their home countries. This system is the Technical Internship Trainee Program (TITP) launched in 1993. Through the TITP, foreign workers could work in Japan in the nearly same employment channel used by low skilled foreign workers in agriculture, fishery, construction, food manufacturing etc. that are the same 14 industrial sectors facing labor shortages even now. This program allows Japanese SMEs to employ short term foreign workers for three to five years as a part of international cooperation for technology transfer to developing countries (Maruyama 2018).

As the Table 3 shows, the most foreign workers come from Asian countries. The majority of foreign technical trainees came from Vietnam with 38.6 percent, China with 35.4 percent, the Philippines with 9.9 percent, Indonesia with 8.2 percent, and others with 4.7 percent. The most of foreign technical trainees stay in remote cities and villages. The total numbers of them accounted for 177,119 in 2007 and declined to 146,696 in 2011, but started to increase again after the Abe government and reached to 230,040 in 2016. Their working condition is regarded as poor because they are cheap workers for the industries; working long hours and receiving lower than the minimum wage (Ministry of Justice 2017) (Fig. 2).

In 2016, the proportion of the foreign technical trainees in the total number of foreigners in Japan accounted for 9.6 percent. Unfortunately, the numbers of institution in illegal treatment to them such as private companies carrying the TITP, supervision organizations, group supervision organizations increased 163 in 2010 to 273 in 2015 and started to decline to 239 in 2016. The illegal cases are mainly no payment of wage, providing no legal document, illegal use of other's name, discordance of technical practice etc. The total number of illegal cases in the TITP in 2016 accounted for 383. Among these, the violation of wage payment to the foreign technical trainees is the highest number with 31.6 percent, and providing no legal document follows with 24.5 percent that are more than a half of the total cases (Ministry of Justice 2017) (Fig. 3).

Along with foreign technical trainees, international students are regarded as potential labors in Japan. Therefore, the government has been actively recruiting international students and allowing them to work part-time during the semester periods and full time during the vacation periods. As a result, the numbers of foreign students increased from 131,789 in 2006 to 257,739 in 2016. The student shares of overall foreign population also increased from 6.3 percent to 11 percent during the same period. Special resource allocation and strong initiative by the Ministry of Education (MOE) enabled to bring more international students to Japan (Green 2017).

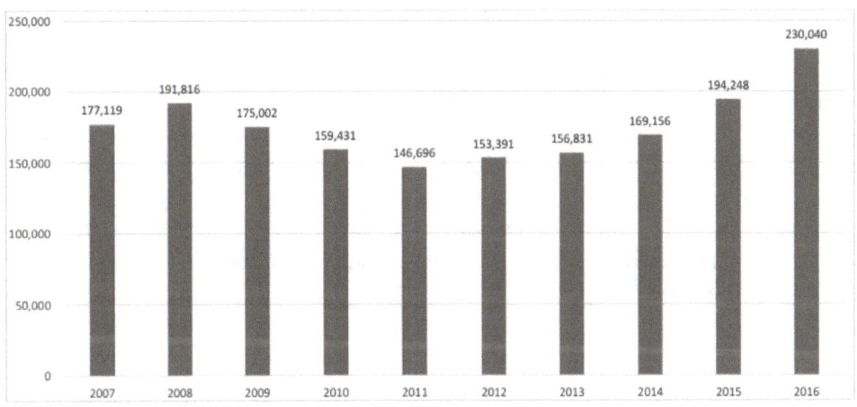

Fig. 2 Trend of the number of foreign technical trainees between 2007 and 2016 (*Source* Ministry of Justice 2017)

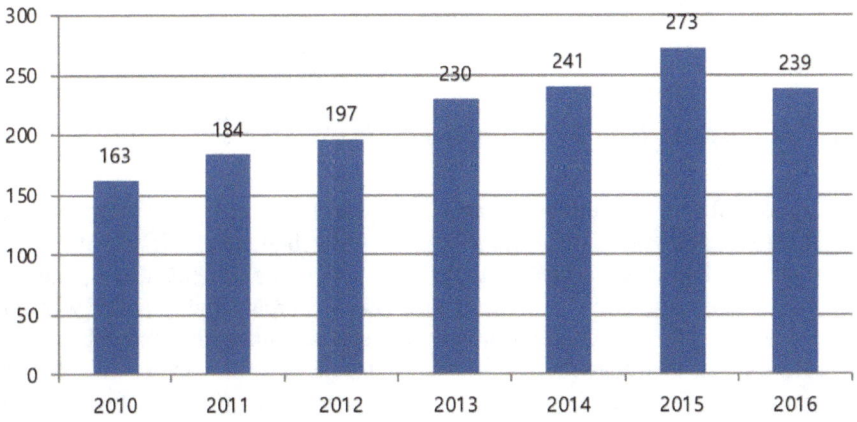

Fig. 3 The numbers of violated institution to the foreign technical trainee program from 2010 to 2016 (*Source* Ministry of Justice 2017)

The MOE adopted the Plan for 100,000 International Students from 1983 to 2000, and an extension, the Plan for 300,000 International Students since 2008 that meets the goal in 2020. Generally, the international student policy deals with higher education institutes. However, it soon needs to consider lower levels of education because educational institutions and industries face the problem to lose students and workers. It is the reason why schools start to accept Chinese students and industries have tried to find labor forces from other countries.

Education and training system seems to solve the problem of labor shortage for a short term. However, more structural change and value shift must be required for the society to keep its sustainability for a long term. Otherwise, keeping the same approach and the same assumption can hardly attract new international labors and students because international rankings of Japanese universities start recently to fall although the MOE has required universities promoting several international programs including English-medium courses within their campus and developing partnerships with foreign universities (Maruyama 2018).

Foreign migrant workers played important roles in contributing to generating economic growth in Japan along with the development of transnational networks, rising value of its currency etc. The number of people overstaying their visas comprising the bulk of immigrant workers grew from 100,000 in 1990 to 300,000 in 1993 and stood around 207,000 in 2005. They mostly came from Asian countries such as Korea, China, the Philippines, Thailand, Malaysia, and Indonesia (Kashiwazaki and Akaha 2006).

Despite the economic contribution of migrant workers, the 1990 revision to the Immigration Control and Refugee Act (ICA) excluded unskilled labors in principle and permitted working visas only for high skilled work and family based visas. However, the revision opened its side door to unskilled labor for Nikkeijin of Japanese heritage and their immediate families. As a result, the population of Nikkeijin grew rapidly throughout the 1990s and 2000s peaking at 375,000 in 2007 that was around 20 percent of the whole foreign population (Green 2017).

3.3   Highly Skilled Professional Foreign Workers

Highly skilled foreign workers in Japan started to come to Japan since the 1990 revision to the ICA. Officially, there are three paths to build the professional careers in Japan. The first is to transfer from a student visa to a professional visa, and the second is to apply directly for a working visa. Finally, foreign highly skilled workers can apply for highly skilled foreign professional status. Additionally, foreign workers are able to switch their status during their stay in Japan. As a result, there were 280,000 student visas in 2016 and transferred to working visa with 270,000. However, the number of highly skilled professional accounted only for around 5500 that are around two percent of foreign workers approved by the government in the same year (METI 2018).

Japanese companies also encourage foreign workers to exercise their abilities fully. They try to develop ideal workplaces for foreign employees by establishing globally standardized personnel system, providing assignment of high level positions depending on competency regardless of their nationality. Furthermore, they try to correct long hour labor practices and develop competency and performance based personnel evaluation system instead of Japanese seniority system.

The Japanese government also emphasizes to attract foreign highly skilled professionals at the central government level. Prime Minister Abe addressed in Invest Seminar in New York in 2016 that the number of professionals working in Japan from overseas had increased 20 percent from 2014 to 2016. In order to accelerate this trend, the Japanese government will create the Japanese Green Card recognized as a permanent residency for Highly Skilled Foreign Professionals, which is the world fastest level of approval process between three and one year. Additionally, waiting time for visa applications will also be shorten within ten business days (METI 2018) (Fig. 4).

The Japanese government also focuses on improving living environment for foreign highly skilled professionals by reducing their language barriers in daily life and improving educational opportunities for their children. Additionally, it improves working environment for foreign highly skilled professionals by clarifying employee's career track and contents of work as well as encouraging companies' mindset change. Last, but not least, the government facilitates immigration procedures by launching the online application system for status of residence in April 2018.

Highly skilled professional foreign workers in Japan declined during the global financial crisis in 2008 and Fukushima disaster in 2011. However, the number of them has started to increase since the Abe administration in 2012. Foreign professionals in the field of engineering, humanities, international services and other specialists

Fig. 4 Change of Japanese green card for highly skilled professionals (As of 2018) (*Source* METI 2018)

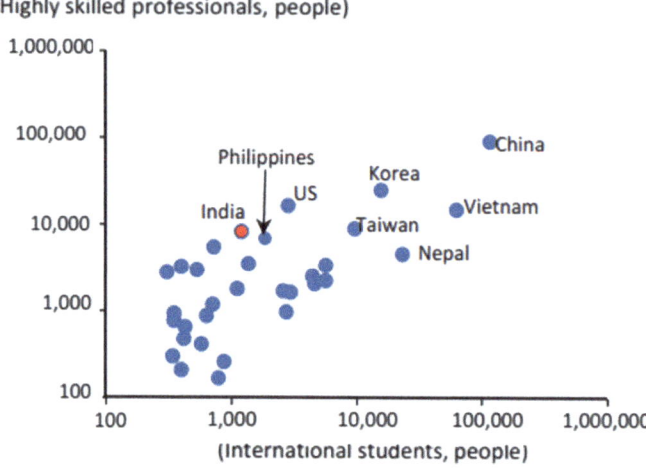

Fig. 5 International student and highly skilled professionals in Japan (As of 2016) (*Source* Ministry of Justice 2017)

from China are the main source of the growth. Although the current volume of highly skilled professional foreign workers is still small, the government aims to enhance the entry of them through the point based system, which started in 2012 and revised in 2018 (Kumagai and Rana 2017; METI 2018).

In 2016, about 5500 foreign highly skilled professionals gained professional visas. Among them, the Chinese share accounted for 65 percent, and the US, India, Vietnam, and the Philippines followed. The Japanese government aims to increase the number of foreign highly skilled professionals to 10,000 by 2020. China was still the leader of the share of total number of aggregated foreign highly skilled professionals in 2016, and Korea, Vietnam, and Taiwan followed. Even in the total number of international students, China was the main drive force in the same year, and Vietnam, Nepal, and Korea followed (Kumagai and Rana 2017) (Fig. 5).

4 Analysis on Japanese Immigration Policy

4.1 Background

Japanese immigration policy has created its positive and negative results since the government has implemented its ICA in 1989. The former is to educate and train foreign workers particularly from developing countries in line with official development aid (ODA) programs while the latter are various challenges not only for immigrants, but also Japanese companies. As a whole, the immigration policy has faced several problems and difficulties for immigrant and Japanese society. These must be solved in order to attract foreign labor forces properly and sustainable. Otherwise, Japanese immigration policy may fail.

4.2 Major Challenges and Difficulties

Mainly there are four issues in the Japanese immigration policy that are regarded as problems and difficulties. These are as follows.

Firstly, dualistic character between Technical Trainee Interns (TTI) and highly skilled foreign professionals.

The Japanese immigration policy has focused on the two immigration groups. The one is the low skilled labor forces mainly from the developing countries particularly in East Asia. The other group is highly skilled foreign professionals from all over the world possessing specialized knowledge and skills and having better working condition and environment than the low skilled workers. Their roles are for strengthening strategic competitiveness of Japanese large sized companies, research institutes, universities etc. The low skilled labor forces are mainly for SMEs facing labor shortage, and they come to Japan in the TTIP that is a part of ODA programs. Additionally, foreign students are included for utilizing labor forces by allowing short term working permission during their semester periods. The low skilled labor forces in TTI and foreign students use to face improper working condition and environment that violates Japanese labor law. The total number of legal violation particularly in TTIs has continuously increased since 2010 (Green 2017; Ministry of Justice 2017).

Secondly, difficult working condition and environment.

General working condition and environment for foreign workers are not only valid for the low skilled labor forces, but also highly skilled foreign professionals. The former group uses to suffer from legal violations, while all foreign workers face generally long working hours, Japan's unique communication style, unclear promote system, slow promotion, requirement for higher Japanese language skill, and complicated recruitment process (Fig. 6).

Thirdly, educational difficulty for immigrant students.

The total number and ratio of immigrant children are only small volume in Japanese schools. There are 82,000 immigrant students out of 13 million students in Japan in 2016 that accounts only for 0.61 percent. The official educational system lacks the same conditions for the small numbers of immigrant students, and few teachers have experiences in working with immigrant students in isolated areas. In Japan, formal compulsory education, both primary and lower secondary, focuses only on Japanese citizens. Therefore, the curriculum is not generally designed for intercultural educational needs such as mother tongue education and religious education (Maruyama 2018).

As a result, Japanese education policy and system indicators for immigrants and preparedness are below average compared with other countries. Migrant Integration Policy Index (MIPEX) categorizes education as access, targeting needs, new opportunities, and intercultural education for all. Japan's scores in these categories were all below average and ranked 29 place among 38 nations in 2014. In order to improve the education system, it is needed to support language education and create intercultural education (http://www.mipex.eu/key-findings) (Fig. 7).

Last, but not least, various challenges for foreign professionals and Japanese companies.

Japanese companies and institutes do have several difficulties to recruit highly skilled foreign professionals because of various reasons. Challenges for utilizing foreign professionals are characterized as lack of Japanese manager, lack of Japanese communication skill, perception gap about career development, cost and time for utilizing foreign professionals, mindset for receiving foreign professionals to department (Kumagai and Rana 2017) (Fig. 8).

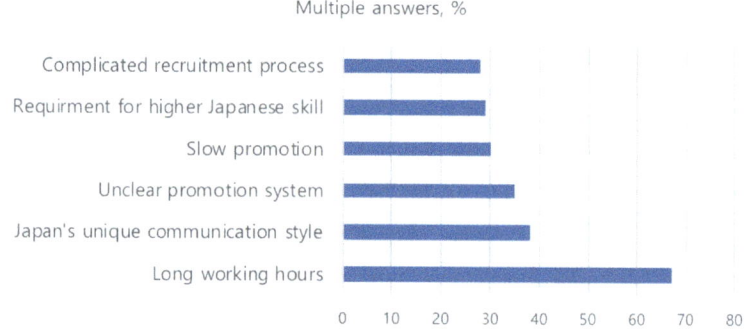

Fig. 6 Difficulties for working in Japanese companies as foreigners (As of 2016) (*Source* Japan Association for Promotion of Internationalization 2017)

1	Sweden	77	14	Denmark	49	27	Slovakia	24
2	Australia	76	15	Luxembourg	48	28	Iceland	23
3	New Zealand	66	16	Austria	47	29	Japan	21
4	Norway	65	16	Germany	47	30	Romania	20
4	Canada	65	18	Switzerland	42	30	Poland	20
6	Portugal	62	19	Czech Republic	38	32	Malta	19
7	Belgium	61	20	Spain	37	33	Lithuania	17
8	Finland	60	21	Greece	36	33	Latvia	17
8	USA	60	21	France	36	35	Croatia	15
10	Estonia	58	23	Italy	34	35	Hungary	15
11	South Korea	57	24	Ireland	30	37	Turkey	5
11	United Kingdom	57	25	Cyprus	27	38	Bulgaria	3
13	Netherlands	50	26	Slovenia	26			

Fig. 7 MIPEX education ranking (As of 2014) (*Source* www.mipex.eu/)

Fig. 8 Challenges for utilization of foreign professionals (*Source* Disco's Survey about Highly Skilled Foreign Professional Recruitment 2017)

5 Conclusion

Migration is regarded as a part of human history. Therefore, it is natural and rational that Japan has been a migration country from the historical point of view. Such a historical heritage had even continued to the end of the twentieth century, and Nikkeijin called as new comer migrated mainly from the South America to Japan, while migrants came to Japan from other Asian countries during the colonialism and their descendants are called as old comer. In the beginning of the twenty-first century, Japan has tried hard to attract foreign work forces due to its labor shortage.

It means that Japanese migration has a clear character to migrate mainly because of economic reasons in the modern history. Japanese people mainly migrated to North and South America in the early twentieth century due to the economic reasons, and the Japanese government received foreign migration during the colonialism and after the Second World War period for its economic growth. After Japan became an industrialized nation, Japanese migration abroad returned to home and foreign workers rushed to Japan to participate in their advantages from the growing economy.

Japan has never been an open immigration country, but the government has always controlled strongly the total number of foreign migration based on its own economic interests. Therefore, it did not control strongly illegal migrants during the economic peak period in the 1970s and 1980s because Japanese industries particularly in SMEs needed labor forces, and the Japanese society accepted it implicit. Additionally, the Japanese government started to launch the Technical Internship Trainee Program (TTIP) in 1993 owing to the structural labor shortage in SMEs providing humble working environment with dangerous, dirty, and difficult jobs that was called as a 3D job category. In the 3D jobs, Japanese workers did not prefer so that a structural labor shortage has remained as a socio economic problem since then.

Through the TITP, foreign workers could work in Japan in the nearly same employment channel used by low skilled foreign workers in agriculture, fishery, construction, food manufacturing etc. that are the same 14 industrial sectors facing labor shortages even now. This program allows Japanese SMEs to employ short term foreign workers for three to five years as a part of international cooperation for technology transfer to developing countries. However, they are not allowed to bring their family members to Japan.

At the same time, Japan tries to attract highly skilled foreign professionals and provide them the permanent residency if they fulfill the condition in order to maintain Japanese competitiveness in the global market after amending Immigration Control Act (ICA) in 2018. Compared to low skilled foreign workers, they are also allowed to bring their families to Japan. Despite such an advantage, the total number of highly skilled foreign professionals was only around two percent of the low skilled workers in 2016.

Overall, Japanese migration policy is regarded as a dualistic function and challenging condition and environment for foreign work force and Japanese companies. Additionally, it has to cope with problems and difficulties in school issues for immigrant students. Japan has carried out the migration policy for low skilled foreign workers in the name of the TITP due to the labor shortage in SMEs since 1993. However, over 380 cases violating the Japanese legal system took place in 2016, and the government has not provided them the equal working condition compared to highly skilled foreign professionals' working condition. It is rather visible that the Japanese government and society do prefer to attract the latter foreign working group instead of the former working group. However, it is not clear that the Japanese dualistic and conditional migration policy can cope with chronic social economic problems in Japan such as rapidly aging society, low birth rate, distorting rural areas, chronic labor shortage, and excessive agglomeration etc. in the future.

References

Green, D. (2017). *As its population increases, Japan quietly turns to immigration, migration, information source.* https://www.migrationpolicy.org/article/its-population-ages-japan-quietly-turns-immigration. Accessed on 10 Nov 2019.

Hamaguchi, K. (2019). How have Japanese policies changed in accepting foreign workers? *Japan Labor Issues, 3*(14), 1–7.

Immigration Bureau, MOJ. (2017). *Points-based preferential immigration treatment for highly skilled foreign professionals.* https://www.lb.emb-japan.go.jp/Points-Based-Immigration-Treatment.PDF. Accessed on 03 Nov 2019.

International Organization for Migration (IOM). (2017). *World migration report 2018.* Geneva: IOM.

Kashiwazaki, C., & Akaha, T. (2006). *Japanese immigration policy: Responding to continuing pressures, migration information source, Nov 1.* https://www.migrationpolicy.org/article/japanese-immigration-policy-responding-conflicting-pressures. Accessed on 09 Nov 2019.

Kumagai, S., & Rana, R. (2017). *How to attract highly skilled Indian professionals to Japan, Japan-India human exchange research series No. 4, Aug.* https://www.jri.co.jp/MediaLibrary/file/english/periodical/rim/2017/66.pdf. Accessed on 13 Nov 2019.

Maruyama, H. (2018). *Challenges for immigrants for formal and informal education settings in Japan, the 2019 global education monitoring report.* New York: UNESCO.

Ministry of Economy, Trade, and Industry (METI). (2018). *Working in Japan: Open for professionals.* https://www.meti.go.jp/english/policy/external_economy/professionals/pdf/recruitment201803.pdf. Accessed on 13 Nov 2019.

Ministry of Justice. (2017). *Sairyu Sinsani Zzide (in Japanese).* http://www.moj.go.jp/content/001 228761.pdf. Accessed on 9 Nov 2019.

OECD. (2019). *2019 international migration and displacement trends and policies report to the G 20.* Paris: OECD.

PWC. (2019). *Japan relaxes immigration policy and processes.* https://www.pwc.com/jp/en/tax news-international-assignment/assets/gms-20190419-2-en.pdf. Accessed on 19 Oct 2019.

Statistics Bureau, Ministry of Internal Affairs and Communication. (2015). *Heisei 27 nen Kokusei Chousa, 2015 census.* http://www.stat.go.jp/data/kokusei/2015/kekka/kihon1/pdf/gaiyou1.pdf. Accessed on 5 Nov 2019.

Tsuneyoshi, R., Okano, K. H., Karoi, H., & Boocock, S. (2011). *Minorities and education in multicultural Japan: An interactive perspective.* London: Routledge.

UN DESA. (2015). *Trends international migrant stock: The 2015 revision.* https://www.un.org/en/ development/desa/population/migration/data/estimates2/docs/MigrationStockDocumentation_ 2015.pdf. Accessed on 18 Oct 2019.

Websites

https://www.jitco.or.jp/en/.
http://www.mipex.eu/key-findings.

Political Rights of Immigrants in Korea

Minjeoung Kim

Abstract An important variable in immigration policy is the immigrant's regime. Korean immigrants are divided into three types; guest workers, foreign wives of Korean men, foreign compatriots mostly with Chinese passport. South Korea's immigration policy is based on the guest worker regime, which basically allows foreigners to live for a certain period of time and they are supposed to return back after an acceptable period of time. However, with the recent increase in married migrant women and the increasing number of their children, Korea should now be interested in social integraion policy of immigrants. It is the political right of immigrants that begins this discussion. South Korea was fairly proactive in granting suffrage in local elections for immigrants with permanent residency. However, their turnout is low and has no practical significance. In order to integrate Korean society more efficiently, a variety of integration methods are needed, such as the granting of political rights, participation in advisory bodies, and participation in programs that can encourage understanding of Korean society.

Keywords Immigrants · Political rights · Guest worker regime · Married migrant women

1 Introduction

Today is called the "age of migration," which means that migration is so common and migration has become a global phenomenon. With the development of transportation, the development of capitalism no longer bound not only capital, but also labor, was not bound to geographic limits. The development of technology became more and more meaningful as borders, interacting with each other so much that the world is almost a culture, is making mankind live in the times. In this situation, countries tend not to sustain the traditional role of the national borders and try to protect their

M. Kim (✉)
University of Seoul, Seoul, Korea
e-mail: rosny07@gmail.com

© The Author(s), under exclusive license to Springer Nature Singapore Pte Ltd. 2021
C.-P. Chu and S.-C. Park (eds.), *Immigration Policy and Crisis in the Regional Context*,
https://doi.org/10.1007/978-981-33-6823-1_3

markets in a broader sense rather than in a limited sense. In this context, countries have to worry seriously about how to treat the immigrants who live in their territory.

Long-term foreigners live in a foreign country but keeping their nationality, but their political rights are seriously affected by political decisions of their residing countries. On the other hand, according to the idea of the human rights concept that all nations must guarantee the basic rights of people as human beings, even if they are non-citizens living within the border, it is argued that even if their nationalities are different, they should guarantee their basic rights. In view of the role of the state defined so far, it seems obvious that the principle of national sovereignty is that the right of suffrage is not recognized to foreigners. Therefore, the argument is that the right to participate in politics should be granted only to those who are recognized as the people according to the principle of national sovereignty, or that migrants should be guaranteed the same rights as the people who are seriously affected by political decisions. In the meantime, recently the concept of a nation-state has been fairly limited since modern times, and the principle of national sovereignty has been shaken by the emergence of arguments for reinterpreting the broader role of the nation. Political participation at the local level is also important, especially given that this is an era of decentralization. Given the nature of local governments, a growing number of foreign cases are giving suffrage to residential foreigners as "residents" in that policy decisions should be made that represent the interests of "residents" living in the provincial unit and reflect their positions. In this regard, it has been argued that it can be a clear discrimination not to grant voting rights to foreigners and furthermore, it is unreasonable that to grant voting rights does not come with the right to be elected. To develop the debate, we need to start with a discussion what is political rights and what political rights include. Speaking of citizenship, Marshall explains civil rights by dividing them into civil rights, social rights and political rights (Marshall 1950). Civil rights are the basic rights necessary for individual freedom, which means freedom of speech, freedom of thinking, freedom of religion, etc. that an individual should enjoy as a citizen. Social rights are basically enjoyed as a member of society, such as economic welfare and social heritage, including the right to enjoy various benefits such as social security, health insurance, work pension, child support deduction, and public housing, which foreign residents should enjoy as a new member of society. Political rights are the right to participate in the partipation of political power, including the right to vote, the right to vote, the right to be elected, and right to join a party, and the right to engage in political activities. Civil rights represent the right to be protected regardless of nationality as an individual, and social rights are the right to be protected from poverty, fear and so on. Studies show that political rights are divided into the right to vote, the right to vote, the right to association and political activities, the right to civil rights and civil service. From the 18th century, it was a key argument of many philosophers that individual freedom should be protected by the state, first meaning only civil rights, but then gradually expanding that right to social rights. Here, regardless of nationality, the state should guarantee individual civil rights and, more recently, social rights should be guaranteed in terms of human rights.

Ensuring these rights is international human rights norms, among them the International Covenant on Economic, Social and Cultural Rights (ICESCR) is a good example which was adopted at the General Assembly of the United Nations on December 16, 1966. It is also called the Social Rights Convention or the Code A. These include the right to work, the right to work in a good environment, the right to create and join trade unions, the right to receive social security, the right to enjoy proper living standards, the right to receive the maximum protection available for physical and mental health, the right for everyone to be educated, and the right to participate in cultural life. In addition, the Covenant on Freedom (ICCPR) provides that everyone has the right to be free from torture, inhumane treatment, slavery, forced labor, child labor, unfair trials and invasion of privacy (Lee 2013: 269–290).

These conventions include much more and comprehensive rights such as economic, social and cultural rights than the Universal Declaration of Human Rights. By doing so, migrants can claim that civil rights and social rights, regardless of nationality. However, there is still discussion on political rights.

From this perspective, this paper will look at foreign countries' cases of migrant political rights and look at the implications for Korean case after looking at factors affecting the political rights of migrants. To this end, first of all, if we look at what political rights mean, we will divide the cases into four types as we move around and try to find out about political rights. Lastly, we will try to understand the implications of Korea through these examples.

2   The Meaning of Political Rights for Immigrants

The rights of migrants are undergoing considerable change in a free and democratic country. Up until the early 20th century, immigrants who had long lived in countries like the United States could be denied re-entry and excluded from welfare benefits. They were also denied ownership of land or employment of public officials, and these rights were only granted to the citizen. There are few countries where these policies are maintained today. For foreigners with permanent residency, a variety of rights are applied, in fact, just like the citizen. However, political rights are only allowed to the citizen. Now, in many countries, migrants share many of the same rights as citizen, but political rights still remain off the table.

So how have the rights of immigrants expanded through so many changes so far? Because the modern state is a nation state, only the members of the nation state were given the rights guaranteed by the state and that was the identity of the nation state. Gradually, what was there in the background for immigrants to have so many rights except political ones? First, Soysal (1994) emphasizes the influence of international norms and international organizations, and argues for the concept of transnational citizenship. He argues that the rights of immigrants expand as international organizations actively expand the international human rights norms set by the international community, which are outside the nation state. Soysal believes that in the context of this argument, the influence of the nation states is weakening and that the criteria for granting rights within political communities through concepts such as transnational citizenship have changed from belonging to the state to universal human beings. Therefore, it is understandable that migrants have rights within the political community, although they do not have citizenship. Secondly, Gurowitz (1999) emphasizes that international human rights norms and the influence of international organizations do not directly work in determining the subject of rights, but through domestic political processes. While paying attention to the process of domestic appropriation, she emphasizes that the differences in the national identity security and international identity strength of each country result in differences in the domestic use of international human rights norms. Thirdly, Joppke (1998) argues that, in a slightly different context, the domestic legal grounds should be explored, expanding the rights of migrants by domestic influences such as the influence of national interest groups and the influence of the judiciary. It stressed that the judiciary's ruling that values migrant human rights and civic groups' activities that emphasize migrant human rights have a significant impact on their rights.

So can political rights be understood in the same context? Can political rights be said to be a right recognized by international law or international norms? It is difficult to reconcile with the inherent characteristics of international law that regulates the political participation of individuals or groups by intervening in the domestic political process. The domestic political process is a typical aspect of the exercise of national sovereignty, and noninterference in domestic affairs is one of the established principles of international law. Political rights are not recognized by foreigners due to the traditional interpretation of the Constitution, but have been understood as the citizen's unique rights that foreigners can enjoy when they become naturalized and acquire nationality. In reality, however, the global trend is that the number of foreigners, including permanent residents, is increasing, and the number of countries is increasing too to grant the right to vote in local elections to foreigners who satisfy certain requirements, such as the length of their residence. According to the table below, Commonwealth countries recognize all citizens of Commonwealth aged 18 or older with the right to vote in both local and national elections, while Portugal gives both foreigners from Brazil or who speak Portuguese to vote in both local and national elections. EU member states also grant the right to vote to migrant foreigners from EU member states in local elections. The main reason for granting the right to vote to foreigners is the expectation that they can become members of a society with a sense of ownership through the vote and that participation in politics will contribute to social integration of multicultural societies (Table 1).

Political rights define their importance in various international norms. In Article 25 of the International Human Rights Code, which went into effect in 1976, the right to political participation is recognized in the name of the Article 25, stipulating that the right to participate in democratic politics shall be prohibited from discrimination, guaranteed participation in public offices and guaranteed free election rights. However, there is no indication to whom to guarantee this right, but admits that restrictions can be allowed if there is "reasonable reason." These reasonable reasons may include minors, criminals, mentally weak people, and those who fail to meet the

Table 1 Political rights of immigrants

	Right to vote			X
	Local assembly		National Assembly	
All countries	Greece Namibia Netherland Norway New Zealand Korea Denmark Morocco USA (several states) Venezuela Belgium Sweden Slovakia	Slovenia Argentina (several States) Iceland Ireland Uruguay Israel Chile Columbia Finland Philippines Hungary Australia (several States) Hong Kong	Namibia New Zealand Slovenia Uruguay Chile Philippines	Republic of South Africa Luxembourg Malaysia Bolivia North Korea Bulgaria Swiss Ukraine Japan China
Specific countries	EU member countries	Others	Commonwealth States	
	Germany Malta Austria Italy Czech Cyprus France	Spain (to Brazil, Spanish speaking countries) Canada (Commonwealth States) Portugal (to Brazil, Portuguese speaking countries) Brazil (to Portugal)	Grenada Dominique Mauritius Babeados St. Kitts and Nevies UK Jamaica Australia Ireland	
			Others	
			Portugal (to Portuguese and spanish speaking countries) Brazil (Portugal)	
All countries	Greece Namibia Netherland Norway New Zealand Korea Denmark Morocco USA (several States) Venezuela Belgium Sweden Slovakia	Slovenia Argentina (several States) Iceland Ireland Uruguay Israel Chile Columbia Finland Philippines Hungary Australia (several States) Hong Kong	Namibia New Zealand Slovenia Uruguay Chile Philippines	Republic of South Africa Luxembourg Malaysia Bolivia North Korea Bulgaria Swiss Ukraine Japan China

(continued)

Table 1 (continued)

	Right to vote			X
	Local assembly		National Assembly	
Specific Countries	To EU member states	Others	Commonwealth countries	
Germany Malta Austria Italy Czech Cyprus France	Spain (Brazil, Spanish speaking countries) Canada (Common Wealth Countries) Portugal (Brazil, Spanish speaking countries) Brazil (Portugal) Australia (Commonwealth Countries)	Grenada Dominique Mauritius Barbados Saint Kitts and Nevies UK Jamaica Australia Ireland Antigua and Barbuda		
		Others		
		Portugal (to Portuguese and spanish speaking countries) Brazil (Portugal)		

Source https://en.wikipedia.org/wiki/Right_of_foreigners_to_vote

qualification of their residence (Summary Record of the 363rd Meeting 1953: 12–16). In this case, the migrants are those who fail to meet the residential qualification and may be a reasonable reason for the suffrage restriction. This is a restriction on individuals, not on groups: restrictions on individual migrants, not on migrants as a whole.

The second is the European Convention on Human Rights, which provides that "the Contracting State guarantees free elections by secret elections on a regular basis, and that the exercise of the right to vote should be done on the condition that the free will of electors who choose the legislator is guaranteed." It is not clear with this clause alone whether the suffrage includes migrants. This provision can be interpreted that the state cannot restrict the political activities of minorities in the country or the political platform of political parties from including the development and spread of political programs based on the identity of minorities. In this regard, the clause obliges the state to guarantee their political activities and participation in politics if migrants reside in a country and meet the requirements of residence or become eligible voters by obtaining nationality.

The third is the Inter-American Convention on Human Rights. Article 23 of the Convention is almost similar to the International Covenant on Human Rights, which has developed its own practice in keeping with regional characteristics. It is that the Inter-American Commission on Human Rights has investigated and dealt with violations of provisions in the form of reports. There is no particular comment on who is given suffrage here, and it clearly states that it is human rights for the nation to guarantee its participation in politics and achieve democracy.

In this regard, while international norms so far agree that the nation should guarantee its members' participation in politics, no progress has been found on whether the membership includes migrants. The international norms on suffrage do not reflect the highly developed international migration situation of the 21st century, as they regard contemporary international order based on the nation state.

3   Migratory Regime and Political Rights of Immigrants

There exists a variety of national disputes over the political rights of migrants, and different approaches appear to the suffrage issue. Some countries only grant the right to participate in politics to foreigners who obtain nationality, while others only grant suffrage to foreigners who have special relationships regardless of nationality, while others grant suffrage partly to a set of countries. In this regard, one of the factors influencing the various ways of ensuring political rights for migrants is how migration took place in that country (Kofman et al. 2000: 44).

When it is called a broad-concept migration regime, the nature of the migration regime affects the political empowerment of migrants. By looking at how the political rights of migrants were granted in the process of migration formation, approaches to the issue of recognizing the political rights of migrants in country are expected to gain a number of implications.

In the case of European countries with a long history of migration by accepting immigrants, migration regimes are divided into three main categories. They are guest worker regime, colonial regime, hybrid regime. The guest workers were invited because of the lack of labor force that led to the beginning of the migration, and they were assumed that they would come to work temporarily without thinking of permanently staying in the country and then return back to their motherland. This is the case with Germany. Korea is also very similar with this case.

In the case of Germany, a guest worker's legacy, the roots of the German people from Eastern Europe and the Soviet region accepted many immigrants, even though Germany did not have colonies unlike other European countries at the end of World War II. They included many former citizens of the German Democratic Republic who were deported. In the early 1950s, nearly 12 million Germans, or Germans who lived in Eastern Europe, formerly part of the German Empire, moved to Germany. Between 1953 and 1987, these migrations decreased rapidly to around 37,000 a year. So, post-war Germany, where labor was needed, began to accept foreign migration, especially after the Berlin Wall was built in 1960, when this trend became clearer and based on a bilateral guest worker agreement. The majority of migrant workers entered Germany through state agencies and were placed in workplaces. Initially, labor permits were issued on the basis of a set period of time for a particular job, and they had to work at a designated workplace for a period of time and return home after a set period of time. Even after family reunions were allowed, the dependents of workers who entered Germany for reunion were not given the right to participate in the labor market because temporary residence permits were given, and of course political rights were not given.

The second is the colonial Regime. Before 20th century, many people of colonized countries of Africa came to colonial countries and after the Second World War and the independence from colonial homeland, ex-colonized countries used to have a special relationship with their colonial countries so the people of ex-colonized countries could easily come to colonial countries. In this case, the colonial country tends to guarantee the political rights to immigrants as its citizen. A good example is the United Kingdom, which recognizes various political rights to migrants, like the British people, when they move from a Commonwealth country or Ireland to the United Kingdom.

In the case of colonialism shown in Britain, many Europeans have been accepted due to a lack of labor in Britain since the end of World War II. About 120,000 Polish soldiers who fought in the war during World War II remained in the U.K. after the end of the war, and nearly 100,000 workers from the Baltic and Eastern European countries also remained in the U.K. They were given a one-year work permit and were able to bring along their dependents in the beginning, but soon afterwards they were banned from bringing in their dependents after 1947. Since then, labor migration has been allowed from Austria, Germany, Italy, Spain, etc. in the capacity of foreigners, and work permits have been granted on condition that are somewhat better than those left after the war. The Irish have already continued their labor migration to the UK as it has been in the past. Under the British Nationality Act in 1948, citizens of Caribbean and Commonwealth countries near the Indian Ocean came to Britain to stay and have family. Under the law, citizens of Commonwealth countries could be treated the same as British nationals.

Lastly it is the hybrid regime. This type is represented by France. This type is mixed with colonial regime and guest workers. When the migration occurred at the beginning, the colonialism was affected but the social status of migrants from the colony is like guest worker. It was right after World War II in 1945 that the Office for Immigration in France was established. Here it took care of all the problems with the migration, labor and residence of foreigners. In the early days, because of the care of the decline of population, there was an active policy on migration as a means of addressing the population shortage. As immigration surged, it began to regulate foreign migration since 1955. In the 1970s, when the French economy slowed down, it shifted to a policy that strictly regulated foreign labor migration and allowed only family reunion. French foreign migration policy does not have a single system, but it begins with the immigration from ex-colony, and various systems coexist, including migration from French expatriates and migration under bilateral contracts. By 1962, Algeria was considered part of France, so no work permit or residence was required to move from Algeria to France under the Evian Agreement even after Algeria gained independence. The bilateral agreements with Tunisia, Morocco, Portugal and Spain have therefore been accepted for migration from these countries. With the passage of the Single European Act in 1987 in the European Community, workers from

European Community member states were allowed to move to France without special permission, and then the Maastricht Treaty was signed in 1992, giving EU member states the right to be elected and to vote in local elections. In the process, however, there was considerable debate on granting political rights to non-French nationals.

In this regard, I would like to look at how political rights are recognized in these countries of the three types of migrant regime, plus the political rights in the United States, which are all centered on migrants without the original inhabitants, to find implications for the political rights of Korean immigrants.

3.1 Immigrant State: USA

3.1.1 General Status and Recent Policy Changes

The first thing to think about before we learn about the rights of immigrants in the United States is that America is basically an immigrant nation built by immigrants who came from Europe. Until the 19th century, most people who moved to the U.S. immigrated for the purpose to work, and until the mid-19th century, there was virtually no explicit immigration policy at the federal level (Kim 2017: 93–97). The immigration policy of the British mainland was applied as early as this was, in fact, the migration from Europe to the British colonies rather than immigration. Anyone could immigrate with a simple physical examination, an immigration review and an immigration stamp. From the early 19th century to the early 20th century, the federal government enacted three immigration laws. It enacted a decree prohibiting the entry of socially disadvantaged people such as the disabled, the elderly and the homeless, the Chinese Exclusion Act, or the Act to block the naturalization of Chinese immigrants, and an additional quota system in 1924 under the original nationality of new immigrants. From this conservative immigration policy, the 1965 'Immigration and Nationality Act' was enacted, eliminating all racist elements and establishing an immigration policy based on the concept of immigrant expertise and family reunion.

Secondly, the U.S. is a federal state that begins with 13 states in the east and becomes expanded to the west, prompting states to join the U.S. federal government. That is why the founding process is different from that of a modern nation-state, where a decentralized institutionalized order such as in Europe is consolidated into a centralized state. This is why in USA states have a strong autonomy and have a highly independent political system from the federal government. Therefore, the political rights of immigrants also differ considerably from state to state.

25% of the total American population, or 80 million, are the first or second generation of immigrants and 13% of the total population of foreign-born people. According to 2012/3 statistics, 1.9 million immigrants are naturalized, 13.3 million are legal permanent residents, 11.4 million are illegal aliens and 1.9 million are visa holders. Family members are still the most important legal way to immigrate to permanent residence, and two-thirds of new arrivals from 2011–13. But in 2017, the Trump administration is trying to get rid of such a direct family guest visa.

Despite the implementation of the integrated immigration reform policy after Trump's rule, minors among immigrants without documents are expected to benefit from the labor market through the Defeated Action for Childhood Arrivals (DACA) and related administrative orders. Ordinary immigrants have been approved by Congress to receive job-related English and vocational training programs. Another recent policy change could benefit from a spouse support program for homosexual couples, just like heterosexual couples. The U.S. law enforcement agency confirmed this as an indication that a gay spouse can be invited in the family reunion policy.

3.1.2   Immigrant's Political Rights

Looking at suffrage of immigrants,[1] the immigrants are entitled to vote according to their respective legal status. For example, immigrants who have become naturalized in the United States and obtained citizenship have voting rights for all kinds of elections (federal, state, and local) just like native citizens of the United States. On the other hand, permanent residents are not given the right to vote in most elections. In the case of federal elections—for example, presidential elections—there is no right to vote for permanent residents, whereas in some states and local elections the right to vote is exceptional.

The right to run for office in various kinds of elections is granted in part to citizens only. With regard to the right to vote, the U.S. Constitution specifies that the president is a citizen born in the United States (US Constitution art. II, § 1, Cl. 5), that the federal House of Representatives is "more than seven years after the acquisition of U.S. citizenship," and that the federal Senate is "more than nine years after the acquisition of U.S. citizenship" (US Constitution art. I, § 2, Cl. 2). Therefore, the granting of the right to be elected to non-citizens (e.g., permanent residents) is fundamentally restricted. There has been a political move to give the immigrant group the right to be elected.[2] A case in point is the "Equal Opportunity to Government" or "Hatch Amendment" proposed by Orrin Hatch, a former U.S. senator in 2003, which calls for granting the right to be eligible for the president even to those 20 years after gaining U.S. citizenship.

---

[1] The political rights of groups of immigrants in the U.S. are generally discussed in terms of suffrage and voting rights. Rights such as freedom of assembly and association, for example, other political activities except for them, are regarded as rights as workers rather than as migrants, and are therefore features that are being discussed in the mix with the political rights of ordinary American workers.

[2] It is not too much to say that the expansion of the immigrant's right to be elected as president of US has been fueled by the victory of Arnold Schwarzenegger in the governor's recall election on October 7, 2003 which was started by the fiscal deficit of 340 billion. The qualifications for the U.S. presidential election are as follows: First, age 35 or older based on the time the president takes office; secondly, living in the U.S. for more than 14 years; thirdly, born in the U.S.; fourthly, an American citizen. Schwarzenegger is a U.S. citizen who immigrated to the U.S. in 1968 at the age of 21 and was born in Austria, Governor Schwarzenegger. He received great attention for his speech at the Republican National Convention on August 31, 2004, and he raised a big debate about his eligibility for the presidential election.

American nationality acquisition is based on the principle of territoriality and birth in the United States has American nationality regardless of the nationality of the parents. On the other hand, in the case of foreigners whose parents are not U.S. nationals born abroad, they must first receive legal permanent residency before applying for naturalization. Permanent residency can be applied if the immediate family is an American citizen, or if they are married to an American citizen, and can be applied through a job. After the acquisition of a permanent residency, the conditions of residence must be met, legally in the United States for at least five years and must have been in the state for at least three months at the time of applying for nationality. Finally, in order to apply for U.S. citizenship, one must pass the English test to prove that speaking, writing and reading are possible in English over the age of 18 and have a good moral character, work life at the time of applying for nationality, and pay good taxes.

3.2 The Regime of Colonialism: UK

3.2.1 General Status and Recent Policy Changes

Britain established a Commonwealth system after World War II, establishing relations with existing colonial states in a new framework. The Commonwealth system served as a guarantee for former colonists if they wanted to immigrate to Britain, meaning that until 1962 when the Commonwealth Resident Act was enforced, there was no legal mechanism to restrict the immigration of ex-colonists to Britain. Prior to the implementation of the Commonwealth Resident Act in 1962, ex-colonists were allowed to immigrate from the old to the United Kingdom without any legal restrictions, and since the implementation of the Commonwealth Resident Act, the country has already become a multicultural society in 1962, as the immigration was freely made from the former colonists for nearly two decades since World War II. Since then, the United Kingdom's policy of integration of immigrants has been developed based on two basic principles: cultural diversity and equality of opportunities, which appear in the establishment of a series of racial equality-related legal systems and Commission for Racial Equality (CRE) (Kim 2011: 201–228).

Britain granted political rights to migrants from countries of Commonwealth states such as South Asia, the West Indies, and Africa. Britain not only acknowledged the voting rights in British elections to the people of those former colonies, but also mutually recognized these political rights among the people of Commonwealth member states. In New Zealand, only British soldiers were allowed to vote before 1975, but after one year of residence since 1975, members of the Commonwealth of Nations were registered to participate in parliamentary elections, and Ireland allowed all immigrants who lived for more than six months to vote.

3.2.2   Immigrant's Political Rights

Britain grants immigrants from member-states of the Commonwealth of Nations the right to vote as well as the electoral eligibility in the House of Representatives elections, at the same time, guaranteeing their political rights in local elections to immigrants from EU member states. With the signing of the Maastricht Treaty in 1992, Article 19 of the treaty stated "The right to vote and the right to be elected, in European Parliament elections and the local elections of the country where they reside." As stated in the article, the voting right and the right to be elected in European Parliament elections and the local elections are granted to migrants from European Union member states, while such rights are not granted to those in the general elections of national parliament. In Britain, the provision also gives migrants from European Union member states the right to vote in elections of European Parliament and in local elections.

But no voting rights are granted to migrants from non-EU countries who do not have nationality. On the other hand, it actively guarantees participation of foreign cooperative organizations at the local level, such as the labor union and the commission for racial equality.

In fact, during the long history of immigrants in Britain and their political rights, the significant political influence of its immigrant community is well-known (Marticiello 2002: 89). As migrants have the right to vote, political parties have no choice but to pay attention to their votes in cities because of their large number. Political parties have shown great interest in collecting opinions from migrants, with some having organizations within their parties representing the interests of migrants. It also has a regional commission for racial equality to encourage migrants to participate in the formation of regional immigrant policies. As an autonomous and voluntary organization at the local level, the Commission for Racial Equality works closely with the Committee on Racial Equality, conveying the norms and values of British society to immigrants in the Commonwealth, and at the same time, it is used as a channel to reflect the opinions of migrants in its policies.

Nationality in the UK applies differently in two cases, those born in the UK, and those who are not. For the case of one who is born in the UK, if one of the parents of a British birth person is a British citizen or a permanent resident, the British nationality is automatically obtained by applying the territorial principle, and if the parents are neither British citizen nor permanent resident in the United Kingdom, the British nationality shall be granted only if one kept their residence in the UK until the age of 10 after birth. In this case, they continue to reside in the UK until the age of 10, register at the age of 18, and can be granted with the British citizenship. On the other hand, those who were born outside the country automatically have British citizenship if any of the parents at birth are British citizens, based on the principle of personal. Foreigners married to British nationals have no stipulation on the period of marriage, but are granted British citizenship after a minimum of three years of residence. If both parents are foreigners among those born abroad, they may apply for citizenship after five years of residence in the UK.

3.3 The Guest-Worker Regime: Germany

3.3.1 General Status and Recent Policy Changes

Germany has the largest group of foreigners among European Countries. As the economy grew rapidly after World War II, it accepted many migrant workers from other European countries to make up for the shortage of labor. Migrant workers arrived from countries along the Mediterranean coast such as Italy, Turkey and Greece, followed by more foreigners as their families arrived and their families gave birth to a second generation of migrants, under the influence of the family reunion policy. After the fall of the Berlin Wall, the number of Germans living in the former Soviet Union and East Europe returned to Germany en masse, increasing the number of foreigners even more. Moreover, it accepted a large portion of refugees, leading to a surge in the number of foreigners.

As early settlers entered the country after World War II, they basically settled for a certain period of labor and returned to their home country when their contracts expired. This is why they were considered temporary residents, so it was considered rare for them to remain permanent and the government did not consider them permanent residents or naturalists. So the government recognized migrants as objects of control and management, and refused to recognize their political rights (Lee 2011: 66). In addition, because Germany had their basic premise of pedigreeism in obtaining nationality, temporary residents were burdened with difficult naturalization requirements.

When the Maastricht Treaty was signed in 1992, Article 28 of the Basic Law was amended to grant voting rights to immigrants from European Union member states to Germany in accordance with Article 19 of the Treaty.[3] As foreigners from non-EU countries are not entitled to participate in local elections, the debate over foreigners' right to local elections has become an issue as non-European people are claimed to have the same rights as immigrants from the EU. The debate is causing considerable social repercussions, as 64 percent of non-European nationals are foreigners. However, as opinion polls show that only 31 percent of Germans support the introduction of immigrant's political right in local elections, it is unlikely that the introduction of the right to local elections will take place in the near future (Lee 2010: 64).

Launched in 1998, the left-wing coalition of the Social Democratic Party and the Green Party revised the Nationality Act to make it easier for the children of migrant workers to acquire German citizenship. According to the revised nationality law, if one of the German-born parents was born in Germany or if any of the parents moved to Germany before the age of 14, they were required to obtain German citizenship at the age of 18 (Jang et al. 2008: 77). The Immigration Act, enacted with the revised

---

[3] In the elections of Article 28 (local constitution) of the German Basic Law (a) …the military (Kreis) and the district (Gemeinde), any person who holds the nationality of a member of the European Community shall also have the right to vote and to vote in accordance with the provisions of the European Community Act.

Nationality Act, includes the immigration of workers, expropriation of asylum based on the guarantee of human rights, and social integration. It simplified the type of stay permit to be granted either for a certain period or for an indefinite period and added a social integration program that allows students to take free language courses and social integration courses as an early orientation (Ko et al. 2017: 64–65). In addition, federal policies for integration of migrants were organized by the Immigration Office and the main body responsible for implementing the actual programs of the policies was organized by local governments at each level (Gu 2012: 145).

In 2006, the cabinet of the Christian Democratic Party and the Social Democratic Party recognized the integration of migrants as an important task of the nation and invited representatives from all sectors of society to hold the first National Unification Summit. Based on this, it was declared that the utilization of migrants' capacity was absolutely necessary for the development of Germany and that their social integration should be strengthened.

3.3.2 Migrant's Political Rights

Migrants were brought into Germany by the Gästarbeiter system, which, according to the rotation principle, allowed to temporarily employ foreign workers and allowed them to come to Germany without their families and work alone for a set period of contract and move back to their home country when their contracts expire. Accordingly, Germany did not take any policy on the political rights of migrants, thinking in a strict sense that it was not an immigrant state. Foreign workers gradually invited their families from the early 1970s, and the children of foreign workers were born as foreign workers did not return to their home countries after a certain period of stay, which extended after all, resulting in the emergence of the issue of the social status of the second generation of immigrants. Germany had a bloodline tradition, so it recognized the right of second-generation immigrants who are not of German descent, only to the extent to be educated in school, and did not care about all other rights.

As a result, foreigners were not granted any political rights in Germany, but as in Britain, the Maastricht Treaty was signed in 1992 and Article 19 was applied to domestic law, giving only immigrants from EU member states the right to vote and to be elected in local elections. Except for these rights, no political rights are recognized by other foreigners.

However, even foreigners who do not have German nationality are allowed to join the German party and engage in party activities. Germany's Christian Democratic Party admits foreigners from non-European Union countries to be party members if they prove that they have lived in areas where the German Basic Law applies for more than three years. The Social Democratic Party allows 14 years old or older and those who agree with the party's basic line to join the party, indicating that nationality is not the condition to be qualified for the member of the party. However, according to the German Basic Law, active engagements in parties are in fact meaningless to foreigners because foreigners are not allowed to work as public service.

Meanwhile, Germany grants limited voting rights and rights to be elected to foreigners, but at the same time has set up a foreign advisory committee to encourage the participation in politics for those who do not have any right. Heinz Kühn, from the Social Democratic Party, who is the first foreign affairs officer of the federal government and also a governor of the North Rhine-Westphalia state, submitted a report to the government in 1979 titled "The Status of Integration and Future Development of Foreign Workers and Their Families in Germany." In the report, Kühn stressed the need for a coherent migrant integration policy, arguing that long-term residents should be given local elections to enhance their political rights. According to the report, giving local autonomy to foreign residents will not only lead to an open and active attitude toward immigration policy, but also strengthen self-responsibility to migrants, accelerating the integration process. If it is difficult to introduce local elections, it is recommended to have a "foreign advisory committee" as an alternative. In accordance with this recommendation, the Foreign Advisory Committee system was established. The Committee consists of members elected through direct elections of foreign residents living in the area for up to three months, by each region. Since the Foreign Advisory Committee is established under local government ordinances, the composition, work and authority of the Committee vary among local governments. In the case of Hessen, about 110 foreign representatives are active, and through this Committee, they discuss the problems facing foreigners and pending issues in the community (Lee et al. 2010: 167).

3.4   The Hybrid Regime: France

3.4.1   General Status and Recent Policy Changes

France has long been an immigrant country. It has already accepted many immigrants from neighboring countries from the 19th century and began to accept political refugees in the 20th century. This was mainly because in the Republic of France, the national ideology states that all humans are equal, and human rights are taught to be the most important value that the state should respect, but also, because it required an increase of new population economically and militarily. After World War II, France accepted increased number of foreign workers from Italy and Spain for the sake of satisfaction of population shortage and post-war rehabilitation. Moreover, in 1962, Evian Treaty between France and Algeria allowed both French and Algerians to freely travel between the two countries, which led to a surge of Algerian migration to France. In the earlier days, migrant workers from Italy and Spain, culturally similar to France, were easily assimilated into French society in accordance with the French government's republican assimilation policy. But immigrants from North Africa, migrated after the 1960s, who came from Muslim cultures that differed from French cultural context, were not easily assimilated into French society. In particular, they maintained their culture through their families, and in the 1970s, their families moved and settled together with the family reunion policy, separating them from French society like cultural islands within French society. Such a failure of the French government's Republican assimilation policy was seen also in the social conflict over the wearing of hijab in several public schools. The conflict finally erupted in 2005 in a massive uprising by second-generation immigrants, putting French society at great risk, and increasing negative perceptions of immigrants t o the French as well (Kim 2007: 5–34). In the 1990s, parties like the Front National, which had already advocated anti-immigrationism, began to gain support from many voters. In the first round of the presidential election in 2002, Le Pen, a candidate for the National Front, rose to second place, and in the 2017 presidential election, France's anti-immigrant political sentiment was dominant. The National Front holds more than 20 percent of the votes in various elections, and the party won in several local council elections and took power in several city administration. Other parties that understand the anti-immigration sentiment among voters, and even left-wing parties, cannot help but recognize the anti-immigration policy to some extent.

In France, one of the oldest migration countries in Europe, almost 25 percent of its population has a background of either second-generation immigrants or citizens born abroad. Unlike Britain, France does not have the same system as the Commonwealth, so there is no link with formerly colonized nations. Therefore, even immigrants from formerly colonized countries were not granted the same political rights as the French without French citizenship. Instead, migrants from European Union member states have recognized their rights in local councils since 1992.

Of the non-French nationals residing in France, two-thirds are from countries other than the European Union, and more than 90 percent are from underdeveloped countries. Among the migrant population from non-European member countries, 40 percent are low-educated and 31 percent are high-school graduates, but the portion of college graduates has been on the rise recently.

Since 2012, under the 2011 Besson Loi Act, migrants have the same right to move into rental homes and are granted higher benefits for their children's educational support. Moreover, homosexual couples are also entitled to family reunions.

3.4.2 Migrant's Political Rights

France has maintained its policy on the basis of the principle of a "constitutional tradition of granting voting rights only to those with nationality." Articles 2 and 5 of the French Election Act stated that "the qualifications for elections are 'French people' aged 18 or older, who are not deprived by law their rights and are registered in the electoral register," thus granting voting rights only to immigrants who have obtained French nationality.

The tradition of France, which had only given the right to vote to the French people, marked a significant change along with the progress of European integration. Article 88–3 of the Constitution, revised to reflect the domestic application of the European Union Treaty, states, "People who reside in France, with the nationality from European Union countries, have the right to vote and to be elected in French local elections. Those who belong to these citizens cannot be mayors or vice presidents, nor can they be appointed electors in the Senate elections or participate in the Senate elections," allowing a limited guarantee to the citizens of EU member states to participate in the local elections. However, it excludes the right to vote and the right to run in other elections. In France, permanent residents are not granted suffrage, and other than that, the same benefits are offered as citizens in employment and medical insurance benefits (Kwak 2007: 62). The political rights of EU citizens are more strictly enforced in France than in Britain. Britain has partially expanded its voting rights in consideration of past historical relations, while France guarantees only the minimum right to participate in local elections and European Parliament elections contained in the Maastricht Treaty.

Migrants from non-EU countries have the right to vote in local elections only for residents of more than five years, but they are not allowed to run for election. In this regard, in order to be granted political rights in the case of migrants from non-EU countries, 60% of those from non-EU member states were naturalized according to 2012 statistics.

In France, the immigration policy was changed under the Mitterrand Government in 1981 to allow the association of migrants, ensuring that migrants can be organized for their own interests at work and in their daily lives. Through the measures announced on October 9, 1981, the organization of foreigners was granted the same rights as the organization of the French people. Permission to the migrant association provided both the right to represent the interests of the migrants and the right to receive public funding. Prior to 1981, the political and social demands of immigrants were difficult to express. But this change of French government's policy of allowed almost 4200 of immigrants associations to be established in the mid-1980s (Ireland 2000: 38). Major French cities, such as Paris, Grenoble, Nantes and Strasbourg, have local advisory bodies, representing the opinions of migrants, so that migrants have channels to express their opinions in forming municipal policies.

As a policy for immigrants, six hours of compulsory civil education is given for newly migrated foreigners, which gives them the opportunity to understand French institutions and republican values.

In France, the process of nationalization is divided into those born in France and those born outside France. In the case of French-born children, they should be confirmed to have lived in France for at least five years from the age of 11. The length of this period means that the French public education has been completed in a period of five years, and that the immigrant youth had a period of acquiring French values and French culture, which is a policy that realizes France's republican assimilation policy. French nationals born abroad may be naturalized after five years of residence in France, and foreigners married to a French citizen may obtain French citizenship if they meet the conditions of a marriage for one year or two years after marriage, or for less than one year with 3 years since marriage.

Table 2 The number of immigrants in Korea

	2012	2013	2014	2015	2016	2018
Foreign residents	1,445,103	1,576,034	1,797,618	1,899,519	2,049,441	2,291,653
Longterm residents	1,120,599	1,219,192	1,377,945	1,467,873	–	1,198,900
Shortterm residents	324,504	356,842	419,673	431,646	–	664,360
Illegal residents	177,854	183,106	208,788	214,168	–	323,267

Source https://kosis.kr/statisticsList/statisticsListIndex.do?parentId=A.1&vwcd=MT_ZTITLE&
menuId=M_01_01#content-group (accessed Jan.21 2021)

3.5 Korean Regime of Migration

A lot of labor flew out from Korea to Germany, Vietnam and the Middle East in the 1960s and 1970s, but Korea has been transformed into an influx country since the late 1980s. The number of foreigners staying in Korea rose from 269,641 in 1995 to 747,467 in 2005, and this number during the 10-year period increased 12.5 percent to 910,149 in 2006. It then rose to 1,445,103 in 2012 and 1,797,618 in 2014 before rising to 2,049,441 in 2016 and 2,291,653 in 2018, up 9.26 percent over the past five years. As such, the ratio of foreign residents is estimated to be 3.9 percent of the total population at present and 5.82 percent in 2021. The number of children with migration background also increased at a rapid pace, rising to 207,693 (2015).

The reason for this increase in foreigners is due to the low birth rate and an aging society, the influx of foreign workers and the increase of international marriages, the introduction of the visiting employment system for foreign compatriots, and the increase of Chinese tourists and Korean-Chinese following the free travel drive with China (Table 2).

There are three reasons why Korea has witnessed such a rapid increase in the number of foreign residents. One is the labor shortage caused by rapid economic growth in Korean society. Since the 1970s, Korean society has achieved government-led high-speed economic growth, called the Miracle of the Han River. By the end of the 1980s, Korea was able to raise its own cheap and skilled labor force as a developing country with a high birthrate, thus bringing about economic development without the help of foreign workers, unlike in Western countries. However, as the birthrate has plummeted since the 1990s and labor costs have also become more expensive, demand for foreign workers has grown, mainly from small and medium-sized enterprises. Therefore, the government introduced the policy of the employment-permission for foreign workers which brought many foreign workers to Korea in short term. The second is due to the shortage of women in the marriageable age in rural areas. Due to industrialization, urbanization, the rural population had moved to cities rapidly. Many young people left the countryside in search of jobs, and mostly settled in cities. In accordance with the traditions of the Confucian and agrarian societies, usually daughters left their home for jobs but sons remain and keep their home. As this phenomenon has become more common, rural areas have experienced chronic shortages of women in the prime of marriage. Due to the hard work of farming and the burden of living in non-urban areas which are less developed than in cities, many Korean women are reluctant to marry to their rural bachelor. They have to search their spouses in other less developed countries such as South east Asia. Married immigrants have come to Korea from this peculiarity of Korean society.

The third reason is the increased entry of overseas Koreans, or Korean-Chinese. As the Korean economy develops, Koreans living in China come to Korea looking for work and the Korean government grants them visas for overseas Koreans, or F4, to find work in Korea. Currently, there are 694,319 Korean–Chinese out, or 30 percent of the total immigrants. So, roughly 30 percent of the visiting workers, 30 percent of foreign brides (including their children), and 30 percent of the overseas Koreans, show that the migrants are being divided into three parts.

In view of this composition, Korean immigrant regime is very similar to a German-style guest worker regime. The guest workers are staying in Korea for a certain period of work, while overseas Koreans of the same blood are active in Korea based on *jus sainguinis*. The difference, however, is that marriage immigrants are unique type of migrants, as even at the very early stage of their residence in Korea, they are assumed to live here for good and their children also are assumed to be a part of Korean population.

The rights of immigrants living in Korea differ considerably from those who obtained their nationality and those who did not. Naturalized citizen naturally enjoy all rights like Koreans, but foreigners do not. There is controversy over whether the basic rights guaranteed by the Constitution are guaranteed to foreigners, but the Constitutional Court's ruling has recognized the basic rights of foreigners. For example, the right to pursue human dignity and values and happiness, the right to life, the right to physical instability, freedom of body, freedom of expression, freedom of conscience, freedom of religion, freedom of art, etc. may be protected. In this case, it can be argued whether even for illegal aliens, basic human rights are guaranteed. The claim is that illegal aliens are not eligible for stay but are not excluded from the rights they perceive as human rights.

In relation to political rights, the rights of foreigners are quite limited. As a foreigner aged 19 or older, with three years after having the permanent residency are registered on the foreign registration list of the local community where he or she lives, he or she will only have the right to participate in local elections (Article 15 of the Public Election Act). Although the portion of immigrants with suffrage is still very small among the total voters, the number of foreign suffrage has steadily increased to 6,727 in the fourth local elections in 2006, when suffrage was first granted to immigrants, 11,680 in 2010 and 48,428 in 2014. As of December 2015, the number of permanent residents stood at 97,823, which means that about half of the permanent residents had suffrage. In fact, allowing suffrage in local elections for permanent residents in Korea is strongly influenced by the decision of the central government or the president, who is the ultimate decision maker. In the mid-2000s, when the influx of marriage immigrants from Southeast Asia grew rapidly, the debate on multiculturalism began to gain great social attention, but so far, immigration policies, on immigrant rights and obligations were not the topic of discussion in Korean society. The Act on the Elimination of Foreign Residents was the only legislation other than the Immigration and Immigration Act, which was established in 2007 after the Government Official Election Act granted permanent residents the suffrage in the local elections. In the government at that time, which actively dealt with the value of human rights, the revised Public Official Election Act was also able to pass the National Assembly without organized opposition from established political forces or mainstream citizens in the process of highlighting the universal values of democratization and globalization as democratic government policies.[4] It was the first time in Asia that a permanent resident was granted the right to participate in the local elections at that time, but it is clear that the issue of immigrant political participation in Korea began in a hurry, not linked to the progress of immigration policy dealing with immigration policy as a whole. So The turnout for permanent residents is not very high. According to a study that has observed their turnout since 2006 (Cho 2016), 70% of naturalized citizen participated the election, while only 19 percent of permanent residents voted in elections. The reason for their low participation in the vote is that their political apathy is large, but their low level of social integration makes them have low level of knowledge of politics or less interested in politics.

Under these circumstances, what is discussed in the political participation of migrants is that three years after the acquisition of permanent residency is required. The debate is whether it is necessary to allow foreigners who have five years to earn permanent residency and are capable of making a living which is a condition for obtaining permanent residency, to wait another three years. Saying that suffrage is an essential factor in social integration, it is an argument that there is no need to have a three-year grace period to facilitate social integration of foreigners who have obtained permanent residency.

The second is that the turnout for foreigners with voting rights is too low. The reason for this low level is that they have less interest in the community and their vote efficacy is very low. It means that it is hard to expect their vote to change local politics. Given this situation, prerequisites that can enhance their vote efficacy will be needed. For example, it would be more effective to open the way for foreigners who can directly represent their opinions in politics through the organization of consultative committees such as the Foreign Advisory Committee of Germany, which is composed with the direct delegation of foreigners.

4   Conclusion

Since 21st century, international movement accelerates and more and more are residing in foreign countries, their periods vary considerably, their types of settlements diverse and their purposes differ. From an era when the migration was as a

---

[4]The discussion of granting suffrage to permanent residents of Japan in elections for local governments at that time has also developed as a point of criticizing the Japanese government for its lack of suffrage.

result of imperialism in the past or to migration as a movement of manpower for labor, it is becoming an era in which migrants and aborigines from various forms of migration live together. It is true that this change in the characteristics of migration is also changing the rights of immigrants considerably. As shown in the example of the United States, in a country where immigrants are mostly composed of their population, all rights have been granted as a result of the acquisition of citizenship (naturalization) due to immigration. As shown in the example of Germany, it was quite difficult for immigrants who had moved to Germany after born in foreign country to have the same rights as the Germans. However, recent changes in the characteristics of migration are increasingly being given the right in the form of a mix of *jus sainguinis* and *jus Soli*, and the requirements for citizenship acquisition are increasingly being simplified (Joppke 2017: 393). For Western European countries, which already have a long history of immigration, the clear standard between civil rights and non-citizen rights has become quite vague. Basic civil rights 'liberty', 'property.', 'safety'—art.2 of the French Declaration on the human and civil rights— was originally for citizen but they are not any more exclusively applied to citizen and they are assumed to everybody who lives within the reach of state. Social rights, especially in the labor market participation such as insurance for industrial accidents and unemployment benefits or health, pension rights are not any more limited to citizens. The welfare state principle of the Western countries is basically based on its territoriality (Joppke 2017). Personal benefits as a 'right' of the modern welfare state is not 'mercy' of the country but personal 'right.' That is because based on the traditional territory, a given right to all individuals residing in its territory. In this sense in the modern nation state civil and social rights of individual are not exclusively for citizens but for everyone who resides within the territory of the nation state.

So what happens to political rights? In fact, Britain's 'taxpayer government,' political rights were a last safety valve to guarantee civil and social rights of taxpayer. Without political rights, civil and social rights can not be kept. In this regard, it seems unreasonable to guarantee individual rights within the territory only through naturalization, as migration is becoming more prevalent and the nature of migration is diversified today. That is why many countries in Europe are gradually making policy changes to allow non-naturalized foreigners to have political rights.

The argument for granting suffrage to migrants is based on several logics. First, they can promote their assimilation within a living community and they can be recognized basic rights to the extent that they do not harm the assimilative integration of original people. As the Keen Report of Germany revealed, the political participation of immigrants contributes to the social integration of immigrants, and the social integration of immigrants can be used for social development, which is quite positive for the entire nation. The second argument is that the right to express opinions within one's community is a basic human right. Immigrants become members of the community, either working or settling down in the community. They argue that having the opportunity to express their opinions as a member of the community is a basic human right regardless of nationality. Especially between immigrants from European Union member states and non-European immigrants, it is a violation of human basic rights to be discriminated against for the reason of a country from which they did not choose, despite their common status in Europe.

On the other hand, however, foreign examples show that there is still a contestation against foreigner's voting. Their argument is that the right to vote is the basic right exercised only by the people of the country, so if a foreigner truly has an attachment to the country, it is desirable to prove it through naturalization and exercise his or her right to vote after naturalization. In the end, they argue that if foreigners are allowed to vote, the motivation for naturalization will disappear. The second argument is that allowing foreigners to vote could cause the nation to be divided by conflicting interests of foreigners with those of originals. This argument is based on nationalist ideology, which is predicated on the people as a unit and a driving force of the nation.

Given this, giving foreigners full voting rights may be premature in present when the boundaries of the nation state are still clear, as is shown above yet. However, in the local elections, which deal with the issue of a more living-problem and directly community matter in which they reside, it is a matter to be seriously discussed in terms of determining the problems of the community based on residents, transcending their nationality. It is also an advantage to note that granting voting rights to migrants in local elections will give them more interest in their community, and that assimilation and integration into the community can be achieved at a faster pace. In the same vein, it is expected that the granting of suffrage to immigrants with three years after acquiring permanent residency in Korea will have a positive effect on the social integration of immigrants. In addition, through foreign examples, the primary task could be to think about ways to hear the opinions of immigrants by providing them with a way to express their opinions, such as setting up a foreign advisory body.

References

Korean

Cho, Y.-H. (2016). "The Relationship between Election and Voting Participation and Immigration Policy of Immigrants in Korea". *Issue Brief*, IOM.

Gu, C.-K. (2012). "Increase in migration and change in German immigrant policy". *International Area Studies, 21*(1).

Jang, M.-H. et al. (2008). *Building a Policy Paradigm for the Transformation into a Multiracial Culture Society: Policies for the Promotion of Multicultural Competence, Current Status of Social Practices and Direction of Development*, Seoul: Women's Policy Institute.

Kim, M. (2007). "France's Immigration Policy: Success and Failure of the Republican Aging Policy". *Journal of World Area Studies, 25*(3).

Kim, T.-G. (2017). "History and prospect of U.S. immigration policy". *International Social Security Review, 1*.

Kim, Y.-C. (2011). "Study on the political rights of British and French migrants". *Journal of the Korean Political Parties Association, 10*(1).

Ko, S., Kim, M., & Kim, S.-J. (2017). *Live-Cycle Language and Culture Education Policy for Resolving Conflicts of Immigrants*. Seoul: Economic and Human Society Research Council.

Kwak, W.-S. (2007). *Comparison of Diversity Between Countries in Strategies for the Integration of Immigrants*. Master Thesis at Hanyang University.

Lee, B.-H. (2014). "International human rights rules and Korean migrant human rights". *Journal of the 21st Century Political Science Association, 24*(1).

Lee, K.-Y., & Kim, K.-M. (2010). "Germany's policies on migrants and suffrage of migrants". *International Regional Studies, 42*(2).

Lee, S.-W. (2011). "The suffrage of immigrants in the Multicultural Era". *Journal of Daehan Political Science Association, 19*(2).

Lee, Y.-H. (2013). "Studies on the possibility of introducing the elections of Chongju Foreigners". *Digital Policy Studies, 11*(3).

English

Gurowitz, A. (1999). "Mobilizing international norms: Domestic actors, immigrants and the Japanese state". *World Politics, 51*(3).

Ireland, P. (2000). "Reaping What They Sow: Institutions and Immigrant Political Participation in Western Europe". In R. Koopmans, P. Statham (eds.), *Challenging Immigration and Ethnic Relations Politics*. Oxford: Oxford University Press.

Joppke, C. (1998). "Why liberal states accept unwanted immigration". *World Politics, 50*(2).

Joppke, C. (2017). "Citizenship in immigration states". In A. Shachat, R. Bauböck, I. Bloemraad, 7 M. Vink (eds.), *The Oxford Handbook of Citizenship*, Oxford: Oxford University Press.

Kofman, E., Phizacklea, A., Raghuram, P., & Sales, R. (2000). *Gender and International Migration in Europe*. London and New York: Routledge.

Marshall, T. (1950). *Citizenship and Social Class*, Cambridge: Cambridge University Press.

Marticiello, M. (2002). "Political Participation, mobilisation and representation of immigrants and their offspring in Europe". In Rainer Bauböck (ed.), *Migration and Citizenship*, Amsterdam: Amsterdam University Press.

Soysal, Y. N. (1994). *Limits of Citizenship: Migrants and Postnational Membership in Europe*. Chicago:The University of Chicago Press.

Summary Record of the 363rd Meeting, *UN ESCOR Commission on Human Rights, 9th Sess, 363rd mtg (1953)*. http://www.mipex.eu/political-participation. Accessed 2019 Nov 28.

The Nexus Between Foreign Labor Policy and Human Trafficking in Taiwan

Wen-Chih Huang

Abstract Since 1986, the "push" and "pull" factors of "Migration Law" are generally used to explain the flux of immigration. Taiwan began to import guest workers in 1989 to alleviate a labor shortage. Whereas, the Taiwan government is generally reluctant to publicly recognize her dependency on unskilled migrant laborers, foreign labor policy is set for the purpose of fulfilling the economic and social needs of the country. Foreign workers are introduced to "supplement" the labor force in limited trades and quantities instead of "replacing" domestic laborers. Ironically, the total number of guest workers in Taiwan hit a record high of 714,291 in September 2019. Taiwan's National Immigration Agency reported that 1,815 cases of trafficking were uncovered from January 2007 to September 2019. Seven hundred sixty-two of these cases involved forced labor (42%) and one thousand and fifty-three cases (58%) involved sexual exploitation. The nexus between foreign labor policy and human trafficking is evidenced in several articles in which the victims of trafficking were interviewed. They were mostly guest workers or foreign spouses of guest workers from Mainland China and Southeast Asian countries. Although Taiwan was ranked on US Trafficking Victims Protection Act's Tier 1 country since 2010, the mindset and flawed procedures of foreign labor policy continuously depleted the opportunities for guest workers to legally migrate to Taiwan. Using guest workers' desperation to seek better lives, traffickers and brokers exploited them without detection by criminal justice agencies. The commonly used methods are (a) fraudulent marriages, (b) legal work permits, (c) undocumented workers, (d) tourist or student visas, and (e) fishermen working on fishing vessels. Fuchs' study found the factors of foreign labor policy heavily contributing to human trafficking including, but not limited to: (a) high placement fees and security bonds, (b) unreasonable brokers' fees and pay deductions, (c) poor working conditions, and (d) positions of vulnerability. Although the Taiwan government has made legal progress to amend Article 52 of the Employment Service Act, Taiwan government's policy-makers need to change their mindsets about guest workers no longer "supplementing" the shortage of domestic labor, instead they are "replacing" the domestic labors. The Ministry of Labor needs to re-consider and re-shape the philosophy behind guest workers' legal positions

W.-C. Huang (✉)
Department of Border Police, Central Police University, Taoyuan City, Taiwan
e-mail: huang.billyhuang@gmail.com

© The Author(s), under exclusive license to Springer Nature Singapore Pte Ltd. 2021
C.-P. Chu and S.-C. Park (eds.), *Immigration Policy and Crisis in the Regional Context*,
https://doi.org/10.1007/978-981-33-6823-1_4

and take legal actions to more seriously reform the recruitment mechanism, a (the) brokerage system, and the working regulations to prevent and protect the victims of human trafficking in Taiwan.

Keywords Taiwan · Foreign labor policy · Human trafficking · Guest worker · Broker system

1 Introduction

Taiwan is located off the southeast coast of China and north of the Philippine Islands. Its unique geographical location creates a main international transport hub for business and travel in East Asia. Since 1986, there have been indications that Taiwan has been experiencing a rapid increase in immigration. The "push" and "pull" factors originating from the global migration law are used to explain the influx of immigration. Taiwan's economic development and the policies in the labor market act as major pull factors, then turn to push factors—attracting legal and illegal immigration. Taiwan achieved substantial economic growth during the past five decades. Traditional labor-intensive industries are steadily being moved off-shore—replaced with more capital- and technology-intensive, as well as creative, industries. Taiwan underwent a series of economic restructurings which created labor shortages in certain sectors. In addition, expansion of secondary, trade/technical and tertiary education have resulted in sectoral shortages of labor. The supply of transferable labor (from agriculture to either industrial or service sectors) has been depleted. The decline in the birth rate since 1952 means that even fewer workers were available to enter the labor force (Huang 2018, p. 225).

Due to globalization effects, the growing inequality of wealth within and between countries is increasing both the push and pull factors—thus leading more people to make the decision to immigrate and emigrate. Labor migration thus grew fast in Southeast Asia in the 1980s, as workers from poorer countries sought difficult, but low-paid, jobs in neighboring countries. Remittances the guest workers send home have often helped their home countries' economies (*The Economist*, January 2007). In 1989, driven by the strong demand of economic growth, Taiwan started importing more guest workers to alleviate labor shortages in the manufacturing sectors. In Article 42 of Taiwan's Employment Service Act (ESA) of 1992, it states "*For the purpose of protecting nationals' right to work, no employment of foreign workers may jeopardize nationals' opportunities in employment, their employment terms, economic development or social stability.*" Furthermore, according to the Bureau of Employment and Vocational Training, Taiwan's foreign labor policy is set "*for the purpose of fulfilling the economic and social needs of the country; foreign workers are introduced to meet the labor shortages in limited trades and quantities*" (Fuchs 2011, p. 17). Based on *Fuchs*' doctrine, Taiwan's government has continuously promoted "limited trades and quantities" for foreign workers, reducing the opportunities for regular migration—thereby resulting in opportunities for traffickers to operate.

Specifically, this paper introduces a series of statistics to provide background information on foreign labor policy and human trafficking in Taiwan. To better appreciate our point, we first define the key concepts of human trafficking as defined by the UN Palermo Convention and Taiwan's Human Trafficking Prevention Act (HTPA). The following provides empirical findings in literature which shed light on trafficking's patterns and trends and the methods used by the traffickers. These factors of foreign labor policy drafted by the Taiwanese government not only limit the sectors in which and quantities of what the guest workers can do, but also are flawed in the recruitment procedure which heavily contributes to the vulnerability positions of human trafficking's victimization. Although the Taiwan government has made some progress in preventing trafficking, prosecuting perpetrators, and protecting the trafficked victims, the most difficult part of reducing human trafficking in Taiwan is to challenge foreign labor policy which is that which the government is most reluctant to do. Finally, there is a canvass of the challenges and the transformation of them into our policy recommendations for the future research.

1.1 Statistics of Guest Workers in Taiwan

Currently Taiwan is facing an aging population and low birth rate—as well as the need for high-quality manpower in a globalized economy. To address Taiwan's needs and to establish a mechanism to gain and retain high-quality foreign labor, Taiwan's foreign labor policy and immigration policy has been amended several times. The number of guest workers has continued to increase since 1989, according to Taiwan's Ministry of Labor (MOL). The total number of guest workers in Taiwan registered at the end of September 2019, climbed to 714,291, an increase of 2.2% over the same period last year (see Table 1). Among the top three nationalities are guest workers from Indonesia, numbering 273,605 (38%), from Vietnam, numbering 224,040 (31%), and from the Philippines numbering 156,248 (22%). These top three nationalities comprise 90% of guest workers. In terms of gender, women account for the majority, at 386,000 workers (54.3%), while there are 325,000 male workers (45.7%).

Guest workers are mainly divided into two categories: production workers and service workers. According to subparagraph 8–10, paragraph 1, Article 46 of Taiwan's Employment Services Act (ESA) of 1992, the work that a foreign worker may be employed to engage in within Taiwan is limited to the following sectors: (a) marine fishing/netting work, (b) household assistant and nursing work, and (c) workers designated by the Central Competent Authority in response to national major construction project(s) or economic/social development needs. The sectors of production which used guest workers include four categories of agriculture, forestry, fishing, animal husbandry, and manufacturing. The detailed sectors of manufacturing for which guest workers can be recruited are illustrated on Table 2—which includes guest workers' population distribution in each sector and their nationalities.

As for production workers, 454,266 (63.6%) work in manufacturing, construction, and agriculture. Over 70% of workers in these sectors are male and 75.9% are

Table 1 Nationalities of guest workers in Taiwan

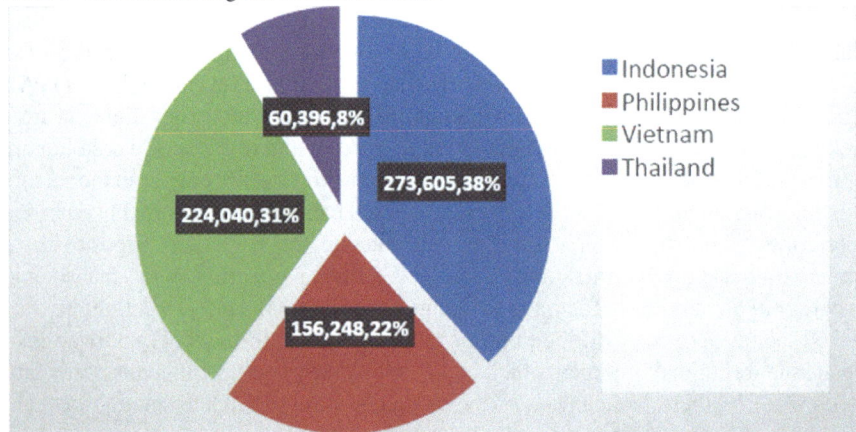

Data Source Statistics from Taiwan's Ministry of Labor, dated September 30, 2019

under the age of 35. The top three nationalities in order of population numbers are Vietnamese at 195,469 (43%), Filipinos at 124,910 (27.4%), and, Indonesians at 73,929 (see Table 3).

Service work mainly provides domestic care and service, accounting for 260,025 (36.4%) workers. Of this group, 99.3% are women, and 44.1% are aged between 35 and 44. Top three nationalities in order of population numbers are Indonesians at 199,676 (76.7%), Filipinos at 31,338 (12%), Vietnamese at 28,571 (10.9%) (see Table 4).

Taiwan's cities with the most guest workers involved in manufacturing, construction, and agriculture were Taoyuan (93,000), Taichung (79,000), and, New Taipei City (56,000). The cities with the most guest workers involved in domestic care and services were Taipei at 44,000 and New Taipei City at 43,000 (Taiwan DGBAS 2019).

1.2 Statistics of Human Trafficking in Taiwan

Human trafficking is said to be the fastest growing source of income for organized crime—exceeded only by drugs and arms trade (Obuah 2006). A study estimates that at least 12 million people worldwide are trapped in conditions of forced labor. Around a fifth of these are being exploited as a result of human trafficking (ILO 2005). As stated in US Trafficking in Persons Report (TIP Report 2010), most trafficking victims in Taiwan are workers from Vietnam, Indonesia, Thailand, and the Philippines—employed through recruitment agencies and brokers to perform low-skilled work in Taiwan's manufacturing industries and as home caregivers and domestic workers. According to the report, Taiwan is considered a destination country for

Table 2 Guest workers in production and service by industries and nationality

Unit: Person

Industry	End of September 2019						
	Grand total	Indonesia	Philippines	Thailand	Vietnam	Others
Grand total	714,291	273,605	156,248	60,396	224,040	2
Agriculture, forestry, fishing and animal husbandry	12,382	9,223	1,699	30	1,430	–
Manufacturing	437,592	64,275	123,199	57,253	192,864	1
Food products and prepared animal feeds	29,063	5,295	4,348	3,333	16,087	–
Beverages	954	180	168	129	477	–
Textiles	25,467	5,026	4,826	5,090	10,525	–
Wearing apparel and clothing accessories	4,715	348	631	413	3,323	–
Leather, fur and related products	2,368	388	104	485	1,391	–
Wood and of products of wood and bamboo	3,037	946	266	142	1,683	–
Paper and Paper products	6,655	1,789	849	827	3,190	–
Painting and reproduction of recorded media	4,073	552	444	502	2,575	–
Petroleum and coal products	39	13	2	1	23	–
Chemical materials, fertilizers, and nitrogen compounds, plastic, and rubber materials, man-made fibres	4,736	505	1,756	799	1,676	–
Other chemical products	3,351	847	804	321	1,379	–
Pharmaceuticals and medicinal chemical products	1,075	250	407	34	384	–
Rubber products	10,890	1,731	985	2,072	6,102	–
Plastic products	30,019	5,165	4,024	4,451	16,379	–
Other non-metallic mineral products	12,062	2,419	2,150	2,768	4,725	–

(continued)

Table 2 (continued)

Unit: Person

Industry	End of September 2019					
	Grand total	Indonesia	Philippines	Thailand	Vietnam	Others
Basic metals	20,104	4,454	3,627	6,076	5,946	1
Fabricated metal products	100,141	17,627	14,456	13,993	54,065	–
Electronic parts and components	71,445	1,344	56,268	3,447	10,386	–
Computer, electronic and optical products	15,463	113	11,698	215	3,437	–
Electrical equipment	9,248	1,516	1,769	1,340	4,623	–
Machinery and equipment	40,521	5,685	6,484	4,642	23,710	–
Motor vehicles and parts	14,963	2,802	2,742	2,704	6,715	–
Other transport equipment and parts	9,988	1,809	919	2,096	5,164	–
Furniture	5,294	1,380	714	431	2,769	–
Others	11,910	2,091	2,758	942	6,119	–
Construction	4,292	431	12	2,674	1,175	–
Human health and social work activities and other service activities	260,025	199,676	31,338	439	28,571	1

Source Workforce Development Agency, MOL

Note 1. Data series from 2016 refer to Standard Industrial Classification System of R.O.C., Rev.10

2. "Others" in Nationality includes Malaysia, Mongolia, and other countries

3. "Others" in manufacturing includes Other manufacturing, manufacture of Tobacco products and materials recovery

Table 3 Nationalities of production guest workers in Taiwan

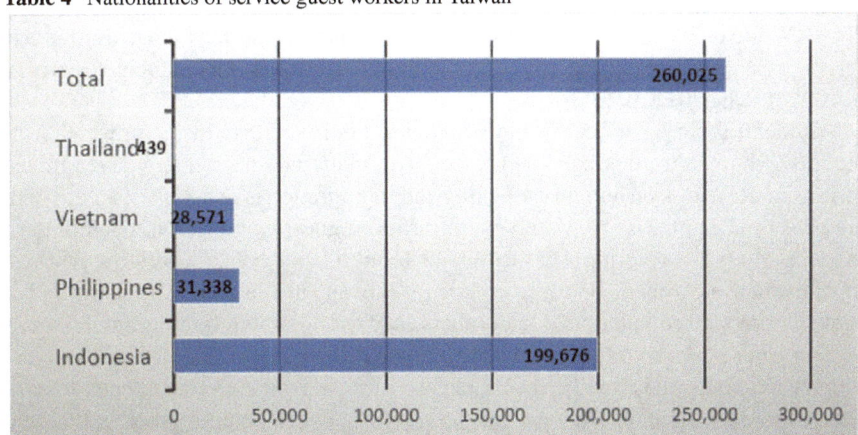

Data Source Statistics from Ministry of Labor, dated September 30, 2019

Table 4 Nationalities of service guest workers in Taiwan

Data Source Statistics of Ministry of Labor, dated September 2019

human trafficking. Women and men are trafficked for the purposes of forced sexual and labor exploitation.

The statistics of Taiwan National Immigration Agency (NIA) reported that 1,815 cases of trafficking were uncovered from 2007 until the end of September 2019. 762 of these cases involved forced labor (42%) and 1053 cases (58%) involved sexual exploitation (see Table 5). Unfortunately, it is not known how many of the cases prosecuted finally were found to be cases of human trafficking and what laws were applied.

Table 5 Trends of human trafficking between 2007 and 2019 in Taiwan

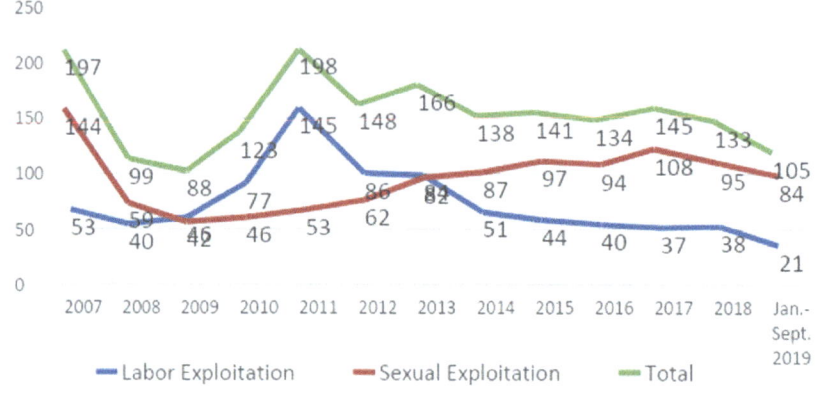

Source National Immigration Agency, Taiwan, dated September 30, 2019

Meanwhile, looking at the convictions of human trafficking cases in 2009, around 68% of the prison sentences were of less than 6 months duration (compared to 63% in 2008). While in 2008 only two out of 287 defendants in suspected human trafficking-related cases were sentenced to prison terms of 7–15 years; this number rose to 13 in 2009 (Fuchs 2011, p. 3).

Although there have been some significant improvements in the prevention of victims of human trafficking (VoT) since 2010, many victims remain unrecognized in Taiwan. Research on human trafficking and immigration is relatively scarce. There are no estimates of possible numbers of trafficked guest workers. On the ground of that, this study is exploring what factors of foreign labor policy lead guest workers (documented as well as undocumented) in Taiwan into human trafficking and if some workers more vulnerable than others. A close look will be given to Taiwan's foreign labor policies to see how these might contribute to the risk for guest workers to become VoT. And, finally, this paper will provide policy recommendations to address these problems arising with the nexus between foreign labor policy and human trafficking in the end.

2 Literature Review

2.1 Definitions

Trafficking in human beings is a complex term that includes trafficking for sexual exploitation as well as forced labor and the removal of organs. In Taiwan, trafficking in persons was criminalized by enacting Human Trafficking Prevention Act (HTPA) in 2009. Taiwan's trafficking legislation is formulated to a large extent, according to the Palermo Protocol adopted by the United Nations in 2000 in Palermo, Italy. This became effective in December 2003, and, up to now, has been signed b y 117 countries to "Prevent, Suppress and Punish Trafficking in Persons, especially Women and Children." This UN protocol is the first global legally-binding instrument with an agreed definition of trafficking (Fuchs 2011, p. 2). In Article 3 (a) of the Protocol, trafficking in persons means as follows:

> "Trafficking in persons" shall mean the recruitment, transportation, transfer, harboring or receipt of persons, by means of the threat or use of force or other forms of coercion, of abduction, of fraud, of deception, of the abuse of power or of a position of vulnerability or of the giving or receiving of payments or benefits to achieve the consent of a person having control over another person, for the purpose of exploitation. Exploitation shall include, at a minimum, the exploitation of the prostitution of others or other forms of sexual exploitation, forced labor or services, slavery or practices similar to slavery, servitude or the removal of organs.

In accordance to the Palermo Protocol, Taiwan's HTPA enacted on January 23, 2009 and effective since June 1, 2009, has similar definitions on means, processes, and purposes of human trafficking:

> To recruit, trade, take into bondage, transport, deliver, receive, harbor, hide, broker, or accommodate a local or foreign person, by force, threat, intimidation, confinement, monitoring, drugs, hypnosis, fraud, purposeful concealment of important information, illegal debt bondage, withholding important documents, making use of the victim's inability, ignorance or helplessness, or by other means against his/her will, for the intention of subjecting him/her to sexual transactions, labor to which pay is not commensurate with the work duty, organ harvesting; or to use the above-mentioned means to impose sexual transactions, labor to which pay is not commensurate with the work duty, or organ harvesting on the victims.

2.2 Drivers of Human Trafficking

As mentioned above, the growing, but unsatisfied, demand for legal migration options has created a breeding ground for smuggling networks and other criminal organizations, which have learned to make a huge profit from people's desire to work abroad. A fundamental breeding ground for trafficking and exploitation is the economic situation of people in poorer regions of the world, pushing vulnerable people to emigrate and seek better opportunities abroad (Bruckert and Parent 2002; Chand 2008).

Migration has become a multibillion-dollar industry that can be particularly lucrative for criminals willing to use physical violence and restraint. By stressing the close link between trafficking and migration, many recent media and policy reports frequently point to lack of legislation and law enforcement, poor border controls, bribery and corruption, or insufficient education as drivers of human trafficking. These factors certainly exacerbate the trafficking problem, but may not explain it at its core. Trafficking occurs where migration flows are largest—not in remote regions with little or no migration. More specifically, regional migration prevalence rates and other proxies of migration pressure are the key predictors of the incidence of human trafficking on the household level. The prevalence of illegal migration patterns appears to increase trafficking risks and awareness campaigns can play a successful role in reducing trafficking risks (Mahmoud and Trebesch 2009).

Using a unique new dataset of 5,513 households from Belarus, Bulgaria, Moldova, Romania, and Ukraine, Mahmoud and Trebesch (2009) found migrant families in high-migration areas and with larger migrant networks are much more likely to have a trafficked victim among their members. They argued that migration pressure, combined with informal migration patterns and incomplete information, are the key determinants of human trafficking.

2.3   Research Findings

Wang (2011) asserts that Taiwan's current immigration policy is based on three ideologies: the patriarchal *jus sanguinis* principle, population quality, and national security. The result is a contradictory policy for marriage and labor migration. As regards the former, many Taiwanese men try to find wives from overseas, while the government strictly controls the entry of 'low quality' women from China and Southeast Asia. In the same manner, the policy allows high-skilled labor to move freely in and out of Taiwan, while it restricts the stay of blue-collar guest workers.

The National Immigration Agency conducted a study in 2006 which found that victims were trafficked to Taiwan through legal work permits, marriages, fraudulent marriages, illegal immigration, or tourist visas (Huang 2007). In order to further explore the means and types of exploitation traffickers used, two studies were later conducted. *Chen* collected data on 81 female VoT in Taiwan between November 2007 and June 2008, while Fuchs (2011) collected data on 74 suspected VoT who were either residents in *NGO* shelters in Hsinchu, Zhongli or Kaohsiung or they were being held in detention centers between December 2009 and February 2010. The two studies reported similar findings concerning the patterns of human trafficking. While Chen found more patterns of human trafficking in Taiwan, the most commonly used methods of traffickers reported by the two studies were alike. In Fuchs' study, out of the 74 persons, 62 are women and 12 are men. 48 workers (all of them female) entered Taiwan with a legal work contract, 26 persons (14 women and 12 men) came to Taiwan using fraudulent marriage certificates or tourist/student visas or with no visa at all. Out of those 48 women, 39 came to Taiwan as caregivers or domestic workers, 8 as factory workers and one as a fisherman. Also, of these 48 women, 14 were identified as VoT during a period of legal employment, while the other 34 were undocumented workers. Of the persons who came to Taiwan without a legal work contract, nine used fraudulent marriages to obtain visas, eight (five women and three men) entered Taiwan as students or tourists and nine (all men) came without any visa. When looking at trafficking-related employment, Fuchs found that the biggest group is in the entertainment/prostitution sector. Other employment areas include farming, care-giving, hotel/restaurant work and fishing. Four of the women were found to be VoT not because of their work but because of debt bondage. Not all the 74 study participants were recognized as VoT by Taiwan's government agencies. Seven

Indonesian fishermen who were considered VoT by the NGOs were not officially recognized as such. Fuchs assumes the data may not reflect a complete picture of the human trafficking situation of guest workers in Taiwan but rather may give a partial impression and some general insights (Fuchs 2011, pp. 4–5).

Huang (2017) categorizes different patterns of existing trafficking in women and girls in Taiwan by using the court proceedings of prosecuted trafficking in women and girls under Taiwan's *HTPA* from 2009 to 2012. Her analysis is based on 37 court cases, involving 195 victimized women and girls and 118 perpetrators. She identifies six forms of Human Trafficking victims according to their country of origin, vulnerability status, and means of transport. This study found that women and girls suffer from both labor and sexual exploitation, from mainly—domestic male perpetrators. While sexual exploitation is more evenly distributed among citizens and immigrants and affects both adults and minors, labor exploitation seems to be an exclusive phenomenon among women guest workers in the data. Human Trafficking cases in Taiwan share many of the similarities of human trafficking, which is highly associated with gender inequality and gender-based vulnerability, in other regions.

Goehrung (2019) examines data on 1,342 human trafficking apprehensions and 2,908 prosecutions from 2009 to 2018. Trends in this data are compared with demographic characteristics of 269 victims of trafficking and the results of interviews with immigration officials, police, and legal professionals conducted by other scholars from 2010 to 2015. Goehrung found that low conviction rates, relatively minor punishments, and an under-emphasis on labor trafficking indicates that the criminal justice approach may have limited efficacy in cases beyond foreign sex trafficking. He concludes with an exploration of potential immigration reforms that might better situate Taiwan and other similar states to more effectively address this pandemic.

3 Human Trafficking in Taiwan

3.1 Trafficking in Persons Report

The U.S. Congress passed the Trafficking Victims Protection Act (TVPA) in October 2000 to declare that trafficking in persons is a serious violation of human rights. TVPA proposes severe punishment of the traffickers, protection of the victims, and prevention of future offences. According to Section 110 of the TVPA (2000), the U.S. Department of State needs to send a Trafficking in Persons Report (TIP Report) to the U.S. Congress annually, describing foreign governments' efforts to eliminate severe forms of trafficking in persons. The US Department of State evaluates whether a country fully complies with the TVPA's minimum standards for the elimination of trafficking and places it into one of four ranks: Tier 1, Tier 2, Tier 2 Watch List, and Tier 3. Countries which fully comply with the minimum standards are ranked as Tier 1, while countries that do not fully comply with the minimum standards but are making significant efforts to do so are ranked Tier 2. A Tier 2 Watch List was added to the tier rankings in the TVPA of 2003. Countries are ranked as Tier 2 Watch List when their governments do not fully comply with the minimum standards but are making significant efforts to do so when one of the Tier 3 criteria exists: "*(a) the absolute number of victims of severe forms of trafficking is very significant or is significantly increasing; (b) there is a failure to provide evidence of increasing efforts to combat severe forms of trafficking in persons from the previous year; or, (c) the determination that a country is making significant efforts to bring themselves into compliance with minimum standards was based on commitments by the country to take additional future steps over the next year...*" (TIP Report 2013, p. 47). Lastly, countries are ranked as Tier 3 when they do not comply with the minimum standards and are not making significant efforts to do so (TIP Report 2013).

Taiwan was a Tier 1 country from 2001 to 2004 (TIR Reports 2001, 2003, 2004). However, Taiwan became a Tier 2 country in 2005 because Taiwan did not properly identify victims of trafficking and placed some victims in detention centers (TIP Report 2005). The TIP Report (2005) also indicated that Taiwan did not provide legal alternatives other than repatriation, and lacked a comprehensive anti-trafficking law to protect and assist victims (TIP Report 2005). Taiwan fell to Tier 2 Watch List in 2006 mainly because the government had not yet drafted a comprehensive anti-trafficking law to prosecute all forms of human trafficking (particularly forced labor) and to protect VoT (TIP Report 2006). Taiwan's brokers and/or employers used workers' large recruitment fees as a tool to coerce them into forced labor, and if the brokers and/or employers were later found guilty of exploiting guest workers, they received only administrative fines (TIP Report 2006). Moreover, over half of the guest workers in Taiwan were caregivers and domestic helpers but they were not protected by the Labor Standards Law (TIP Report 2006). Lastly, victims of trafficking were not properly identified, were even punished for their criminal acts which were direct results of being trafficked, and there were no shelters specifically designed for them (TIP Report 2006).

The poor ranking spurred the Taiwan government to take actions. Taiwan returned to Tier 2 in 2007 and remained so until 2009. Although Taiwan passed the National Action Plan (NAP) to show its determination to combat human trafficking, the 2007 TIP Report criticized Taiwan for being in need of a comprehensive anti-trafficking law to criminalize all forms of trafficking and related acts. The TIP Reports (2007, 2008, 2009) indicated that Taiwan did not properly identify victims, not only categorizing them as illegal immigrants or workers but also placing them in over-crowded detention facilities in which very limited services were provided. "Runaways" (i.e., guest workers who decided to escape from their legal employers) were treated as criminals and subjected to punishment and deportation without being considered victims of trafficking (TIP Reports 2007, 2008, 2009). The Council of Labor Affairs (CLA, the predecessor of the Ministry of Labor) often viewed exploitative work situations as labor disputes, rather than trafficking, and did not refer the incidents to law enforcement agencies for further criminal investigation (TIP Report 2007). Despite the fact that Taiwan passed an anti-trafficking law in 2009 and built shelters to better assist victims, the law has not been fully implemented to prosecute traffickers and to protect victims (TIP Report 2009).

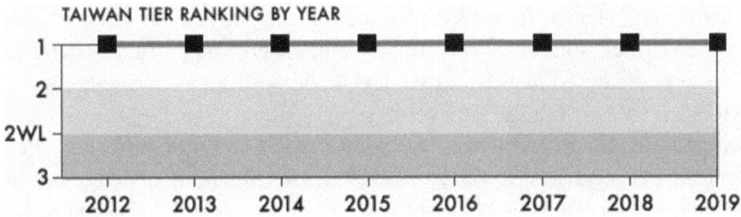

Chart 1 Taiwan TIP tier ranking by year from 2012 to 2019 (*Data Source* 2019 TIP Report, US State Department)

Taiwan was finally ranked Tier 1 in 2010 and has kept Tier 1 rating since then (see Chart 1). Taiwanese authorities fully met the minimum standards for the elimination of trafficking. Authorities continued to demonstrate serious and sustained efforts during the reporting period (TIP Reports 2010, 2011, 2012, 2013). They have consistently stated that Taiwan has implemented the anti-trafficking law, stringently prosecuting and punishing traffickers, improving victims' protection, and continuing to train law enforcement personnel, officials in the CLA, and labor inspectors on victim identification and the anti-trafficking law. Taiwan has also been encouraged to improve efforts by US Department of State to more effectively use the anti-trafficking law to investigate, prosecute, and convict trafficking incidents. In addition, the U.S. Department of State suggests that Taiwan continues to train personnel who may come into contact with victims, raise awareness among victims to ensure that they know what their options are, and increase public awareness of all types of trafficking (TIP Reports 2010, 2011, 2012, 2013).

In 2019, the TIP Report said Taiwan authorities fully met the minimum standards for the elimination of trafficking. Authorities continued to demonstrate serious and sustained efforts during the reporting period. These efforts included investigating significantly more traffickers and labor recruitment agencies than in previous years—for the first time, conducting random inspections of fishing vessels on the high seas, repatriating an increased number of foreign victims, and amending legislation to improve protections for guest workers. Although Taiwan met the minimum standards, separation of purview between the Ministry of Labor (MOL) and the Fisheries Agency (FA), coupled with insufficient inspection protocols, continued to impede efforts to address forced labor on Taiwan-flagged and/or -owned fishing vessels in the highly vulnerable Distant Water Fleet (DWF) (TIP Report 2019).

4   Patterns and Trends of Trafficking in Taiwan

In January 2009, Taiwan's Human Trafficking Prevention Act (HTPA) was passed and was implemented in June of the same year. Since the law was enacted, the situation has improved for some trafficking victims. Recognized VoT are now allowed to apply for a temporary visa and work permit while they wait for their legal cases to be closed. The chance to work and send some money home to their families is helping to ease their sorrows. Previously, victims were caught in a system in which they were kept sheltered as their cases developed but they were unable to earn any money to send to their families. Nevertheless, the lengthy process until a legal case is closed and the person can leave the country creates a lot of suffering. It can take only a couple of months for the court case to be closed but the majority of trafficked persons have to wait one year or longer before the case is sealed. For many, the court trial is disappointing and disenchanting: Up to now, none of the victims has received compensation; many even had to leave without their outstanding salaries or savings. On the other hand, the traffickers leave the court with mild sentences (Fuchs 2011).

The TIP 2013 stated that Taiwan is a destination country for guest workers who become victims of sex trafficking and forced labor. Victims are mostly guest workers from Vietnam, Thailand, Indonesia, China, Cambodia, and the Philippines. The guest workers are recruited by the employment agencies or brokers to perform low-skilled and difficult jobs in the production sector (i.e., manufacturing, construction, and fishing industries) as well as the domestic sector (i.e., home caregivers and domestic workers). In addition to forced labor, some women and girls from China or Southeast Asian countries were deceived into coming to Taiwan for the purpose of sexual exploitation (TIP Report 2013). While the population of guest workers has been on the rise, the procedures for recruiting guest workers have been regarded as flawed and as contributing to human trafficking. The majority of guest workers came to Taiwan via private employment agencies or brokers, which often asked migrants to pay large sums of money before coming to Taiwan (Migration News 2007). Traffickers usually take advantage of these flawed procedures and of guest workers' desperation to seek better lives, abusing and exploiting workers without being detected by criminal justice agencies (Fuchs 2011). These commonly used methods are as follows: Chen (2014).

4.1 Fraudulent Marriages

Traffickers lure women from China and Southeast Asian countries to Taiwan through fraudulent marriages and deceptive employment offers for purposes of sex trafficking. Many trafficking victims are guest workers from Indonesia, the Philippines, Thailand, Vietnam, and to a lesser extent, individuals from China, Cambodia, and Sri Lanka (TIP Report 2019). Human Trafficking gangs often focus on young persons from rural and poor areas, those with few employment opportunities and low educational levels. Those youths are recruited by employment agencies, brokers, or matchmakers in their home countries and come to Taiwan through fraudulent marriages. Dated to the end of 2018, Taiwan has received 543,807 foreign spouses, including 359,461 mainland Chinese women who marry Taiwanese men and 184,346 foreign brides from other countries (NIA 2018). Since 2003, the government has required an interview with the foreign spouse before immigration. As a result, the share of marriages that involve a foreign spouse dropped from a third to a sixth of total Taiwan's marriages (Migration News 2007). If there are fraudulent marriages, brokers or employers forced those women to work after arriving in Taiwan. The victims are subjected to forced labor or sexual exploitation.

4.2 Legal Work Permits

Guest workers are recruited by employment agencies or brokers in their home countries and come to Taiwan through legal work permits. Their contracts are typically for fixed two-year terms, extendable for one year. Almost all legal guest workers come to Taiwan via recruitment agencies. The agencies or brokers charge workers huge sums in recruitment fees, so they were deep in debt while working in Taiwan. Workers were forced to work over 10 h every day to repay the debts, and might also be subjected to verbal threats, physical violence, confinement, and/or the confiscation of travel documents. They are then subjected to forced labor or sexual exploitation.

4.3 Undocumented Workers

These guest workers came to Taiwan through legal work permits. However, they decided to run away from their legal employers when they cannot accept or stand working overtime, low wages, and/or bad employers. Another reason for becoming undocumented can be that the contract term is finished but the worker doesn't want to return to his or her country. Two often-heard explanations for becoming undocumented are: (1) that the loans are not yet repaid because the money earned was insufficient, and (2) guest workers simply could not afford to leave and then pay the placement fee again to come back to Taiwan to work here for another term. They were subsequently recruited by friends or others, and were subjected to forced labor or sexual exploitation (Fuchs 2011, p. 10). Currently there are 47,885 undocumented guest workers counted on August 30, 2019 by the NIA. Top three nationalities in order of undocumented population are Indonesians at 22,856 (48%), Vietnamese at 21,861 (45%), and Filipinos at 2,366 (5%). The increasing number of caregivers/domestic workers corresponds to the rise of undocumented female workers and it can be assumed to be a direct correlation between the kind of employment and the decision to become undocumented (National Immigration Agency 2019) (Table 6).

Table 6 Top three nationalities of undocumented workers in Taiwan

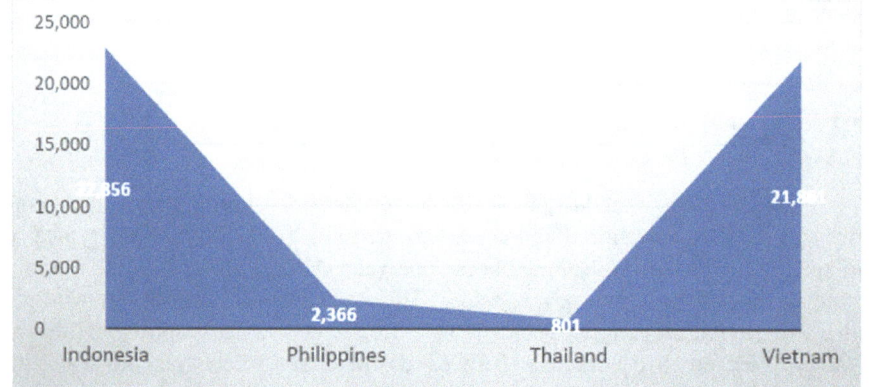

Data Source National Immigration Agency, Taiwan, dated August 31, 2019

4.4   Tourist or Student Visas

The method of tourist visas is used primarily to recruit women or girls for the purpose of sex trafficking, while using student visas is popular to recruit men for labor trafficking. Women and men are recruited by friends or through advertisements in the newspapers and come to Taiwan through tourist or student visas. After they arrive in Taiwan, traffickers use verbal threats, physical violence, confinement, and confiscate travel documents to force them into prostitution.

4.5   Fishermen Working on Fishing Vessels

Documented and undocumented Chinese, Indonesian, Filipino, and Vietnamese fishermen working on Taiwan-flagged and -owned fishing vessels experience non- or under-payment of wages, long working hours, physical abuse, lack of food or medical care, denial of sleep, and poor living conditions while indebted to complex, multinational brokerage networks. Migrant fishermen have reported senior crewmembers employ such coercive tactics as threats of physical violence, beatings, withholding food and water, and pay deductions to retain their labor. These abuses are particularly prevalent in Taiwan's Distant Water Fleet comprising over 2,000 Taiwan-flagged and -owned fishing vessels operating thousands of miles from Taiwan and without adequate oversight (TIP Report 2019).

There were two lesser-used trafficking subterfuges: real marriages with the guest spouse forced into prostitution or smuggling (Chen 2008). No matter how guest workers were trafficked to Taiwan, they all faced at least one of the before-mentioned conditions: verbal threats, physical abuse or violence, sexual assault, confinement, and confiscation of travel documents. In addition to malicious employment agencies or brokers, legal employers can also become traffickers. If the employers ask guest workers to perform work that is not within the scope of their contracts and/or subject them to poor working conditions, employers' acts constitute trafficking in persons (Fuchs 2011). Sometimes brokers in Taiwan help employers deport guest workers who do not live up to their expectations, thus allowing the brokers to recruit more new guest workers to fill the empty quota (TIP Report 2013). These bad practices have left guest workers trapped in abusive working environments.

5   Factors Contributing to Taiwan's Human Trafficking

In 1992 the Employment Services Act (ESA) was promulgated to give human labor imports a firm basis in Taiwan law. The government's foreign labor policy has always included a licensing system that limits both the job categories in which guest workers can be employed and the total number of them. Industries currently permitted to employ foreign labor include manufacturing, construction, maritime fishing, slaughterhouses, institutional and outreach nursing and home nursing and nurses' assistants. They primarily work in factories and as domestic workers and caregivers, with smaller numbers working as fishermen and in construction. Most legal guest workers come to Taiwan via recruitment agencies. Even though there have been some significant improvements in prevention of human trafficking in Taiwan, this study assumes that many victims remain unrecognized. Law enforcement agencies, as well as the judiciary, generally lack an awareness of trafficking offenses and they are not very clear about many migration-linked problems.

Without evidence-based knowledge and a better understanding of trafficking patterns, initiatives might be inadequate and anti-trafficking policies could be ineffective. Despite the policy relevance, academic research on the nexus between immigration policy and human trafficking remains scarce. Therefore, this paper seeks to illuminate the migration-linked factors which potentially contribute to the human trafficking of guest workers. The pitfalls commonly seen in entering Taiwan's foreign labor market are as follows: (Fuchs 2011; Chen 2014; Huang 2017).

5.1   High Placement Fees and Security Bonds (on Home Country Side)

The recruitment agencies demand high commissions which they term "placement fees." Most guest workers have to take out loans to pay the placement fee in their mother countries. Although some countries set limits on these fees, the placement fee finally paid by the workers is usually higher than conceived. If they want to return to Taiwan for work, either they again have to shoulder the placement fee or their employers need to agree on the direct hiring scheme in which there are no recruitment agencies involved (Fuchs 2011, p. 6).

In addition to placement fees, Indonesian caregivers and domestic workers have to pay a US$ 800 security bond. This bond was implemented by the Indonesian government in reaction to the high number of Indonesians becoming undocumented in Taiwan. If the bond deposit is not paid before departure, it is deducted from the worker's salary and is returned only after fulfillment of the contract. Consequently, a worker who becomes undocumented loses this money. A similar deposit is also paid by many Vietnamese, although in their cases it is currently not a government regulation. For them the amount of the deposit varies from US$ 500 to US$ 1000. A third group, Indonesian fishermen, also have reported that security bonds ranging between US$ 700 and US$ 900 were deducted from their salaries.

5.2   Unreasonable Brokers' Fees and Pay Deductions (on Taiwan Side)

After arriving in Taiwan, the indebted workers are under pressure to pay off the loans for high placement fees and security bonds. With regular payments, it takes a migrant worker, on average, from 19 months (Philippines) to 44 months (Vietnam) to pay off their debts. Aside from repaying any money borrowed, they have to pay a broker's fee that equals US$ 1,900 for a 3-year contract. This is usually collected in monthly installments. In many cases, the monthly installments are directly deducted from the workers' wages—a practice not mentioned in advance. This is extremely difficult, because for many workers the monthly take-home pay during the first contract year is only about US$ 50–US$ 150. Not being correctly informed about the extent of their pay deductions their resulting low net income is troublesome (Fuchs 2011, pp. 8–9). For example, in 2007 guest workers but at the behest of employers, NT$4,000 a month can be deducted for room and board. A 2006 survey found that almost 60% of employers were deducting room and board at an average N$2,300 a month (Migration News 2007). Guest workers, therefore, were heavily indebted and might [afterwards] be coerced or threatened by brokers or employers to repay their debts in Taiwan (TIP Report 2013).

5.3   Poor Working Conditions

The working contract system in Taiwan often supports poor working conditions. First, there are the high pre-departure costs on one side; then there is the inadequate protection of foreign workers, especially of caregivers and domestic workers, on the other. Foreign factory workers are covered by the Labor Standards Law, but caregivers and domestic workers (local as well as foreign) in private households are not. Confiscation of personal documents by the broker or employer is fairly routine. Foreign caregivers often are expected not only to take care of a person, as stated in their working contract, but also to perform other household duties or even to clean the houses of the employer's relatives or to work at other businesses the employer may own. Workdays may easily consist of 12–15 h without any regularly scheduled day off. This taxing and unhealthy schedule is often combined with restrictions on personal freedom. These types of exploitative working and living conditions are characteristic of human trafficking. Having little bargaining power, many workers do not even dare to complain about bad working conditions or unjust payment terms because they fear that it could endanger their employment and result in their repatriation. For guest workers, to be sent back home is the worst-case scenario. Currently, no control mechanisms or regular and independent inspections of work places of foreign workers in private households or nursing homes are in place. The abuse and exploitation of these workers stays widely undetected. Also, because a private household is an isolated work place, these workers remain mainly invisible to the outside world and this makes them even more vulnerable to psychological and physical abuse and sexual harassment. Although there are no data available about the number of guest workers in Taiwan who face abuse and exploitation, NGO workers often hear about these problems when talking to caregivers/domestic workers (Fuchs 2011, pp. 6–9).

5.4 Positions of Vulnerability

In accordance with Taiwan's foreign labor policy, a foreign worker's work permit and visa are bound to the employer. A change of employer or work is possible only under certain circumstances. This condition of extreme vulnerability applies to more-or-less all guest workers and the problem is made worse by the fact that many workers are not aware of their rights. Employers and brokers can take advantage of this lack of knowledge by giving false information about laws and the attitude of authorities or simply by threatening that workers who complain will be sent home. In this context, workers view reporting an abusive situation to the police as synonymous with returning home. This kind of vulnerability and dependence created through the brokerage system can be seen as a possible starting point of human trafficking (Fuchs 2011, pp. 8–9).

The vulnerability is particularly true for undocumented workers. First, it is usually hard for undocumented workers to find work without the assistance of an illegal broker. Second, there is also a reporting scheme at the NIA rewarding people who inform law enforcement agencies about undocumented workers. Third, undocumented workers are very afraid of being caught by the police and of being repatriated. Due to this fear, they try to keep their movements to a minimum. Illegal brokers act as middlemen for factories, nursing homes and private households, as well as for brothels and KTV-bars. Besides an introduction fee, paid upfront and ranging from US$ 150 to US$ 600), the worker also ends up paying a monthly broker's fee. While some workers may earn more money during their undocumented period, for others, meeting the illegal broker is the beginning of a nightmare. Some illegal brokers turn out to be traffickers who force undocumented workers into abusive work conditions with very low or no income. This often is combined with restrictions on their movement and physical abuse (Fuchs 2011, p. 11). For people from impoverished families, becoming a migrant worker is a once-in-a-lifetime chance and they will do anything to take advantage of it. Of course, it is even easier to threaten undocumented workers, for example, by saying that they will be reported to the police and repatriated if they do not follow given rules and instructions. The isolation of guest workers also creates a situation in which the victim is dependent on the trafficker. The trafficker becomes the main source of information and, therefore, is able to control the worker's perception by creating views according to his needs. By telling trafficked persons that the Taiwan police and other government agencies are very bad and corrupt, that officials would harm them, put them into prison, beat them, etc., traffickers enhance the often already low trust in police and other agencies. This psychological and physical violence is used to extend control over persons. The self-confidence of a trafficked person can be broken by constant oppression and insults. These conditions of vulnerability and low bargaining power, which apply to more or less to all guest workers, can become the starting point for human trafficking (Fuchs 2011, p. 15).

6   New Policy Adopted

In pursuant to amendments to Article 52 of the ESA promulgated on May 13, 2003, a migrant worker was required to leave Taiwan for at least one day upon completing the term of his/her contract. That provision prevented foreign laborers from establishing long-term residence as part of a covert scheme to immigrate to Taiwan. Since there is no longer any concern that foreign laborers will establish long-term residency and thereby immigrate to Taiwan by covert means, the Taiwan government proposed draft amendments to Article 52 of the ESA. Those amendments passed a third and final reading in the Legislative Yuan on October 21, 2016, eliminating the requirement that foreign laborers leave the country for one day upon expiration of their employment permit and then re-enter the country to work. Another new provision allows foreign laborers to request leave to visit family in their native country during the term of their employment permit and requires employers to grant such requests. These amendments were promulgated by the President and entered into on November 5, 2016–benefitting 600,000 guest workers now in Taiwan. Under the amended Act, employers are permitted to directly renew employment contracts, reducing potential gaps in the labor supply as well as reducing training costs and making manpower deployment more flexible. Under the amended Act foreign laborers are permitted, during the term of their employment contract, to apply to their employer for leave to return to their home countries. By law, the employer cannot refuse that application. An employer who refuses such a request—and fails to rectify the situation within a specified period of time—will be subject to a fine of not less than NT$60,000 and not more than NT$300,000, and their permission to recruit and hire foreign labor will be revoked. The amendments are expected to simplify labor contract renewal procedures and reduce the financial burden imposed on laborers by foreign brokers (Executive Yuan 2016).

7 Conclusion and Recommendations

7.1 Change the Mindset of Policymakers in Foreign Labor Policy

Three decades have passed since 1989 when Taiwan began allowing foreign workers. There are now nearly 1 million blue- and white-collar foreign workers in the nation. However, the labor ministry is stuck in the mindset of 20 years ago (Kuan 2019). Guest workers were originally aimed at helping Taiwan finish infrastructure projects and to serve as a bridge to a more automated manufacturing sector. By 2007, half of the foreign workers were being admitted to fill service jobs. Some economists say that Taiwan's guest worker program has shifted from providing supplemental production workers to admitting cheap workers (Migration News 2007).

Fuchs said that there are three main areas related to the human trafficking of guest workers in Taiwan that need improvement. For classification of doing what needs to be done, the "3 P" paradigm (prevention, protection and prosecution) can be applied. The first area requiring attention is Taiwan's foreign labor policies and protection of guest workers; the second is rationalizing the brokerage system; the third is a better understanding of human trafficking and the labor migration approach of all involved government agencies. Taiwan government's ideology in the importation of foreign laborers remains a strategy designed to supplement the domestic labor market and will not impact the rights of domestic laborers (Fuchs 2011, pp. 25–26).

Taiwan faces a serious basic labor shortage—the main reason that the number of blue-collar foreign workers in Taiwan has doubled to 700,000 over the past decade. Taiwanese companies, not finding enough domestic workers—hire foreign workers and spend large amounts of money training them. However, when the maximum employment period expires, those foreign workers have to leave and employers have to recruit and train new workers. This not only wastes Taiwan's trained human resources, but also delivers skilled workers into the hands of other countries. Consider the example set by Singapore, where foreign workers initially work on two-year fixed-term labor contracts. After working there for four years, foreign workers are eligible to take qualification exams recognized by the Singaporean Ministry of Manpower. Those who pass the exam are qualified to work in Singapore continuously until the age of 55 while those who fail must leave after a maximum employment period of 12 years. As Taiwan's foreign labor policies are largely modeled on those of Singapore, its example could be followed in this respect. Taiwan Commerce Associations suggest that the Taiwan's government issue three-year work permits to foreign workers. After working here for six years, they would be eligible to take qualification exams recognized by the labor ministry—testing them on subjects such as language, law, professional skills and Taiwanese culture and customs. They could take the tests at vocational training centers or at private institutes recognized by the MOL. If workers pass, they would be permitted to work in Taiwan until the age of 60. If they fail, they must leave after a maximum employment period of 12 years. This would enable businesses to retain basic skilled workers without getting stuck on the question of salaries. Employers would certainly be willing to pay foreign workers according to their skills and ability in order to retain such talent. On the other hand, excessive government intervention would only confuse local employers and cause needless displacement into human trafficking (Kuan 2019).

7.2   Reform of the Brokerage System

Although Taiwan is host to more than 700,000 foreign workers, Taiwan's law enforcement agencies, as well as the judiciary, generally lack awareness of trafficking offenses. Clearly, they are not very cognizant of many migration-linked problems. For example, most guest workers are hired in home countries through recruitment agencies and brokers. To pay brokers' often exorbitantly high recruitment fees, some foreign workers incur substantial debts which brokers or employers use as tools of coercion to obtain or retain their labor. After recruitment fee repayments are garnished from wages, many foreign workers in Taiwan earn significantly less than the minimum wage (Fuchs 2011, pp. 25–26). Currently, they are at particularly high risk of trafficking because they have lost their immigration status and access to formal sector employment by absconding from contracted positions. Although some initially fled due to abusive work conditions, including forced labor, they have no choice but to be in the same position again.

Domestic workers and home caregivers are also especially vulnerable to exploitation. They often live in employers' residences, making it difficult to monitor their working and living conditions. Brokers in Taiwan sometimes assist employers in forcibly deporting "problematic" foreign employees should they complain, enabling brokers to fill the empty positions with new foreign workers facing continued debt-based coercion. Some traffickers use Indonesian-owned stores in Taiwan as illegal remittance channels, confining Indonesian workers and subjecting them to sex trafficking. Traffickers reportedly take advantage of Taiwan's "New Southbound Policy" visa-simplification program to lure Southeast Asian students and tourists to Taiwan and subject them to forced labor and sex trafficking. Without evidence-based knowledge and a better understanding of trafficking patterns, initiatives might be inadequate and anti-trafficking policies ineffective.

In order to amend the serious pitfalls of brokerage system, when foreign workers with good moral character and skills reach the end of a maximum employment period of 12 years, they should be granted long-term residence of 20–30 years so that they can continue contributing to Taiwan's industries. The MOL long ago introduced a measure in this regard, namely that outstanding foreign workers recommended by their employers could obtain a long-term residency permit after working in Taiwan for six years. However, this measure only applies to those who earn a monthly salary of more than NT$40,000, which is far higher than the basic monthly wage in Taiwan and much higher than the average starting salary for Taiwanese workers. Although the ministry introduced this requirement with good intentions, it is more than most employers could afford (Kuan 2019).

References

Bruckert, C., & Parent, C. (2002). *Trafficking in human beings and organized crime: A literature review*. Mimeo: Royal Canadian Mounted Police.

Chand, S. (2008). *Economics of human trafficking: A survey*. Mimeo: The Australian National University.

Chen, Y. (2008). *Patterns of human trafficking and assessment of victim services needs in Taiwan: Final research report* (in Chinese). Taipei, Taiwan: Taipei Women's Rescue Foundation.

Chen, Y. (2014). Human trafficking in Taiwan. In W. Hofmeiser & P. Rueppel (Eds.), *Trafficking in human beings: Learning from Asian and European experiences* (pp. 65–74). Konrad-Adenauer Stiftung and European Union: Singapore.

DGBAS, Directorate-General of Budget, Accounting and Statistics. (2019, October 4). *National Statistics*, No. 187. https://www.dgbas.gov.tw/public/Data/910485923A8RC8SAF.pdf.

Directions of the Employment Transfer Regulations and Employment Qualifications for Foreigners Engaging in the Jobs Specified in Items 8 to 11, *Paragraph 1, Article 46 of the Employment Services Act (2004)*. Ministry of Labor. Taiwan. https://law.moj.gov.tw/ENG/LawClass/LawAll.aspx?pcode=N0090027.

Employment Service Act. (1992). *Ministry of Labor*. Taiwan. https://law.moj.gov.tw/ENG/LawClass/LawAll.aspx?pcode=N0090001.

Executive Yuan. (2016, November 15). *Employment Services Act amendments strengthen labor Rights, Department of Information Services*. Executive Yuan. https://english.ey.gov.tw/News3/9E5540D592A5FECD/4a00f610-1f94-4a94-b5b2-2ad35ae21760.

Fuchs, R. (2011). *Human trafficking of legal and illegal guest workers in Taiwan*. http://www.mfasia.org/component/simpledownload/?task=download&fileid=ZnVjaHNfaHVtYW50cmFmZmljja2luZ19mZWIyMDExLnBkZg%3D%3D.

Goehrung, R. (2019). Evaluating the criminal justice approach to human trafficking in Taiwan. *Journal of Human Trafficking*, 1–16. https://www.researchgate.net/publication/334222398_Evaluating_the_Criminal_Justice_Approach_to_Human_Trafficking_in_Taiwan.

Huang, F. (2007). *Patterns, causes, and prevention strategies for transnational human trafficking*. Taipei, Taiwan: National Immigration Agency.

Huang, L. (2017). The trafficking of women and girls in Taiwan: Characteristics of victims, perpetrators, and forms of exploitation. *BMC Womens Health, 17*, 104. Published online November 9, 2017. https://doi.org/10.1186/s12905-017-0463-2, https://www.ncbi.nlm.nih.gov/pmc/articles/PMC5679141/.

Huang, W. C. (2018). Immigrant crime in Taiwan: Perspectives from Eastern Asia. *Forensic Research & Criminology International Journal, 6*(3), 225–236. https://pdfs.semanticscholar.org/8293/6769dd65b7ff2bbc41ad07cf7875ecad796b.pdf.

Human Trafficking Prevention Act. (2009). *Ministry of the Interior*. Taiwan. https://law.moj.gov.tw/ENG/LawClass/LawAll.aspx?pcode=D0080177.

ILO. (2005). *A global alliance against forced labour*. Geneva: ILO.

Kuan S. (2019, October 14). Taiwan foreign labor laws outdated. *Taipei Times*. http://www.taipeitimes.com/News/editorials/archives/2019/10/14/2003723886.

Mahmoud, T. O., & Trebesch, C. (2009). *The economic drivers of human trafficking: Micro-evidence from five Eastern European countries* (Kiel Working Paper No. 1480/February/2009). Kiel Institute for the World Economy. https://www.files.ethz.ch/isn/97165/kap1480.pdf.

Migration News. (2007). Taiwan: Migration policy evolution. *Migration News*, 14. http://migration.ucdavis.edu/mn/more.php?id=3307_0_3_0.

National Immigration Agency. (2018). *Ministry of the Interior*. Taiwan. https://www.immigration.gov.tw/5385/7344/7350/8887/?alias=settledown&sdate=201801&edate=201812.

National Immigration Agency. (2019). *Ministry of the Interior*. Taiwan. https://www.immigration.gov.tw/5385/7344/7350/8943/?alias=settledown&sdate=201901&edate=201908.

Obuah, E. (2006). Combating global trafficking in persons: The role of the United States post-September 2001. *International Politics, 43,* 241–265.

The Economist. (2007, January 18). Wandering workers. *The Economist.* http://www.economist.com/node/8565050.

Trafficking Victims Protection Act of 2000 § 108, 22 U.S.C. § 7106 (2000).

Trafficking Victims Protection Act of 2000 § 110, 22 U.S.C. § 7107 (2000) (amended 2003).

U.S. Department of State. (2001, July). *Trafficking in persons report.* https://2001-2009.state.gov/g/tip/rls/tiprpt/2001//index.htm.

U.S. Department of State. (2003, June). *Trafficking in persons report.* https://2001-2009.state.gov/g/tip/rls/tiprpt/2003//index.htm.

U.S. Department of State. (2004, June). *Trafficking in persons report.* https://2001-2009.state.gov/g/tip/rls/tiprpt/2004//index.htm.

U.S. Department of State. (2005, June). *Trafficking in persons report.* https://2001-2009.state.gov/g/tip/rls/tiprpt/2005//index.htm.

U.S. Department of State. (2006, June). *Trafficking in persons report.* https://2001-2009.state.gov/g/tip/rls/tiprpt/2006//index.htm.

U.S. Department of State. (2007, June). *Trafficking in persons report.* https://2001-2009.state.gov/g/tip/rls/tiprpt/2007//index.htm.

U.S. Department of State. (2008, June). *Trafficking in persons report.* https://2001-2009.state.gov/g/tip/rls/tiprpt/2008//index.htm.

U.S. Department of State. (2009, June). *Trafficking in persons report.* https://www.ait.org.tw/2009-trafficking-persons-report-taiwan-tier-2/.

U.S. Department of State. (2010, June). *Trafficking in persons report.* https://www.ait.org.tw/2010-trafficking-persons-report-taiwan-tier-1/.

U.S. Department of State. (2011, June). *Trafficking in persons report.* https://www.ait.org.tw/2011-trafficking-persons-report-taiwan-part-tier-1/.

U.S. Department of State. (2012, June). *Trafficking in persons report.* https://2009-2017.state.gov/j/tip/rls/tiprpt/2012//index.htm.

U.S. Department of State. (2013, June). *Trafficking in persons report.* https://www.ait.org.tw/2013-trafficking-persons-report-taiwan-tier-1/.

U.S. Department of State. (2019, June). *Trafficking in persons report.* https://www.ait.org.tw/2019-trafficking-in-persons-report-taiwan/.

Wang, H.-Z. (2011, June). Immigration trends and policy changes in Taiwan. *Asian and Pacific Migration Journal: APMJ.* https://www.researchgate.net/publication/276324983_Immigration_Trends_and_Policy_Changes_in_Taiwan.

Did China's Soft Power Seduction Lure Taiwan's Youth? Preliminary Evidence for Overseas Employment

Ya-chi Lin, Chan-hui Lin, and Kuo-chun Yeh

Abstract Taiwan's brain drain has been the main concern due to China's strong economic gravity, and the situation might have worsened over the past decade. Based on Yeh (2019), we explore the determinants for Taiwan's youth overseas employment using the questionnaire administered in 2015 for residents between 20 and 45 years old. An empirical model is derived to investigate the push and pull factors directing Taiwan's youth to go abroad. The empirics do not show clear evidence to support Taiwan's brain drain by 2016. In contrast, personal considerations, such as broadening international vision and encountering career bottlenecks are more important influences for Taiwan's youth to be employed in China.

Keywords Taiwan's brain drain · Youth employment · China · Southeast Asia

1 Introduction

The brain drain has been a serious concern for Taiwan due to China's strong economic gravity over the past decade. China's "soft-power seduction" of Taiwan has been widely reported by the international media (e.g., BBC 2018; *Washington Post* 2018). Some consultancies (e.g., IMD 2017; Oxford Economics 2012) warn that by 2021 Taiwan will face "talent deficits," even worse than India, China, and some serious aging societies as Japan and S. Korea.

Original data from Taiwan's Ministry of Labor is acknowledged.

Y. Lin
Department of Economics, Feng Chia University, Taichung, Taiwan
e-mail: yaclin@fcu.edu.tw

C. Lin · K. Yeh (✉)
Graduate Institute of National Development, National Taiwan University, Taipei, Taiwan
e-mail: kuochunyeh@ntu.edu.tw

C. Lin
e-mail: chlin1211@gmail.com

© The Author(s), under exclusive license to Springer Nature Singapore Pte Ltd. 2021
C.-P. Chu and S.-C. Park (eds.), *Immigration Policy and Crisis in the Regional Context*,
https://doi.org/10.1007/978-981-33-6823-1_5

In theory, human capital outflow increases overseas employment and entrepreneurship, which in turn decreases domestic productivity. But there might be some positive contributions to some emerging economies with aging problems in macro- and micro- levels. The macro-level includes improvement to domestic unemployment and economic growth (Mountford 1997; Vidal 1998; Beine et al. 2008), remittances (Bredtmann et al. 2019), technology transfers, and institutional quality such as democracy and economic freedom (Djajić et al. 2018). Micro-levels relate to accumulated working experience to improve an individual's independent problem-solving skills, creativity, courage, and flexibility (Frändberg 2015; Leung et al. 2008; Maddux et al. 2014).

The individual decision to work overseas is based on push and pull factors in source and destination countries, respectively. If countries share common languages, cultural similarities, and various communities or channels, individuals could more easily integrate into foreign labor markets and societies (Kaplan and Höppli 2017). Furthermore, personal characteristics, such as adaption, communication, entrepreneurship, creativity, responsibility, ambition, intelligence, and leadership, affect individuals' decisions.

Based on Yeh (2019), this study uses a questionnaire (Chen et al. 2015) administered by Taiwan's Ministry of Labor in 2015 to Taiwan residents aged between 20 and 45. We investigate the determinants driving Taiwan's youth to work abroad. We mainly focus on China (including the mainland, Hong Kong, and Macao) and Southeast Asian economies (including ASEAN, Australia, India, New Zealand, and Oceanic countries), most of which are not as advanced as Taiwan in terms of per-capita GDP. This can indicate the attitude of Taiwanese young adults toward working in China or Southeast Asia before and after Taiwan's 2016 presidential election campaign and China's countermeasures since 2018.[1]

This paper is structured as follows. Section 2 describes the data, presents descriptive statistics, and outlines the empirical methodology. Section 3 discusses the empirical results and Sect. 4 concludes.

2 Model and Data

The 2015 questionnaire sponsored by Taiwan's Ministry of Labor (Chen et al. 2015) surveyed the interest of Taiwan's youth in overseas employment or entrepreneurship. Following the "Directions for Youth Entrepreneur Loan" by Taiwan's Ministry of Economic Affairs, youth defined as residents between 20 and 45 years old are the survey objects. The questionnaire had passed two tests before the launch of the formal investigation, and then the research platform was constructed for controlling the survey process, which is responsible for the consistency of the questionnaire

---

[1]In February 2018, the Chinese government in Beijing unveiled a package referred to as the "31 Measures" encouraging people and businesses from Taiwan to move to China, including tax breaks, subsidies, research grants and access to government contracts.

survey sample. The samples are uniformly distributed among the four main regions of Taiwan (north, middle, south, and east) according to the regional youth population ratios. A total of 1070 valid samples were collected. Details are shown in the original data (Chen et al. 2015) and the appendix of this paper.

To identify determinants for Taiwan's youth interest in overseas employment, we estimate a model in which the willingness of youth overseas employment is a function of push factors in Taiwan and pull factors in destination countries. Corresponding to Taiwan's current diversification strategy mentioned above, we focus on overseas employment and entrepreneurship in China and the Southeast Asian economies. In our baseline specification, the model is constructed as follows:

$$C_i = AX_i + BZ_i + \varepsilon_i \tag{1}$$

where C_i represents whether the respondents of the questionnaire are willing to work in the destination countries, X_i and Z_i the determinants for overseas employment and the personality characteristics, respectively, A and B the matrices of corresponding estimators including constant terms, and ε_i the residual vector. Destinations in the questionnaire were not limited to China and Southeast Asian economies, but we here focus on these two largest trading and investing areas since they are related to issues of Taiwan's authority.

Here, $C_i = \begin{bmatrix} Ccnee & Cseaee \end{bmatrix}'$, which includes two variables: the willingness of Taiwan's youth to seek employment ($Ccnee$) in China and employment in Southeast Asian economies ($Cseaee$), respectively. In the questionnaire, respondents were asked to fill in their first three choices for overseas employment destinations. The value is one if a respondent chooses China or Southeast Asia, and otherwise zero. Here, China includes the mainland, Hong Kong, and Macau; while Southeast Asia includes ASEAN, New Zealand, Australia, Oceania, India, etc. Table 1a presents descriptive statistics of the explanatory variables.

For Taiwan residents between 20 and 45 years old, the determinants for overseas employment, X_i, can be divided into pull factors from overseas destinations, and push factors in Taiwan. The pull factors from destination areas include better payment (*pay*), industry potential development (*industry*), better living environment (*environ*), respect for the profession (*respect*), better division of specialties (*division*), learning a different culture (*learn*), pursuing the challenge (*challenge*), upgrading language ability (*language*), broadening the international vision (*intl*), increasing working experience (*workexp*), future career development (*future*), building social links (*link*), having local connections (*friend*), introduction by relatives o r fiends (*introd*), and migration (*migration*). The push factors in Taiwan include encountering an employment bottleneck (*bottleneck*), having no job in Taiwan (*nochance*), and emigration assistance from Taiwan's government (*twpolicy*), etc. All of these variables are dummies. Table 1b shows the descriptive statistics of the factors for overseas employment X_i.

Table 1 Descriptive statistics of explained and explanatory variables

(a) Descriptive statistics of the explanatory variables

	Cseaee	Ccnee
Number of $C_i = 1$	355	216
Number of $C_i = 0$	715	854
Mean	0.33	0.20
Std. Dev.	0.47	0.40
Observations	1070	1070

(b) Descriptive statistics of the determinant factors for overseas employment

	pay	industry	environ	respect	division	learn	language	intl	workexp	link	friend	introd	bottleneck	nochance	twpolicy
Number of $X_i = 1$	580	284	292	270	94	385	361	467	379	218	60	40	125	52	214
Number of $X_i = 0$	145	441	433	455	631	340	364	258	346	507	665	685	600	673	511
Mean	0.80	0.39	0.40	0.37	0.13	0.53	0.50	0.64	0.52	0.30	0.08	0.06	0.17	0.07	0.30
Std. Dev.	0.40	0.49	0.49	0.48	0.34	0.50	0.50	0.48	0.50	0.46	0.28	0.23	0.38	0.26	0.46
Observations	725	725	725	725	725	725	725	725	725	725	725	725	725	725	725

(c) Descriptive statistics of the determinants factors for the personality characteristics

	male	eduh	fin	hitech	build	eating	retail	transport	estate	public	bio
Number of $Z_i = 1$	455	252	44	229	28	34	71	31	9	71	30
Number of $Z_i = 0$	374	577	785	600	801	795	758	798	820	758	799
Mean	0.55	0.30	0.05	0.28	0.03	0.04	0.09	0.04	0.01	0.09	0.04
Std. Dev.	0.50	0.46	0.22	0.45	0.18	0.20	0.28	0.19	0.10	0.28	0.19
Observations	829	829	829	829	829	829	829	829	829	829	829

The personal characteristics Z_i include gender (*male*), receiving a master's or higher degree (*eduh*) and current occupation. Occupation can be divided into financial sector (*fin*), high technology (*hitech*), construction (*build*), food and beverage (*eating*), retail sale (*retail*), transportation (*transport*), real estate (*estate*), civil service (*public*) and biotechnology (*bio*). Descriptive statistics of the personal characteristics are shown in Table 1c.

3 Empirical Results

As mentioned above, this questionnaire was completed before the most recent political power rotation in 2016. The previous Kuomintang (KMT) government had implemented the Economic Cooperative Framework Agreement (ECFA) and Service Trade Agreement with China, whereas the new DPP government implemented the "New Southbound Policy" to strengthen exchanges with ASEAN and related economies. Therefore, this paper tries to find some evidence for the two main questions presented above.

The estimation by Eq. (1) is presented in Table 2 for these two questions, respectively. H-L Statistics and Andrews Statistics indicate the goodness of fit for the binary models is acceptable. The problem of co-linearity has been taken into account and deleted some insignificant variables.[2] Note that the pull and push factors affecting Taiwan's youth and their characteristics would affect respondents' evaluations of overseas employment and entrepreneurship, but not vice versa. Therefore, the estimation approach proposed by Eq. (1) should have consistent estimators without the problem of endogeneity. Moreover, recent research indicates that statistically insignificant variables in large-sample estimation should not be overlooked (Abadie 2018). We still expect independent variables would support the willingness to go to China or Southeast Asia if they were statistically significant with positive signs; otherwise, variables might not be important to explain the possible youth brain drain in 2016.

3.1 Determinants for Taiwan's Youth Overseas Employment

We start our analysis by estimating the effect of pull and push factors on the willingness to seek overseas employment and entrepreneurship in China, as shown in Table 2. The main results are as follows.

---

[2]Correlation coefficients are lower than 0.5 among all explanatory variables, including those related to overseas employment and to overseas entrepreneurship. Moreover, few coefficients are higher than 0.4. We follow the general to specific principle but include all variables first for the purpose of comparison between the cases of China and Southeast Asia.

Table 2 Determinants for Taiwan's youth overseas employment

Explanatory variable	Explained variable			
	Ccnee	Ccnee	Cseaee	Cseaee
	(1)	(2)	(3)	(4)
c	−0.70 (0.26)***	−0.95 (0.36)***	−0.35 (0.23)	−0.29 (0.30)
pay	0.26 (0.23)	0.41 (0.28)	0.59 (0.20)***	0.38 (0.24)
industry	0.03 (0.19)	0.04 (0.23)	0.04 (0.17)	0.03 (0.19)
environ	−0.96 (0.20)***	−1.16 (0.25)***	−0.08 (0.17)	−0.11 (0.20)
respect	−0.36 (0.21)*	−0.21 (0.25)	0.06 (0.18)	0.20 (0.21)
division	−0.92 (0.37)**	−1.25 (0.44)***	−0.38 (0.26)	−0.35 (0.30)
language	−0.59 (0.20)***	−0.61 (0.25)**	0.05 (0.18)	0.11 (0.21)
intl	0.35 (0.22)	0.43 (0.25)*	−0.27 (0.19)	−0.35 (0.22)
workexp	0.14 (0.21)	0.01 (0.25)	0.09 (0.18)	0.35 (0.22)*
link	0.44 (0.21)**	0.48 (0.26)*	−0.08 (0.19)	−0.12 (0.23)
bottleneck	0.58 (0.25)**	0.83 (0.30)***	0.14 (0.22)	0.20 (0.26)
nochance	−0.13 (0.38)	0.33 (0.53)	0.33 (0.33)	−0.05 (0.44)
twpolicy	0.17 (0.19)	0.17 (0.24)	0.05 (0.17)	0.15 (0.21)
male		0.74 (0.23)***		−0.08 (0.19)
eduh		−0.45 (0.24)*		−0.07 (0.20)
fin		−0.16 (0.45)		0.31 (0.40)
hitech		−0.25 (0.27)		−0.30 (0.23)
retail		0.25 (0.42)		0.86 (0.39)**
public		−1.65 (0.57)***		−0.85 (0.36)**
N	725	551	725	551
McFadden R^2	0.09	0.15	0.02	0.04
H-L Statistic	10.16	9.98	3.38	13.98
Andrews Statistic	11.15	13.29	4.16	15.99

Note Ccnee and Cseaee are binary variables for Taiwan's youth overseas employment in China and Southeast Asia, respectively. Robust standard errors are in parentheses. ***$p < 0.01$, **$p < 0.05$, *$p < 0.1$. Some insignificant variables are deleted. Variables are defined in the Appendix. See Lin et al. (2020)

First, column (1) shows the pull factors for Taiwan's overseas employment in China. Developing social connections (*link*) and broadening international vision (*intl*) are statistically significant with the expected positive sign, but the living environment (*environ*), respect for professions (*respect*), division of specialties (*division*), and upgrading language ability (*language*) are significantly negative. This may be because some push factors were offset by optimistic expectations for cost savings and industrial upgrades due to a series of Taiwan-China agreements by 2016, allowing Taiwan's workers and businesses access to China's growing market without moving to the mainland. Working in China would be helpful to personal links and globalization, but living and working conditions regardless of payment in China are less attractive. Common language may give Taiwan's employees in China a comparative advantage over workers from other foreign countries. The variable *language* representing upgrading language ability is therefore not a reason for Taiwan's youth to go to China. Among the push factors in Taiwan, encountering an employment bottleneck in Taiwan (*bottleneck*) is the main reason to work in China, which implies that most young workers going abroad are not new on the job market. The younger generation might have worked in Taiwan after graduating from college and encountering the bottleneck then decided to go abroad. There is home bias in job choice. Therefore, enhancing the working system is important for the government to block brain drains, such as employee training or advanced compensation and welfare.

Secondly, in addition to the pull and the push factors in China and Taiwan, there are influential, personal characteristics, such as gender (*male*), master's or higher degree level (*eduh*), and current occupations, as shown in column (2). As noted above, in 2018 over 70% of overseas employees have tertiary education. But the most important result here is that *eduh* is negatively significant, implying that the "China lures Taiwan's youth" assumption cannot be sustained before 2016. Furthermore, *male* is positively significant, which means Taiwan's men are more interested in working in China. The variable *public* is negative since civil service sector employees are normally guaranteed a permanent job, so there is no incentive to go abroad.

We can similarly describe Taiwan's youth employment in Southeast Asia according to columns (3) and (4) in Table 2. Payment (*pay*) and increasing work experience (*workexp*) would be the main determinants for working in Southeast Asian countries. Of the personal characteristics, workers in the retail sector are interested in moving to the new destinations. The may be because the threshold for transfer to other industries or participating in the Southeast Asian retail sector is lower than for other industries. As results in column (2) show, Taiwan's civil service employees are not willing to go abroad. Note that the questionnaire was administered before the "New Southbound Policy" was launched in 2016, and the results would be different after the policy encouragement providing preferential treatment for Taiwan's youth to go to Southeast Asian countries.

3.2 Robust Tests

Variables in the robust tests here are almost the same as above, except that the four independent variables become indices rather than binary. The values of two C in Eq. (1) depend on the weighted average of the questionnaire respondents' first three destinations. The weights on the first, second, and third choices are 3, 2, and 1, respectively. Compared with the previous binary logit approach, this method can measure the magnitude and volatility of the respondents' willingness, as

$$C_i = 3 \times 1\mathrm{st}_i + 2 \times 2\mathrm{nd}_i + 1 \times 3\mathrm{rd}_i$$

where 1st, 2nd, and 3rd are a respondent's first, second, and third choice of overseas employment or entrepreneurship destinations in the questionnaire. For instance, $Ccnee = 3$, if a respondent's first three choices of overseas employment are mainland China, Australia, and Singapore, respectively. In contrast, $Cseaee = 4$ if Thailand, Hong Kong, and Singapore, respectively.

The details of robust tests are skipped here but most of the results are similar to Table 2.[3] Variables including environ1, division, language, and migration are still significantly negative, which implies the offset effect caused by the relatively stable situation between Taiwan and China. A series of the cross-strait agreements by 2016 gave rise to optimistic possibilities, including more foreign investment and a reversal of Taiwan's capital. So some personal considerations, such as intl and bottleneck, are more important for Taiwan's youth to seek employment in China.

4 Concluding Remarks

The brain drain problem has been a leading concern in Taiwan due to China's strong economic gravity, so Taiwan has promoted its "New Southbound Policy" since 2016. This paper explores the determinants driving Taiwan's youth to work or to start their businesses in China or Southeast Asia using a questionnaire by Taiwan's Ministry of Labor in 2015. In our binary logit estimation and the robust tests, we do not find clear evidence to support Taiwan's youth brain drain in the case of high tech and financial sector employees with high education levels before 2016. However, some personal considerations, such as broadening international vision (*intl*) and career bottlenecks (*bottleneck*) supported Taiwan's youth to seek employment in China.

Next, we will make an extension and concentrate on Taiwan youth overseas entrepreneurship according to the questionnaire. However, this preliminary analysis at least shows that the brain drain of younger professionals was not serious before 2016. In the future, a new comprehensive questionnaire to evaluate changes since the DPP took power in 2016 is critically needed. And then a pooled data analysis will be possible to show the differences between KMT's and DPP's policies.

Appendix

This questionnaire sponsored by Taiwan's Ministry of Labor surveyed the willingness of Taiwan's youth to seek overseas employment and entrepreneurship. Following the "Directions for Youth Entrepreneur Loan" by Taiwan's Ministry of Economic Affairs, youths defined as residents age 20–45 were the survey objects. Samples were

---

[3] See Yeh (2019) and are also available on request.

uniformly distributed from the four main regions of Taiwan (north, middle, south, and east) according to the regional youth population ratios. 1070 valid samples were collected from August 2014 to July 2015. We retrieve all variables from the original Chinese questionnaire, which is also attached behind the English definitions.

Variable	Definition
Dependent variables	
Ccnee, Cseaee	Willingness to be employed in China (Southeast Asia). *Ccnee* = 1 if the respondents selected mainland China, Hong Kong or Macao as one of the first three destinations of employment, otherwise zero. *Cseaee* = 1 if the respondents selected Southeast Asia includes ASEAN, New Zealand, Australia, Oceania, India, etc. as one of the first three destinations of employment, otherwise zero
Independent variables for overseas employment	The following variables are all dummies, a value of one if answered yes, otherwise zero
pay	Better payment in destination areas
industry	Industry potential in destination areas
environ	Better living environment in destination areas
respect	Respect for professions in destination areas
division	Better division of specialties in destination areas
learn	Learning a different culture
challenge	Pursuing a challenge
language	Improving language ability
intl	Broadening international vision
workexp	Increasing work experience
future	Future career development
link	Developing social connections
friend	Having local connections in destination areas
introd	Introduced by relatives or friends
bottleneck	Encountering an employment bottleneck in Taiwan
nochance	No job in Taiwan
twpolicy	Assistance from Taiwan's government
migration	Motivation for migration
Personal characteristics	Dummies mostly
male	Male = 1
age	Age 20–45
marriage	Marriage = 1
eduh	*eduh* = 1 if having a master's or higher degree
occu	Occupations including financial sector (*fin*), traditional industries (*industry*), high technology (*hitech*), biology (*bio*), construction (*build*), food and beverage (*eating*), retail sales (*retail*), transportation (*transport*), real estate (*estate*), civil service (*public*), other services (*otherservice*)

Source Yeh (2019) and Chen et al. (2015); authors' definitions

References

Abadie, A. (2018). *Statistical non-significance in empirical economics* (NBER Working Paper 24403). http://www.nber.org.

BBC. (2018, July 17). *Soft power seduction: China lures Taiwan's youth.* https://www.bbc.co.uk/mediacentre/proginfo/2018/29/the-documentary-soft-power-seduction.

Beine, M., Docquier, F., & Rapoport, H. (2008). Brain drain and human capital formation in developing countries: Winners and losers. *The Economic Journal, 118*(528), 631–652.

Bredtmann, J., Flores, F. M., & Otten, S. (2019). Remittances and the brain drain: Evidence from microdata for Sub-Saharan Africa. *The Journal of Development Studies, 55*(7), 1455–1476.

Chen, J., Li, S., Liang, S., Zhang, M., Jiang, W., & Liu, R. (2015). *A research on youth's attitude, characteristics and impacts towards working and creating start-ups abroad.* Commerce Development Research Institute (in Chinese).

Djajić, S., Docquier, F., & Michael, M. S. (2018). *Optimal education policy and human capital accumulation in the context of brain drain* (FERDI Working Paper P224). https://hal.archives-ouvertes.fr/hal-01743814.

Frändberg, L. (2015). Acceleration or avoidance? The role of temporary moves abroad in the transition to adulthood. *Population, Space and Place, 21,* 553–567.

IMD. (2017). *IMD world talent ranking 2017.* IMD Business School. https://www.imd.org/globalassets/wcc/docs/talent-ranking/talent_ranking_2017_web.pdf.

Kaplan, D., & Höppli, T. (2017). The South African brain drain: An empirical assessment. *Development Southern Africa, 34*(5), 497–514.

Leung, A. K., Maddux, W. W., Galinsky, A. D., & Chiu, C. (2008). Multicultural experience enhances creativity: The when and how. *American Psychologist, 63*(3), 169–181.

Maddux, W. W., Bivolaru, E., Hafenbrack, A. C., Tadmor, C. T., & Galinsky, A. D. (2014). Expanding opportunities by opening your mind: Multicultural engagement predicts job market success through longitudinal increases in integrative complexity. *Social Psychological and Personality Science, 5*(5), 608–615.

Mountford, A. (1997). Can a brain drain be good for growth in the source economy? *Journal of Development Economics, 53*(2), 287–303.

Oxford Economics. (2012). *Global Talent 2021.* https://www.oxfordeconomics.com/Media/Default/Thought%20Leadership/global-talent-2021.pdf.

Vidal, J. (1998). The effect of emigration on human capital formation. *Journal of Population Economics, 11*(4), 589–600.

Washington Post. (2018, April 15). Taiwan battles a brain drain as China aims to woo young talent. https://www.washingtonpost.com/world/asia_pacific/taiwan-battles-a-brain-drain-as-china-aims-to-woo-young-talent-away/2018/04/13/338d096e-3940-11e8-af3c-2123715f78df_story.html?noredirect=on&utm_term=.d6071052ecbf.

Yeh, K. C. (2019, November 15). *Did China's soft power seduction lure Taiwan's youth?* [Paper presentation]. International Conference on Transnational Immigration Policy and Cross-strait Public Management and Experience, National Dong Hwa University, Taiwan.

Thailand Immigrant Policy: The Challenge and Opportunity Before and After ASEANIZATION

Prateep Chaylee

Abstract Immigrant workers and related issues always have challenged Thai economic development and social policy since late 1980s onwards by the external factors, especially the political Uprising in neighboring country specifically as Burma/Myanmar. Consequently, the influx of Burmese migrants and later become the largest migrant workers in Thailand. Also, in terms of economic terms, they are also the most productive labor force in various economic sectors, especially in fishery industry. However, the official inauguration of ASEAN Economic Community (AEC) in 2015 would be a new platform of Thailand in rethinking and positioning its strengths and long-term economic development policy based on sustainability and accountability. Any economic crimes related to human slavery and trafficking in illegalized migrant workers should be officially and continually promoted and suppressed within the ASEAN networks. Domestically and challengingly, Thai Immigrant Policy should be redefined based on integrated immigrant policy frameworks among various stakeholders in the current and future contexts. Furthermore, ASEAN 2025 would be the new platform of rethinking on policy implementation with the current and future contexts simultaneously.

Keywords AEC · Burmese migrant workers · Integrated policy framework

1 Introduction

Thailand has its geographical advantage in the heart of ASEAN countries, included GMS countries or currently CLMV (Cambodia, Laos, Myanmar, Vietnam). More than 50 decades, Thailand has made remarkable progress in social and economic development, moving from a low-income country to an upper-income country in less than a generation. Thailand, therefore, has been one of the widely cited development success stories, with sustained strong growth and impressive poverty reduction, particularly in the 1980s.

P. Chaylee (✉)
Institute of China & Asia Pacific Studies (ICAPS), National Sun Yat-Sen University, Kaohsiung, Taiwan
e-mail: d076070010@student.nsysu.edu.tw

© The Author(s), under exclusive license to Springer Nature Singapore Pte Ltd. 2021   89
C.-P. Chu and S.-C. Park (eds.), *Immigration Policy and Crisis in the Regional Context*,
https://doi.org/10.1007/978-981-33-6823-1_6

Prior to this great success, Thailand has operated its economic development policy based on *"Export led Growth Economy"* by positioning itself as the industrial manufacturing base of the advanced Industrial Company, especially Japan along with its lower labor cost advantage. Also, it totally transforms Thai Economic and social structures by changing from agricultural labors in rural or remote areas to be the industrial labors instead. Specially, it has supported and developed Thailand to be the business and industry hub in this region since 1960s. However, this policy has mainly focused on Thai labors before widely opening to foreign workers from nearby neighboring countries.

Before officially forming regional economic cooperation as ASEAN Economic Community (AEC) in 2015. But the political instability in these neighboring countries has forced them to cross the borders to work and stay in Thailand thereafter. Obviously, immigrant labors from Myanmar are the biggest group among these neighboring countries is approximately 80% of total immigrants (Chaipanit and Liwa 2011). Likewise, Thailand economic and social structures had been the right position in absorbing these large numbers of migrant labors, whereas Thailand Economic and social conditions was preparing to restructure its economy by preparing to be basic industry as shown in the fifth national economic and social development plan that economic restructuring so that speed up the transformation of primary processing industry into the finished product. Export industries. The government will develop a basic industrial complex around the eastern seaboard. Furthermore, the government will encourage the dispersion of manufacturing activities to outlining regions in order to increase rural development as well as use their local material resources (NESDB 1991).

Later, since the sixth National Economic Development Plan (NEDP) pushed Thailand to official Industrial society since the early 1990s on wards. The high demand for Thai labors on industrial sectors were significantly increased from 11 million persons in 1987 to 16 million persons in 1996, from the sixth to the seventh national economic development plan. At the same time, the demand for labor on Agricultural sectors were slightly decreased from 19 million persons to 16 million persons, respectively (NESDB 1991).

Besides, the advantage of Thailand's Geography that locates in the center of ASEAN particularly are circled by GMS (Greater Mekong Sub-regions) or currently CLMV (Cambodia, Lao PDR, Myanmar, and Vietnam). After the World War II, Thailand is only one country in this region that follow the way of liberalism by opening the diplomatic and economic relations with the US and other western countries. As a results, Thailand got the official development programs from the US since early 1960s and thereafter its miracle economic performance.

Thailand, hence, took advantage of its growth to establish itself as the nexus point of the region, launching an informal initiative in the early 1990s it called the "Baht Economic Zone." The set of policies sought to set up the Thai baht as the currency of choice in the northern peninsula and included relaxed limits on the amount of currency Myanmar, Laos, Cambodia, Thailand and Vietnam would be allowed to carry. At present, the Thai baht is still widely used, often viewed as more trustworthy than other domestic currencies while influencing a vast array of manufactured goods, as many businesses choose to settle their accounts in Thai baht.

Significantly, Thailand also hosts 2 million–3 million migrant workers, mostly coming from Myanmar, Laos and Cambodia. And over the past two decades, Thailand has accrued $124.5 billion in foreign direct investment as opposed to the collective $104.6 billion among Vietnam, Cambodia, Laos and Myanmar (Min Read 2015).

Thailand has been the first destination of immigrant workers in this region as the study of Bank of Thailand (BOT), it found that in ASEAN—Thailand is credited to be the first destination of these immigrant workers as well as more than 54% of regional-labor mobility. Burmese labor group is the first-priority, Laotian and Cambodian labors are the second and third priorities, respectively. In addition, the attractive factors are the plentiful resources and its geographical advantages as the logistic gateways/center of this region.

Comparatively, Thailand has more daily minimum-wage rate higher than nearby neighboring countries at 9.31–9.98 USD, whereas Myanmar, Lao PDR, and Cambodia are 2.56 USD, 3.60 USD, and 5.67 USD, respectively. It, therefore, supports Thailand to be their most attractive country in securing economic opportunity and living quality. On the other hand, the influx of these immigrant workers has been mainly absorbed to Thai manufacturing system and societal structure reciprocally during 1990s in many sectors, included household sector. In addition, Thailand has gradually been a destination country in absorbing both official and unofficial registered immigrant workers simultaneously. Whereas, the policy response of Thai government is mainly looked only in terms of national security within the frame of crime suppression without considering other related issues on human rights, human development and capabilities.

Therefore, since 2015 onwards have been the crucial year of resetting new frameworks on immigrant policy by integrating the regional and international regulations and related commitments to pursue and drive to the goal of ASEAN Community. Not just only in the conventional economic development growth and development within AEC, but also it extends to the new scope of ASEAN Social and Culture Community(ASCC) and ASEAN Political and Security community(APSC) have to participate and commit in the new aspects of new policy in the new global and regional contexts, respectively.

2 Research Objectives

This study would like to review the past and current status of Thai immigrant policy in order to fit the current and future global economic transformation that directly affects Thai immigrant policy determination and appropriately responses. Since two objectives mainly focuses on these two things:

2.1. Review Thai Immigrant Policy Before and After the ASEANIZATION
2.2. Analyze New Opportunities Beyond the ASEAN Framework

3 Research Methodology and Theoretical Framework

3.1 Research Methodology

This study is a qualitative research based on policy review on immigrant policy of Thailand before and after 2015 (ASEAN Economic community/AEC Accession) by using secondary data from official data from the royal Thai government agencies as the National Economic and Social Development board (NESDB),Thai Research fund (TRF), Bank of Thailand (BOT). Also, the data source of various stakeholders in research on immigrant workers included international NGOs, also international organization as International Labor Organization (ILO), ASEAN, respectively.

3.2 Theoretical Framework

The Development State Theory refers to the significance of state as a pivotal role in economic and social development reciprocally. However, this concept has been incorrectly used to describe any state presiding over a period of economic development and improvement in living standards. But describes the state's essential role in harnessing national resources and directing incentives through a distinctive policy-making process (Singh and Ovadia 2018). In practice, the collaboration between and among relates sectors, particularly the roles of state and business sectors, technocrats in guiding the way of development as well as the global economic trends and changes. Therefore, the third-world countries in Asia during 1990s had undertaken in this way. Effectively and hopefully, the Import-Substitution-Industrialization (ISI) in these countries were highly implemented and promoted as to their abundant natural resources, included human resources in catching up with the demand for global markets.

Japan was a main role model of economic development by focusing on market mechanisms for developmental goals for most leading East Asian nations. Furthermore, it has been successfully emulated in South Korea, Taiwan, Singapore, and Hong Kong. A comparative analysis of the Newly Industrialized Countries (NICs) allows variations of the developmental state to emerge from the background of the astonishing economic growth in East Asia. The experience of this region is evidentiary that the success of the developmental state stems from the amalgam 'embedded autonomy,' in which the developmental state is linked intimately with the private sector but preserves sufficient distance for the renegotiation of goals and policies when capital interests are inconsistent with national development.

In East Asia, the developmental state's bureaucracy has several important characteristics. Profits and investment depend on decisions made in the state. There is extensive discourse on 'developmentalism,' the necessity of industrialization and of state intervention to promote it in terms of economic development. However, the Asian development model had existed for decades prior to the crisis, during which the region had experienced spectacular economic growth that lifted 400 million people out of poverty through hard work, the establishment of competitive niche markets internationally, and high household savings that were reinvested into the domestic economy (Kasahara 2003).

Three main characteristics of developmental state could be found in these ways: (Singh and Ovadia 2018, p. 1038).

(1) The impressive transformation of state institutions aimed at generating rapid, sustained industrialization throughout the postwar years. Indeed, the developmental capacities of states—defined in terms of the creation of a Weberian rational bureaucracy—and the choices in economic state-crafting were deemed pivotal in directing economic growth in the region. State capacity is oftentimes linked to economic growth and poverty reduction, political legitimacy and nation-building.

(2) The crafting of a mutually beneficial state–business alliance, whereby the state implements a series of incentives and rewards to persuade domestic capitalists to undertake investments in targeted sectors in the economy. This relationship partly underpins the justification for national ownership. National ownership opens a developmental space for domestic firms to compete with multinational companies through state protectionism.

(3) Capabilities of mobilizing financial resources to pursue ambitious industrial policy had motivations linked to national security and survival of the political ruling class. That elites saw economic growth as the main source of regime legitimacy stems from existential threats and immense vulnerability brought about by structural conditions and historical contexts.

Furthermore, patterns of state-society relations in East Asia are fundamentally different from those in the West. East Asian states pervade into society; as a result, the lines between public and private, government and market, are often blurred. *The concept of the 'developmental state' means that government and private industry are in a mutually beneficial relationship, so that neither state nor enterprise prevails over the other*. The state establishes incentives and disincentives to direct private investment; the success of enterprise in turn reinforces state legitimacy. Therefore, in this case Japan heavily opposes any nations in calling this specific term as *"East Asian Miracle (EAM)"* due to its inapplicable to other nations conventionally, except in East Asia only. Specifically, East and Southeast Asian economic growth also stemmed from special linkage with Japan. Japanese colonialism had created the social foundations for industrialization in East Asia, but also the foundations for dependency relations (Reus-Smit 2001).

According to Johnson, the source of authority in the developmental state is one of 'revolutionary authority': the authority of a people committed to the transformation of their social, political, or economic order. Hence, legitimation stems from the state's achievements, not the way the state came to power. Such attributes of the developmental state model have contributed significantly to the highly successful economic development in Japan and the NICs seen in the recent decades. Likewise, Thailand once had been one of the exemplar of NICS by setting its high dream of being the fifth tiger of ASEAN. Regrettably, the economic crisis in 1997 completely chased its dream to be heavily economic collapse instead.

On the other hand, this approach shows political terms as Singh and Ovadia (2018) emphasized the East Asian experience, this phenomena becomes the primary motivation for state intervention; centralization of patrimonialism and rent-seeking becomes a form of disciplined capital accumulation. Also, growing authoritarianism notwithstanding, the ability of political elites at the apex of power to generate a consensus or 'political settlement' is the glue that holds together the relationships between contending elites—and between states and social forces—that consequently provides an enabling environment for national elites to secure political stability and policy consensus over the trajectory of development planning.

4 Research Outcome

4.1 Thai Immigration Policy Before ASEAN: Late 1980s–2015

In found that Thailand actually doesn't have a formal immigrant policy since the early 1960s, but the political situation in nearby neighboring countries had forced Thailand to accept this issue primarily based on humanitarian, especially the influx of immigrants from Lao PDR, Burma (Myanmar), and Cambodia. Most of them were both legal-registered and non-legal registered immigrants. Adversely, the latter has more than the former and remains the risk group of Thai society in various sectors; politics, economy, and societal.

However, within these foreign workers, Burmese was the first rated immigrants approximately 80% referred to the political instability in their country, especially the grand political suppression—Uprising in 1988 by the Burmese junta. The rising inflation rate greatly devalued the nominal wages of civil servants. Although the remuneration of employees in the private sector was much higher than that paid to public sector employees, wages failed to keep up with the rate of inflation. Consequently, many Burmese were forced to leave the country in search of better-paid employment. In the aftermath of the 1988 uprising, both legal and illegal emigration increased markedly, and Burmese emigrants came to include skilled professionals and technicians, as well as unskilled laborers. The prevalence of forced labor, political instability and systemic human rights violations thus resulted in thousands of people, especially from the rural border areas, fleeing to neighboring countries, particularly Thailand (Mon 2010).

Later, the influx of immigrant workers in that period directly supported Thai Economic structure during late 1980s and has fully absorbed thereafter due to its domestic economic structure had changed. At that time, the Thai economy grew dramatically between 1980 and 1995, and since 1985 total exports have also grown by an average of 10% annually. In terms of the value of manufactured exports, the annual growth rate was a remarkable 25% in the early 1990s. These developments induced very large flows of skilled and unskilled labor from other countries and from rural Thailand (Mon 2010).

In addition, the shortage of unskilled labors in some manufacturers would be highly demand. Consequently, Burmese immigrant workers completely fulfills since then. Positively, Thailand at that time had driven its economic development policy based on economic led-Growth economy. Since most supportive factor is "Excess labors from Agriculture or rural areas." Domestically, labor mobility from rural to urban areas were significantly increased from 14.3% during 1976–1981 to 18.4% during 1985–1990, respectively (NESDB 1991).

Significantly, in 2003 the per capita gross national product of Thailand was US$2238, which was six times higher than the US$351 recorded in Burma in the same year (Mon 2010).

4.2   Thai Immigration Policy After ASEAN: 2015 Onwards

Early 2019, the study of Chandrapong et al. from Bank of Thailand (BOT 2018) found that there are numbers of legalized migrant workers 2.06 million workers (5.5% of the total workers). The biggest groups are migrants from Myanmar, Lao, and Cambodia who are allowed to work adherence to the article 59 of migrant workers. These main groups work in elementary occupations based on labor intensive jobs as well as domestic workers. These are the main grass-root labors of Thai economic development. These are 44.7% of total labors.

In addition, they work variously in all economic sectors, mostly work in industrial sector approximately 12.6% of total industrial workers (as shown in Fig. 1). Moreover, they are found in these sectors: construction, Agriculture and continued processes, service sectors, etc. Obviously, this figure reflects Thai economic structure significantly reflects the low levels of technological production of Thailand. It relies on the many low wage migrant workers.

Challengingly, current Thai labors' attitudes totally divert from specified heavy jobs, especially in the 3D-job condition; *Dirty, Dangerous, and Difficult*. Whereas Thai high skilled labors are hired in the positions of administrator, senior manager/manager, teaching careers, technicians instead. Furthermore, various technicians, architects, and engineers can fulfil the gap of any skills that Thai labors lacked off.

Currently, Thailand's economy even highly relies on the migrant workers, but it lacks of the right policy platform of professional policy implementation between and among related sectors or stakeholders. However, it can learn from the managerial experiences in tackling problems on migrant workers in in terms of integrated migration approach from the leading European countries and the US as the same destination countries, including the case of skilled migrant labors. As the survey in ASEAN countries by the United Nations it found that in these countries have their limitations in management processes on labor mobility more than most developed

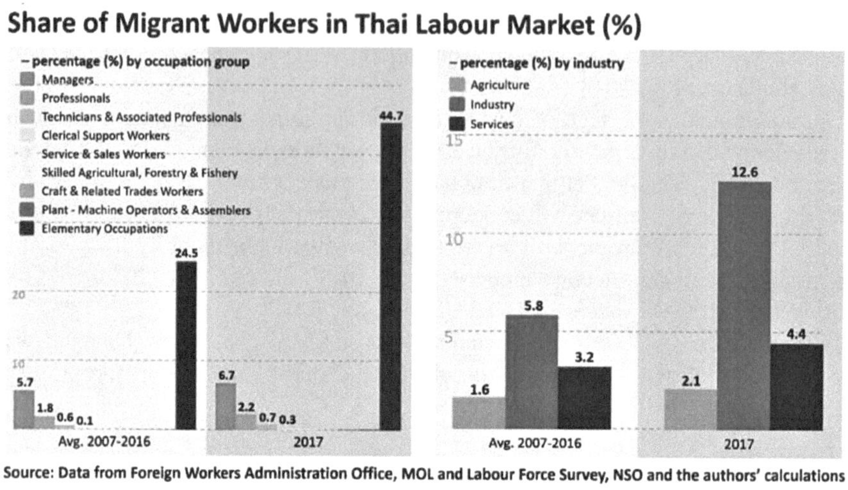

Share of Migrant Workers in Thai Labour Market (%)

Source: Data from Foreign Workers Administration Office, MOL and Labour Force Survey, NSO and the authors' calculations

Fig. 1 Share of migrant workers in Thai Market (%) (*Source* Data from foreign workers administration office, MOL and labour force survey, NSO, and authors' calculations)

countries, particularly in the long-hiring process of migrant workers, the accession of migrant workers' rights and welfares.

However, Thailand has significantly progressive and improved in the rights of migrant workers. Whereas there is no policy on language acknowledgement and career-qualified authorization as shown in Fig. 2.

Thailand even focuses on its economic development and its future transformation. In fact, the heart of economic driven force mainly depends on migrant workers for economic prosperity. However, the challenges of Thailand based on these key issues;

4.2.1 Vagueness of Government policy on migrant worker policy: It dominantly relates to rights on education and public health. The former is the national educational system has solely and highly focused on Thai context more than others without opening new options on cultural and ethnical diversity for better understanding and realization. In addition, there is no clear in education policy of children of migrant and ethnic workers. Whereas the latter is the healthiness of migrant workers and epidemic awareness. Most migrant workers are even the young men without any severe diseases. But in the future, when they are older or the new comers have increased. Any diseased and any risk of public health would be increased that burden its own government budget as well as the well-being of Thailand, reciprocally.

4.2.2 Viewpoints on migrant and ethnic workers: Other than the previous issue, the main problem is the holistic of Thai economy and its real societal aspects both top-down and bottom-up levels, especially government and related organization. They try to separate the economic problems from the social problems completely. But, in fact, both problems are dual faces of coin. As a results,

International Migration Policies

	Policy trends		Measures on integration of immigrants		
	Policy in immigration	Policy on highly skilled workers	Language skills training	Transfer of professional credentials	Protection against non-discrimination
America					
Canada	Maintain	Maintain	●	●	●
USA	Maintain	Maintain	●	●	●
Europe					
Finland	Raise	Raise	●	●	●
France	Lower	Raise	●	●	●
Germany	Raise	Raise	●	●	●
UK	Lower	Lower	●	●	●
Asean-5					
Thailand	Raise	Raise	○	○	●
Indonesia	Maintain	Maintain	●	○	●
Malaysia	Lower	Raise	○	○	○
Philippines	Maintain	Maintain	○	○	●
Singapore	Maintain	Lower	●	○	○

Source: International Migration Policies, Data Booklet, UN (2017) and the authors' preparations

Notes: A black dot ● indicates that policies or strategies were adopted or concrete measures were taken.
A hollow dot ○ indicates that no policies were adopted nor measures were taken.

Fig. 2 International migration policies (*Source* Data migration policies, data booklet, UN (2017) and the authors' preparations. *Notes* A black dot • indicates that strategies or policies were adopted or concrete measures were taken. A hollow dot ○ indicates that no policies were adopted nor measures were taken)

any complicated policy issues, operational and implemented processes have affected related stakeholders, included migrant workers in practice.

4.2.3 Policy and Practical Partnerships: lack of working partnerships between the policy and practical organizations in Thailand is the main problematic functions. However, today there are many Non-Government Organization that highly concentrate and concern more on migrant labors' rights on education, public health, and other rights are located along or nearby the sites of these groups. However, if government accepts the current crisis of this issue. It should open mind to adjust its traditional way of thought and practice. Both parties would get new platform of innovative policy and its operations effectively for a long run.

Furthermore, it is the suitable to set up and balance the standardization domestically and internationally by committing to the international standard as well as reform and reconstruct any shortcomings that detriment to long term capability and competitiveness of the country.

In terms of policy recommendation, Thailand has its options to commit and adherence to follow in this possible practice. Like the case fishery industries that are always the high concerned on International level.

5 The Challenges and Opportunity of Thailand

Prior to penetrate deeper details on the challenges of Thailand, the contributions of immigrant labors to Thai Economy should be the first acknowledgement.

5.1 The Economic and Social Impacts of Migrant Workers: Positive Impact

Registered migrant workers represent about 3% of the Thai labor force; however, in the fishing, fish-processing and domestic service sectors, they account for 25% or more of the total number of employees. Southern Thailand rubber plantations and northern Thailand rice and fruit farms are the biggest employers of migrants in absolute terms, while fruit farms, flower farms (nurseries), rice farms and chicken producers in the northern region of Thailand are the most intensive users of migrant labor. Migrant workers have made and continue to make a significant contribution to the economic growth of Thailand. While their wages are low, their impact on the economy is important because millions of migrants help to produce or process items for export, Including agricultural products, seafood and garments. Migrant labor has different impacts on various sectors of the Thai economy.

A study by the Thailand Development and Research Institute (TDRI) by Chalaemwong & Prugsamatz (2009) estimated that 700,000 unauthorized migrants in 1995 increased Thailand's gross domestic product by 0.5%, but lowered the wages of Thai workers with primary or lower levels of education by 3.5%. The National Economic and Social Development Board (NESDB) estimated that the real income of the poorest 60% of households fell by 0.4% as a result of migrant labor, whereas the real income of the richest 40% rose by 0.3%. The Board has concluded that migrants' benefit mainly the Thai employers and a few government officials (Phillip 2004).

Likewise, a study of Pholphirul and Rukumnuaykit (2010) also found that the capital gains from migrant workers show an increasing trend from around 3% of the real national income (Bt880million) in 1995 to around 5.5% of the real national income (Bt2039 million) in 2005. The net contribution from migrant workers to the entire Thai economy is on average 2.3% of the real national income per year, or around Bt760 million per year. The greatest economic benefit typically derived from international migration by the sending country is the receipt of remittances from migrant workers. For example, in 2005 the remittances of Filipino migrants were estimated at US$16.12 billion, and those of Indonesian migrants at US$2.08 billion (International Labor Organisation 2007).

But while hundreds of thousands of Burmese migrants have been working in Thailand for many years, it does not appear that their remittances have had a significant effect on the national income of Burma. There are a number of reasons for this apparent anomaly. Thai Government regulations prevent undocumented workers from opening a bank account. The banking system is also quite unreliable, and as the official exchange rate is extremely overvalued in Burma, nearly all migrant workers remit their money through private agents, who transfer the money to the senders' families in Burma at the market exchange rates. Some migrants also send gold instead of cash through their close friends or relatives, but if they do so, they run the risk of theft or of the gold getting lost in transit.

According to one source, private agents charge the exorbitant fees of Bt.500–900 to remit just Bt. 3000 to Burma. One estimate of remittances from Thailand to Burma puts the figure at Bt590 million per month, but this is probably a very conservative estimate (Huguet and Punpuing 2005). It is also worth noting that migrants in Thailand transfer their remittances in Thai currency but that their families in Burma receive the remittances in Burmese currency. It may thus be assumed that informal agents also make a profit from the currency exchange rate.

Thai employers often take advantage of undocumented migrants by offering wages lower than they would have to pay to Thai workers. Immigration officers and the police take bribes from factory owners, from brothel owners and, ultimately, from the migrants. As a consequence of all these factors, a large part of the income of Burmese migrants is usually spent in Thailand on food, lodging, clothing and extortion protection.

5.1.1 Negative Impacts: Healthcare & Education for the Migrant Children

It is widely perceived in Thailand that migrants, and particularly Burmese migrants, have diseases that have been eradicated or are rare in Thailand and that they thus pose a public health risk (Huguet and Punpuing 2005). It is true that Burmese migrant workers in Thailand are exposed to many chronic diseases such as pepticulcers, diarrhoea, influenza, pneumonia, skin diseases, malaria, tuberculosis and elephantiasis. In addition, undocumented migrant workers are often forced to accept dangerous working environments. Other serious health issues include drug addiction and HIV/AIDS infection (Mon 2010).

Although Thai public health officials have recognized a need for migrant health volunteers to serve in both public health service and NGOs, there is as yet no official plan to legally employ migrant health volunteers (Mon 2010). The spread of HIV/AIDS among the migrant population is also a burden on the Thai health system. Also, the educational issue for migrant children and children of migrant workers is also a troublesome aspect of cross-border migration to Thailand. Children born to migrants working in Thailand also raise social and legal issues due to current government policies.

These children are illegal migrants under Thai law. Neither the Thai nor the Burmese Government recognizes these children, who have effectively become stateless. Some children migrated with their families or with friends who came to Thailand to sell their labor. Some of the children came by themselves, while others were persuaded or were lured by agents to come to work in Thailand. A few NGOs in

Thailand provide some education to the children of undocumented migrant workers. Social welfare of these children is yet another burden for the Thai Government.

4.3.3 International Law and regulations: International Labor Organization (ILO) measures is an international institutional factor that most countries must be conformed to attain the international standard of international labor laws. Therefore, any country (including Thailand) must commit and follow in these key issues:

4.3.3.1   Strengthen the legal framework based on the ILO Forced Labor Protocol, (ILO 2007) and Work in Fishing Convention, 2007 (No. 188). The Royal Thai Government and Ministry of Labor should, in consultations with workers' and employers' organizations.

4.3.3.2   Set adequate and effective penalties for forced labor and clear guidance to help officials identify possible forced labor victims, including migrants both regular and irregular.

4.3.3.3   Establish clear standards for work hours, health and safety, and other standards for work in fishing, based on ILO Convention No. 188.

4.3.3.4   Propose changes to Thai law for compliance with ILO core labor standards, including worker organizing and collective bargaining rights.

4.3.3.5   Collect and publish independent data on working conditions for migrant workers in fishing and seafood processing to measure impact and value of migration agreements between Thailand and countries of origin.

Crucially, these following main issues should be more oriented

A.   **Ensure effective enforcement of the labor laws and other standards across multiple tiers of seafood supply chains, protecting workers and creating a level industry playing field.**

The Royal Thai Government and the Ministry of Labor should focus on these issues:

- Re-orient inspectorate to investigate, identify and punish violations of labor laws with a focus on proactive investigation of routine violations of recruitment, wage, hours (including overtime), safety standards, and indicators of forced labor, including document retention and wage withholding.
- Set clear enforcement action targets for labor inspectors and defend inspectors against interference as they act to enforce the law.
- Aggressively enforce wage regulations using new electronic payment records in fishing.
- Connect ministry and inspectorate goals to enforcement results in high-risk fishing and seafood processing enterprises rather than to levels of activity or numbers of inspections.
- Conduct private interviews with workers away from workplaces, and monthly meetings with local unions and civil society organizations to accelerate and focus enforcement actions.
- Restrict access to new migrant workers for employers with unremediated labor law violations.

B. **Establish higher industry standards that move beyond benchmarks to measurable improvements in the Thai industry's labor practices, especially between tier 2 and fishing vessels.**

Thai suppliers and industry associations should:

- Treat supplier compliance with labor standards as the floor (minimum level), with support and escalating pressure from industry associations' Good Labor Practices programs to improve practices or face sanction.
- Reward good labor practices using actual due diligence "from boat to bag" by major buyers, including Wal-Mart, Costco, Tesco, Coles, Simplot, Migros, Mars, Nestlé, CPC Foods and Thai Union.

C. **Enhance workers' skills, knowledge and welfare with investments in worker activities through unions and civil society organizations:**

- Initiate massive worker education campaigns by unions, civil society organizations and the Government, in light of the small numbers of workers seeking help and the lack of workers' knowledge about Thai labor standards.
- Establish community support and grievance or complaint channels that are face-to-face for all migrant workers, but Cambodian workers especially.
- Re-orient legal strategies to end widespread and routine violations of wage, work hours and safety standards.

5.2 New Opportunity Through ASEAN VISION 2025

Since AEC has launched in 2015 onwards, it has been a new quick step in developing a new protocol of economic performance based on accountability and sustainability by integrating the related issues among the three ASEAN structures or milestone three pillars: ASEAN Economic Community (AEC), ASEAN Socio-Cultural Community (ACSC), and ASEAN Political-Security Community (APSC) simultaneously. (ASEAN Secretariat 2015) Especially, within the issue of economic development that related to migrant workers. For example: Fishery industry that always has complaints on these issues on human trafficking and human slavery, human rights. Hence, within the framework of ASEAN Community. These three main pillars have set the main protocol in joining solutions and new framework.

As represented in ASEAN Vision 2025 in moving forward with its motto "Forging Ahead Together" (ASEAN Secretariat 2015) Likewise, within the main framework of this vision, these are main key points of satisfactory progress.

4.4.1 Since 2009 in implementing the Roadmap for an ASEAN Community comprising the ASEAN Political Security Community, ASEAN Economic Community and ASEAN Socio-Cultural Community Blueprints, as well as the Initiative for ASEAN Integration (IAI) Strategic Framework and the IAI Work Plan II (2009–2015) and the Master Plan on ASEAN Connectivity has led us to another important milestone in ASEAN development, namely, the formal establishment of the ASEAN Community 2015.

4.4.2 Resolve to consolidate our Community, building upon and deepening the integration process to realize a rules-based, people-oriented, people-centered ASEAN Community, where our peoples enjoy human rights and fundamental freedoms, higher quality of life and the benefits of community building, reinforcing our sense of togetherness and common identity, guided by the purposes and principles of the ASEAN Charter.

4.4.3 Envision a peaceful, stable and resilient Community with enhanced capacity to respond effectively to challenges, and ASEAN as an outward-looking region within a global community of nations, while maintaining ASEAN centrality. We also envision vibrant, sustainable and highly integrated economies, enhanced ASEAN Connectivity as well as strengthened efforts in narrowing the development gap, including through the IAI. We further envision ASEAN empowered with capabilities, to seize opportunities and address challenges in the coming decade.

4.4.4 Underline the complementarity of the United Nations 2030 Agenda for Sustainable Development with ASEAN community building efforts to uplift the standards of living of our peoples.

Therefore, within this framework we can see our new platform of systematic and effective operation in sensitive issue on human crimes on economic and related sectors. Interestingly, along the way to achieve this big goal. Any new platform of collaboration in any issue based on the value of the community as well as the global value simultaneously. Surprisingly, nowadays the global mission through the UN Sustainable Development Goals (SDGs)—the goals and targets are universal, meaning they apply to all countries around the world, not just poor countries (United Nations 2015).

Reaching the goals requires action on all fronts—governments, businesses, civil society and people everywhere all have a role to play. The Goals and targets will stimulate action over the next fifteen years in areas of critical importance for humanity and the planet (United Nations 2015):

a. **People**: We are determined to end poverty and hunger, in all their forms and dimensions, and to ensure that all human beings can fulfil their potential in dignity and equality and in a healthy environment.

b. **Planet**: We are determined to protect the planet from degradation, including through sustainable consumption and production, sustainably managing its natural resources and taking urgent action on climate change, so that it can support the needs of the present and future generations.

c. **Prosperity**: We are determined to ensure that all human beings can enjoy prosperous and fulfilling lives and that economic, social and technological progress occurs in harmony with nature.

d. **Peace**: We are determined to foster peaceful, just and inclusive societies which are free from fear and violence. There can be no sustainable development without peace and no peace without sustainable development.

e. **Partnership**: We are determined to mobilize the means required to implement this Agenda through a revitalized Global Partnership for Sustainable Development, based on a spirit of strengthened global solidarity, focused in particular on the needs of the poorest and most vulnerable and with the participation of all countries, all stakeholders and all people.

Significantly, whether ASEAN or SDGs, the main concepts, the inter-linkages and integrated nature of the Sustainable Development Goals are of crucial importance in ensuring that the purpose of the new Agenda is realized. If we realize our ambitions across the full extent of the Agenda, the lives of all will be profoundly improved and our world will be transformed for the better. Positively, international standard would systematically institutionalized domestic regulations and institutions to the *"global value"* in securing the good governance beyond and within ASEAN and the rest of the world.

6 Conclusions

Thai immigrant policy before the 2015-AEC, it found that it was the new thing for Thailand in tackling the immigrant policy during the late 1985s due to the political instability in neighboring country as Burma/Myanmar. Whereas it was restructured its economic sphere of competition with the global economy with infant industry. Therefore, it was the big turning point of Thailand in absorbing the excess labor forces from the rural areas to drive this great economic force. Likewise, this transformed its old social structure that pushed most Thai labors must significantly shift from general skilled jobs to be any specific skilled jobs-complicated skilled jobs. Therefore, migrant workers have been the key driven force of Thai economy since then.

Crucially, most migrant workers have worked in the specific work conditions in terms of 3Ds: (1) Dirty condition (2) Dangerous condition and (3) Difficult job. However, the big indifferent things have been existed in Thailand is the attitude and viewpoint on migrant workers. There is a negative viewpoint on them despite these group are the main labor force of mobilizing Thai economy since the early 1990. But the traditional viewpoints and thoughts on migrant workers in other new perspectives are limited. In turn, Thailand has gradually improved the rights of migrant workers and their accession significantly.

Hopefully, new opportunities would be the crucial year since 2015 onwards by officially inauguration of another ASEAN cluster-Economic cluster as AEC (ASEAN Economic Community) would be a new platform of these countries to set their common standard among key issues on economy, politics, and security. Fortunately, at the same time this inauguration and its core values are completely fit to the UN-SDG reciprocally. Since it is a new significant platform of learning and practice of Thailand and their members in in the international standard in trade and related issues as migrant labors based on accountability or good governance.

Likewise, policy determination and implementation should be in "integrated policy approach" by linking various aspects on migrant and ethic workers into consideration would be the right thing to commence in the current situation. As the policy band practical partnerships should be strengthened and more opened than government scope.

It highly revitalizes the role of civil society as international and local NGOs in participating in this area so that the effectiveness of policy determination and implementation would serve the well beings of Thailand as well as migrant workers and related sectors in the long run, respectively. Ultimately, these problems on migrant and ethnic workers should highly bear in mind with these three principles: (1) Realization (2) Touch the real problems and (3) Fairness, respectively.

References

ASEAN Secretariat. (2015). *ASEAN 2025: Forging ahead together*. Jakarta: ASEAN Secretariat Office.

Chaipanit, & Liwa. (2011). *The 2nd generation of the Burmese Immigrants: Situation and problems on Public Health issues*. Bangkok: TRF.

Chalaemwong, & Prugsamatz. (2009, 4–8). *The economic role of migration labor migration in Thailand: Recent trends and implications for development*. TDRI. https://tdri.or.th/wp-content/uploads/2012/09/t5s2009001.pdf.

Huguet, & Punpuing. (2005, 30–35). *International migration in Thailand*. ResearchGate. https://www.researchgate.net/publication/265658840_International_Migration_in_Thailand.

International Labour Organisation. (2007). *Labour and social trends in ASEAN 2007: Integration, challenges and opportunities*. Bangkok: ILO Regional Office for Asia and the Pacific.

Kasahara, S. (2013, 18–20). *The Asian development state and the flying geese paradigm*. UNCTAD. https://unctad.org/system/files/official-document/osgdp20133_en.pdf.

Min Read. (2015). *How Thailand hopes to capitalize on its neighbors' success*. Stratfor. https://worldview.stratfor.com/article/how-thailand-hopes-capitalize-its-neighbors-success.

Mon, M. (2010). *Burmese labors migration to Thailand: Governance of migration and Rights*. London: Routledge.

National Economic and Social Development Board. (1991, 33). *The sixth economic and development plan*. NESDB. www.nesdc.go.th/nesdb_en/ewt_dl_link.php?nid=3781.

Phillip, M. (2004, 7–14 & 33). *The economic contribution of migrant workers to Thailand: Towards policy development*. ILO. http://www.ilo.org/wcmsp5/groups/public/---asia/---ro-bangkok/documents/publication/wcms_098230.pdf.

Pholphirul, & Rukumnuaykit. (2010, 17). *Economic contribution of migrant workers to Thailand*. NIDA. http://news.nida.ac.th/th/images/PDF/article2551/.อ.พิริยะ.pdf.

Reus-Smit, C. (2001). *Constructivism in theories of international relations*. New York: Palgrave.

Saovanee Chandrapong et al. (2018). *MPG economic review: International trends on mobility*. Bangkok: BOT Press.

Thailand Research Fund. (2016). *Problems on Burmese migrant workers*. Bangkok: TRF.

Electronic Sources

ASEAN Secretariat. (2015, 06). *ASEAN 2025*. ASEAN. https://www.asean.org/wp-content/upl oads/images/2015/November/KLDeclaration/ASEAN%202025%20Forging%20Ahead%20T ogether%20final.pdf.

ASEAN Secretariat. (2015, 11). *SHIPRIGHTS*.ASEAN. https://www.asean.org/wp-content/upl oads/images/2015/November/KL-Declaration/ASEAN%202025%20Forging%20Ahead%20T ogether%20final.pdf.

Nem Singh, J., & Ovadia, J. S. (2018, 15). The theory and practice of building developmental states in the Global South. *Third World Quarterly, 39*(6), 1033–1055. https://doi.org/10.1080/ 01436597.2018.1455143.

Pholpirun, P. (2012). Labour migration and the economic sustainability in Thailand. *Southeast Asian studies, 31*(3), 59–83. https://doi.org/10.1177/186810341203100303.

United Nations. (2015, 03). *Transforming our world: The 2030 agenda for sustainable development*. UN. https://sustainabledevelopment.un.org/post2015/transformingourworld.

Labor Immigration in Vietnam: Policy and Practice

Ngoc-Tram Dang and Tuan-Duong Nguyen

Abstract After 30 years of reform and the opening up of the economy in an era of globalization, Vietnam has now become a country involved in both the emigration and immigration migrant workers. This paper is a briefing on the status-quo of foreign workers in Vietnam and the policy in regard to them, particularly the long-term application of Non-Immigrant (Temporary) Work Visa policy in Vietnam. Vietnam's immigration policy is primarily based on the labor shortage model and remains almost unchanged in its content. Consequently, it brings instability because of the increasing flow of foreign workers into the country. The decentralization of policy-makers and management's agencies, the high level of sub-state authorities' power, and the increasingly substantial role of foreign investors and contractors within the foreign-capital dependent approach of development, are the main factors which causes the ineffectiveness of immigration policy.

Keywords Immigration · Migration policy theories · Weak state · Vietnam

1 Introduction

The intensive international integration activities have been bringing a lot of opportunities to the Vietnamese labor market that create more job opportunities domestically and internationally. Vietnam has been sending the workers to foreign countries, mostly developed, to work for more than 30 years. There are more than 500 thousand Vietnamese currently working abroad under labor contracts in more than 40 countries and territories. Hence, it is worth noting that this has led to an economic growth resulting in a change: presently, Vietnam is a country that has migrant workers who are both emigrating and immigrating; the number of foreign immigrant workers is on the rise. According to HSBC's Expat 2019 Global Report, Vietnam placed in the top

N.-T. Dang (✉) · T.-D. Nguyen
Deparment of Management, National Sun Yat-Sen University, Kaohsiung, Taiwan
e-mail: dangngoctram129@gmail.com

T.-D. Nguyen
e-mail: tuanduongftu@gmail.com

© The Author(s), under exclusive license to Springer Nature Singapore Pte Ltd. 2021
C.-P. Chu and S.-C. Park (eds.), *Immigration Policy and Crisis in the Regional Context*,
https://doi.org/10.1007/978-981-33-6823-1_7

10 countries for expatriate workers (together with Switzerland, Singapore, Canada, Spain, New Zealand, Australia, Turkey, Germany, the United Arab Emirates—UAE) where foreigners feel most positive about living condition, career opportunity, and family life. It can be seen that Vietnam will likely be an attractive destination for more foreign migrant employees in the near future.

Recently, the Chairman of the Vietnam Communist Party Commission for External Relations Hoàng Bình Quân said Vietnam was among the countries with the most substantial room for investment and commerce in all of ASEAN. Government improved all mechanisms and policy systems related to external affairs and emphasized that trade must be "open and easy" (Vietnam News 2019), to show that Vietnam is more open and welcoming of foreigners coming to the country. However, liberal-inspired policymaking has not been applying in the field of immigration policy yet. The lack of theoretical discussion is obvious, especially in the field of politics.

On the status-quo of foreign workers in Vietnam and policy toward them, this paper aims to point out gaps between purposes and results of long-term applying Non-Immigrant (Temporary) Work Visa's policy in Vietnam. We suggest that decentralization of policy-makers and management's agencies, high level of sub-state authorities' power, as well as more substantial role of foreign investors and contractors within the foreign-capital dependent approach of development, are main factors which causes the ineffectiveness of immigration policy. Therefore, there is the necessity of review national immigration policy altogether, as well as enforce governance capability in the field of immigration for further economic and social development in Vietnam.

2 Foreign Workers in Vietnam: Status-Quo

2.1 Vietnam in the Intensive International Integration and Growth in FDI

After joining the World Trade Organization (WTO) in 2007, Vietnam has been active in entering into several free trade agreements (FTAs). Vietnam has confirmed several bilateral trade agreements, including FTAs with Japan (VJEPA), US (BTA), Eurasian Economic Union (VN-EAEU), South Korea (VKFTA), and Chile (VCFTA). Also, being a member of the Association of Southeast Asian Nations (ASEAN), Vietnam has become a part of the FTAs that this association has signed with countries such as Australia, China, India, Japan, Korea, and Hong Kong (Dezan Shira and Associates 2019). On top of that, the two main FTAs with Vietnam to mention are ASEAN Economic Community (AEC), where skilled labor can freely transfer within the region and Comprehensive and Progressive Trans-Pacific Partnership (CPTPP), which Vietnam entered in 2015 and 2018. International co-operation has enabled Vietnam to get access to the knowledge and technology required to transfer from low-cost to higher value-added production. Not only has the international integration boosted Vietnam's export capacity, but it has also been an opportunity for Vietnam to modernize the legal and tax systems and to improve the business activity facilitation in order to become a competitive hub for foreign investment.

The trade war between the US and China since 2017 has been further attributable to the increase in foreign direct investment (FDI) into Vietnam when investors moved their plants out of China. According to data the Ministry of Planning and Investment, FDI has steadily increased in recent years. In the first ten months of 2019, there were around 30,136 active projects that comprised of an amount of registered capital of US$358.53 billion. It experienced an increase of 6.6% compared to the same period last year. Manufacturing and processing aggregately accounted for 58.8% with US$210.69 billion of total FDI (these numbers in the same period last year were 57.3% and US$192.8 billion, respectively), followed by real estate for 16.3% with US$58.50 billion (this number in the same period in 2018 was US$57.0 billion). The investment came from about 130 countries, and 35% of total FDI was from Korea and Japan. Other major sources of investment in Vietnam were Singapore, Taiwan, and Hong Kong (Foreign Investment Agency, Ministry of Planning and Investment 2018). Besides, with efforts from the government to achieve improvements in tax systems and business activity facilitation, the score of Vietnam in the World Bank (WB) Ease of Doing Business Ranking has increased from 66.77 in 2017 to 68.36 points in 2018, and further to 69.8 points in 2019. This makes investors more confident and attracts more foreign investment (World Bank 2019).

Vietnam is a country with young demographics in a population of over 95 million with an average age of 31, among which 33% are living in nonrural areas. According to the statistics produced by the Ministry of Labor—Invalids and Social Affairs (MoLISA), the workforce in Vietnam increased from 53.3 million in 2016 to 53.7 million in 2017 and came to 54.3 million in 2018. It is predicted that the labor force will hit 56 million in 2019. In addition, the labor market is supplied with approximately 1 million persons every year, in which, a half of Vietnamese workforce in the age ranging from 15 to 39. Furthermore, the male workforce constitutes more than 50% of this population. However, well-trained and skilled employees only make up less than 25% of the total workforce: the unskilled labor constitutes of more than 75% of the total workforce. In the period 2010–2015, the demand of skilled labor in the foreign invested economic sector is always high and accounts for more than 90%, but the capacity of skilled labor supply only responds to 17–22% of its demand. According to the World Bank, there is more than 60% of foreign-invested firms that consider the shortage of qualified workers as one of biggest challenges to their operations in Vietnam. Vietnamese entrepreneurs are working hard to find the right workers for these modern jobs either because of the lack of skills of job seekers (skill gaps) or because of the shortage of workers in certain occupations (professional skills shortages), is particularly acute among applicants in technical, professional and managerial occupations. In contrast, skills shortages or shortages of candidates in certain types of jobs among more elementary occupations are also common (Bodewig and Badiani-Magnusson 2014; World Bank 2013).

2.2 Foreign Migrant Workers in Vietnam

The higher FDI has increased the demand for foreign employees to relocate to Vietnam for work, especially high skilled workers that are required for top management positions or new technology. Currently, Vietnamese labor market relies on skilled workers from foreign migrants to fill vacant positions in which the domestic employees fail to meet the requirements (Trinh 2016).

According to the statistics of MoLISA, the number of migrant workers in Vietnam has experienced a sharp increase for the last ten years. In particular, this number was 83,500 in 2015 from more than 12,600 in 2004. This figure reached to 91,200 by the end of July 2019, of which 81,900 were subject to licensing (MoLISA 2019). Among more than 100 sending countries, China, South Korea, Taiwan, and Japan placed top positions of countries having citizens working in Vietnam. This is compatible with the origins of FDI to Vietnam, which accounted for 30.9, 18.3, 12.8, and 9.5%, respectively. Concerning the gender of migrant workers, men account for the majority with 89.9%. And there are 86% having age of more than 30 years. However, there are no official statistics on the number of foreign migrant workers in Vietnam because some localities do not compile statistics on foreign workers. The main source of the number of foreign employees in Vietnam is the examination and the granting of work permits for foreigners, and most of them are expats (Hang 2017).

The number of foreign migrant workers in Vietnam is summarized the Table 1 below:

Among foreign migrant workers in Vietnam, the proportion of expatriates in managerial and director positions is increasing while the proportion of technical labor is decreasing. Concerning the working field, at the end of July 2012, there was 25.0% of foreigners working in technology, education, and management industry where there was a shortage of skilled employees from the local labor market while 22.2% of foreign employees were working in the manufacturing and processing industry, followed by 13.0% in construction. In addition, Ho Chi Minh City, Ha Noi and Binh Duong, which are the three biggest locations for FDI companies—accounted for 23.4, 12.7, and 11.2% of total foreign employees in Vietnam, respectively (Nguyen and Nguyen 2015).

In order to explain this trend, it is clearly recognized that Vietnam has become a desirable location for foreign employees to live and work in some recent years because of its low cost of living, high level of security, many job opportunities, and traveling easily to neighbor countries. In particular, according to HSBC Expat Explorer annual survey, Vietnam ranked 23rd place in the overall league table in 2017, then moved up to 19th place in 2018. In 2019, Vietnam was within the top10 best

Table 1 Number of Foreign migrant workers in Vietnam Unit: Person

	2004	2008	2010	2011	2012	2015	First 7 months 2019
Total	12,600	55,000	56,900	78,440	77,000	83,500	91,200

Source The Ministry of Labor—Invalids and Social Affairs

places to live and work for foreign employees, with 58% of surveyed people saying that they can adapt to the local culture within the first few months. Besides, 57% of migrant employees admitted that the living quality in Vietnam is more favorable than their home countries. Notably, the average annual income of surveyed expatriates living in Vietnam is higher disposable income because of lower living costs and increased salary while some of the living costs are included in employment contracts. All of the significant factors attributing to this, the growth of the Vietnamese economy and the stability of politics played critical roles when over 70% of the surveyed expatriates agreed to.

It is undeniable that foreign workers in Vietnam have contributed to the process of improving the productivity and competitiveness of the Vietnamese workforce associated to international standards. Most of the managers, senior and medium technical experts in foreign organizations and enterprises in Vietnam are foreigners (Pham 2011). And the presence of foreign migrant workers has positive influence on the productivity of the local workers. Specifically, according to the reported published by General Statistics Office of Vietnam, every 01% increase in the number of migrant workers at the skilled level causes 0.91% increase in the total labor productivity in the organizations (GSO 2016).

Apart from mentioned considerable advantages of foreign migrant workers in Vietnam, there are still several limitations in terms of the management of them. In which, the most significant issue relating to the illegal foreign migrants who taking manual jobs in Vietnam without the working visa. This group has increased in some recent years which was reported to be 44% of the total foreign workers (Trinh 2016). But this number might be much higher in reality, and most of them came from African countries and China.

3 Vietnamese Labor Immigration Policy: A Typology Analysis

3.1 Vietnam's Policy for Foreign Workers

In the economic opening and reforming after *Doimoi 1986*, the previously centrally planned and mostly closed economy needs opened flows of capital, technology and trade with the world's market. But there was a critical shortage of skilled workers who could handle these tasks. Accordingly, Vietnamese's State legally allowed FDI enterprises to hire foreigners for jobs requiring high skills by Article 16 of Law on Investment 1987, which could be considered as the first legal rule in the field of foreign workers management (Hang 2017). According to a report released by the National Assembly's Foreign Affairs Committee recently, the management of foreigners in Vietnam is now performed on the basis of legal documents in different realms, ranging from immigration and management of foreign workers to housing, marriage, family, and child adoption involving foreigners. In the field of immigration, the legal system consists of 11 texts, and 10 sub-laws. In the realms of management of foreign workers, a total of 14 legal documents, including laws and sub-laws, have been issued. The Labor Code moderates the matters of labor conditions of foreigners working in Vietnam, conditions of employing foreign workers, work permits related process; when the others confer on some rights and obligations, including social insurance, individual tax, visa granting, or temporary residence.

Previously, the term "foreign worker" was defined more widely, which referred to the foreigner who does not hold the Vietnamese nationality but was narrowed by the 2012 Labor Code. Accordingly, a "foreign worker" is defined by law as a foreign citizen who enters Vietnam to work on behalf of work permit scheme, while other types of foreigners as stateless persons or refugees are excluded. Foreign workers are neither entitled to the same social and economic benefits of Vietnamese citizens, nor have the right to join the ranks of government authorities at all levels. It is critically challenging for foreigners to obtain permanent residency in Vietnam or a status of Vietnamese nationality.

Since 1987, the work permit policy has not changed. In accordance with Vietnamese labor regulations, foreign workers are only to take over positions of top management, expert, technician, and manager, where Vietnamese workers are not able to meet requirements. The enterprises are able to employ foreigners with limited quota in the short-term, but only with plans of training Vietnamese staff to replace foreign workers later. The State has also gradually enlarged the categories of employers who shall be entitled to employ foreigners on three types as State agencies, family households, or individuals permitted by law to engage in business. Foreign workers can be employed in several ways such as labor contracts, internal transfer between offices within multinational firms, or contracted for a specific scope of work.

For the sake of enforcing the management of foreign workers in Vietnam, the State has enacted a more comprehensive legal framework for foreign workers. The New Labor Code is expected to give the labor authorities greater power to regulate and review the status of foreign workers employed by Vietnamese employers, while the Amended Law on Immigration is expected to provide more convenience for foreign workers with valid work permits to apply for/transfer to resident permits in Vietnam. These changes will require employers to review and update the current status of their foreign employees for the work permit and immigration procedures and planning. New regulations, which apply sanction on both employers who employ illegal foreigners and the foreigners who are working illegally in Vietnam, are also issued (Vietnam News 2019).

3.2 Typology of Vietnam's Immigration Policy

Transnational migration study requires an interdisciplinary approach, but a knowledge of politics is central to its analysis. Mostly migration policy theories are bases on the perspectives of Western societies, and almost neglect the other side of the contemporary global migration flow: that is, from developed countries to developing countries. This reality has placed policy-makers from developing countries in a more difficult position to deal with this emerging trend, both in terms of theoretical knowledge and practical skill.

The labor markets in developed countries need high-skilled migrants for innovation and low-skilled labor for vacancies that many locals lacking interest to apply. However, immigration policy in developing countries clearly focus on recruiting high-skilled migrants only. Countries could choose their actions following approaches: human capital approaches or labor shortages approaches, or a hybrid model of them (Papademetriou et al. 2008). Endogenous growth theory explains that the growth of human capital stock will lead to dynamic growth and spillover effects: countries adopting this approach have used immigration to increase their human capital stock, therefore consider highly skilled immigrants as permanent. Under the labor shortage approach, countries have always been interested in temporarily recruiting highly skilled immigrants in order to give them enough time to training their workers, or to fill labor shortages in specific sectors (Cerna 2016).

Migration policy theories point out the relationship between policy and politics: policies vary by purposes and consequences. As Zolberg observed: "All the countries to which people would like to go restrict entry. This means that, in the final analysis, it is the policies of potential receivers which determine whether the movement can take place, and of what kind" (Zolberg 1989), Freeman suggests that certain types of policies are related to certain political modes (Freeman 2006) (Table 2).

Freeman's Non-immigrant (Temporary) Work Visa migration policy indicates the cost-benefit effects of work visa program depend on their duration, flexibility, specificity, and size. In practice, the temporary work plan is designed for short-term residence, whose advantages are faster at modifying than a permanent visa program and targeting specific skills of labor. The temporary character makes them more acceptable than permanent visa schemes in terms of politics and security. There may be cases where casual temporary workers can fill a sudden shortage of labor that has a detrimental effect on the income of local people. Recruitment of highly skilled talent

Table 2 Four types of policy and politics

Policy type	Migration type/policy	Mode of politics
Concentrated distributive (concentrated benefits/diffuse costs)	Permanent residence visas	Client
Diffuse distributive (diffuse benefits/diffuse costs)	Non-immigrant visas for purposes other than work	Majoritarian
Redistributive (concentrated benefits/concentrated costs)	Non-immigrant visas for work, welfare for immigrants, non-immigrants, and asylees	Interest group
Regulatory (diffuse benefits/concentrated costs)	Asylum claims	Entrepreneurial

Source Freeman (2006)

has been successfully sold as a no-cost policy that brings vast (or even decentralized) benefits to society while integrating into innovation-driven global economy.

Nevertheless, mostly migration policy theories are based on the perspectives of Western societies, therefore almost neglect the other side of the contemporary global migration flow: from developed/democratic countries to less-developed/non-democratic countries. Because of lower possibility being subject to public demand for closure than a liberal democratic regime, illiberal or authoritarian regimes can more easily adopt an open immigration policy when these meet their priorities, which was named as an 'illiberal paradox' hypothesis (Natter 2018). Non-democratic regimes also need to maintain their legitimacy and survival (Bueno de Mesquita et al. 2003). They also negotiate decisions with economic and political participants within and outside state-controlled institutions.

In the case of Vietnam, despite the adoption of a welcoming policy toward foreign investment, Vietnam has maintained a long-term strict immigration policy for several reasons: mostly to protect domestic labor market, but also to prevent potential political and security challenges brings by foreigners within one-party ruling regime. However, as the statistics showed, the percentage of expats holding managerial and executive posts are on the rise while the percentage of technical workers is declining. Expecting spillover effects bring by foreign expats are also hardly to be meet. Empirical study also points out sources of spillovers from technology transfer in Vietnam do not come from foreign in the case of worker turnover just as in the case of new technology, among the firms for which skills and experience of new employees are an important source of technology transfer, only 15.5% from foreigners working in Vietnam over the 2009–2013 period, compared with 84% from Vietnamese nationals (CIEM et al. 2015).

The State has affirmed that high quality human resources is one of the three pillars of Vietnam's economic growth and sustainable development. The quality of human resources is also one of three breakthrough steps to implement the Socio-Economic Development Strategy for the period of 2011–2020. However, the role of immigrant labor force remains unnoticed. Trinh argues, although the Vietnamese labor immigration policies and laws have undergone positive changes, on the one hand, they still cannot meet the country's demand for highly skilled workers cause by lacking flexibility to attract skilled permanent residents, on the other hand, they lack ability of protect the human rights of foreign workers (Trinh 2016). Passive, not proactive, issue of immigrant labor is seen as a derivative one of attracting foreign investment and expanding trade, but not seriously considered as a strategy at national level. Additionally, the emphasis of high-level social control within an authoritarian political environment leads Vietnam's policy to dealing with a short-term human shortage model. There are also no significant or typical discussions about moving towards a longer-term and broader policy.

Without an Act or Law for foreign workers, preferring rather to migrant foreigners in few categories of workers and not fully recognizing rights for them as residents or citizens, in a less positive perspective, we could even describe Vietnam's policy-maker as a typical newly industrialized country that is completely void of an "immigration policy" (Massey 2009).

3.3   Main Factors Influence the Performance of Immigration Policy in Vietnam

Thayer applied Bertelsmann Sustainable Governance Indicators for Southeast Asian countries, which emphasizes Vietnam as a "weak state" primary because the relatively high degree of actual autonomy at the subnational levels of government. Competition for resources, especially private and foreign investment capital, has leading power conflicts between the central government and sub-central agencies (Thayer 2016). Stallings and Kim suggest that it's unrealistic to consider Vietnam as developmental state, which brings miraculous success to East Asian industrializing countries. The East Asian approach emphasizes macroeconomic stability and efficiency as important components of a successful economy; such an approach expects substantial and coordinated institutions within the state, together with the ability to formulate development policies appropriate to the situation (Stallings and Kim 2017). Governance in the field of immigration in Vietnam, again, points out its goals were not fully reached, for both stability and efficiency within a foreign-capital dependent approach of development.

3.3.1   Weak Coordination Among Related Agencies in the Management of Foreigners

The State management weakness is one of the main reasons for increased illegal migrants. There remains a lack of coordination in the implementation of the law on foreigners' entry in, exit from, and residence in Vietnam. Related agencies fail to build a shared database on the management of foreigners, leading to difficulties in sharing and exchange of information among them. For the time being, the task of managing foreigners in the country is assigned to numerous ministries and sectors, but the competent agencies cannot coordinate with each other in the governance of foreign workers in Vietnam, thus there is no authoritative body in Vietnam that bears primary responsibility for the weaknesses of handling foreign workers.

3.3.2   High Degree of Sub-Central Agencies' Power

Since 2001, radical changes have been made in Vietnamese state administrative decentralization. The Resolution of the 9th Plenum of the 9th National Assembly's task setting and commitment have been defined as *"Urgently completing decentralization and assignment of powers from the central to local levels in each branch, each field in a synchronous manner, ensuring effective unified management of the Central over localities while encouraging the creativity and self-responsibility of localities."* (Nguyen 2018) As a result, sub-central agencies have implemented the policy in a unified manner, improving their autonomy in managing and using local resources.

However, control and inspection of the central government toward sub-central agencies are showing a low level of strictness; several sub-central governments have taken advantage of decentralization to enhancing their power by making decisions and implement policies in favor of local interests or being ready to violate regulations issued by central agencies.

There were a number of local authorities ignoring the practices of recognizing illegal foreign workers in pursuance of attract more foreign investment, as well as belittling the significance of controlling foreign visitors, in their respective localities. There are no official statistics on the number of foreign migrant workers in Vietnam because localities do not complete statistics on them. Some still fail to issue regulations on coordination in the management of foreigners in localities, causing difficulties to the operation of responsible authorities and the maintenance of social order.

3.3.3 Substantial Role of Foreign Investors and Contractors

Temporary arrangements may be seen as more easily manipulated by employers; in the case of Vietnam, there are FDI's investors and contractors for infrastructure development projects. The widespread phenomenon of FDI firms whose recorded long-term negative earning but continuously extent their business in Vietnam suggests state should not rely on numbers of labor shortages claiming or surveying by employers. In many cases, these exaggerated numbers allow employers get cheaper labor, and definitely not-local ones so far.

Whether or not they have been investing and operating in Vietnam for a long time or recently, foreign investors are more likely to employ foreign workers at the management level than local ones, which is especially true for FDI firms of largest investor community in Vietnam from Japan, Korea or Taiwan. Studies on the relationship between nationality and management rank in FDI enterprises (Kim 2004; Wang and Tsai 2007) have shown the fact that low and middle level of managers can be given opportunities for Vietnamese indigenous or mainland Chinese, but they have almost no hope of reaching the senior management position of Taiwan FDI's firms. When more than half (86%) of Taiwanese in the enterprise held a middle to senior management position, their education level was only ½ at the university level, their majority of work experience abroad (over 80%) is less than 5 years (Chong et al. 2010). The human resource approach of firms that does not rely on qualifications but rather on nationality, illustrates how the policy of accepting hiring foreign employers for positions that indigenous people cannot meet the requirements for is, in many cases, non-existent. These continuously circumstances are significantly reducing the labor market's ability to create a healthy development, as well as the ability to meet a spillover effect through technology transfer (especially in management skill).

Although most employers of foreign workers strictly abide by the laws, many contractors and businesses have taken advantage of dodging regulations. By inviting or granting a guarantee for foreigners to work in Vietnam for a period of under three months, then bring workers to the nearest border gate after that to carry out the re-entry procedures, they could make those foreigners continuing to work in Vietnam without having to apply for a work permit. Foreign contractors also listed schedule and quality requirements as the main reason for violating the regulations on the enrollment of local employees. There are also cases where foreign investors only commit small amounts of investment thanks to lack of minimum investment requirement in investment and enterprise laws which allows them enjoy work permit waivers and long-term temporary residence permits.

The problem of illegal foreign workers has not been resolved, especially regarding unskilled workers. Since 2000s when the Chinese government launched the strategy of "Going Global", Chinese contractors have brought into Vietnam a large number of contract workers when they won construction contracts of infrastructure projects (mostly under the form of EPC), and they were more willing to hire Chinese workers. Vietnam's data showed that between 2005 and 2010, the number of Chinese workers in Vietnam had jumped from 21,217 to 75,000 persons. For more detail, data from the field study of Nguyen showed a low rate of Chinese workers legal registered, from minimum 7% to maximum 38% only (Nguyen 2013).

As the result, those circumstances have negatively affected the employment of local workers. Vietnam's labor market has been pushed into a situation in which neither highly skilled nor low skilled occupations are more available and foreign workers are able to make better-earnings than natives.

4 Findings and Conclusions

The increasing number of foreign employees in Vietnam in recent years has contributed to improvements in labor productivity, created a competitive environment with local employees, and transferred the cutting-edge technology to Vietnam. In the medium-term, Vietnam's economy is expected to continuously expand, with GDP growth to be projected at a moderate rate of around 6.5%. Together the undergoing negotiation process for further international trade agreements, the efforts of the state in increasing transparency in custom and tax procedures, and applying technology in public services to streamline the business the business activities, Vietnam will remain to be an attractive FDI destination in the upcoming years, especially when the US—China trade war is still on-going. Besides, the booming of new business models such as e-commerce, fintech recently has escalated the demand for high skilled specialists, which the Vietnamese labor market has not enough supply for. It is expected that the demand for foreign employees will rise by more than 20% annually in the near future. It can be seen that Vietnam will be an attractive destination for more foreign migrant employees in the near future.

Immigration policy-making and management emphasize the character of 'strong authoritarianism, weak management' of the Vietnamese regime. Vietnamese authority strengthens its legitimacy by its economic performance with the help of advantages brought from the external environment. Nevertheless, those advantages are undermining the necessity of enhancing the State's internal governance capacity.

There is a lack of theoretical discussion about immigration policy while attempting to resolve the long-term issues of the Non-Migrant Work Visa, Vietnam's policy-makers are not able to carefully consider the purposes and consequences of the policy, especially the manipulation of FDI' s investors in the labor market in particular and in the economy in general. Furthermore, weak governance capacity, characterized by weak coordination among related agencies in the management of foreigners, together with high degree of sub-central agencies' power have distinct negative effects. On the one hand, these weaknesses limit willingness of immigrant workers to contribute more effort to their employers; on the other hand, these weaknesses also bring serious challenges to well-functioning labor market, as well as stabilizing social order.

To sum up, the Vietnamese State are facing the dilemma over thoroughly welcoming foreign capital for bolstering economic growth on the one hand and pursuing authoritarian social controlling on the other hand. In order to keep its competitiveness in the global (or regional) labor market, there are critical necessaries for either theoretical review long-term migration policy, and also to enforce practical skills in the field of governance toward foreign workers in Vietnam.

References

Bodewig, C., & Badiani-Magnusson, R. (2014). *Skilling up Vietnam: Preparing the workforce for a modern market economy.* The World Bank.

Cerna, L. (2016). *Immigration policies and the global competition for talent: The International series of public policy.* London: Palgrave MacMillan.

Central Institute of Economic Management CIEM, General Statistic Office GSO & University of Copenhagen UnC. (2015, April). *Firm level technology and competitiveness in Vietnam evidence from 2010–2014 surveys* (Report). https://www.wider.unu.edu/sites/default/files/Public ations/Report/PDF/Tech%20report%202009-2013%20April%202015.pdf.

鐘憶慈,余明助,何正得. (2010). *外派幹部之海外適應與留任意願關係研究-以越南台商為例.* 工程科技與教育學刊, 7(1), 頁1–15 [Chong, Y., Chu, Y., & Ho, C. (2010). 外派幹部之海外適應與留任意願關係研究-以越南台商為例. *Journal of Engineering Technology and Education, 7*(1), 1–15].

De Mesquita, B. B., Smith, A., Siverson, R., & Morrow, J. D. (2003). *The logic of political survival.* Cambridge: MIT Press.

Department of Employment, MoLISA. (2019). *Hội nghị truyền thông về việc làm.* http://doe.gov. vn/News/Detail/1/226.

Dezan Shira & Associates. (2019). *Vietnam's free trade agreements—Opportunities for your business.* https://www.vietnam-briefing.com/news/vietnam-free-trade-agreements-opportunities-for-your-business.html/.

Foreign Investment Agency, Ministry of Planning and Investment. (2018). *FDI attraction in the first 10 months of 2018.* https://dautunuocngoai.gov.vn/tinbai/6073/Tinh-hinh-thu-hut-Dau-tu-nuoc-ngoai-10-thang-nam-2018.

Freeman, Gary P. (2006). *National models, policy types, and the politics of immigration in liberal democracies. West European Politics, 29*(2), 227–247.

General Statistics Office of Vietnam (GSO). (2016). *Labour productivity in Vietnam: Practices and solutions.* https://www.gso.gov.vn/Modules/Doc_Download.aspx?DocID=19551.

Hang, T. T. (2017). *Report on Vietnam's rules regulating foreign workers. Japan Labor Issues, 3*(1), 77–82.

HSBC. (2019). *Expat 2019 global report.*

Kim, J. H. (2004). They are more like us: The salience of ethnicity in the global workplace of Korean transnational corporations. *Ethnic and Racial Studies, 27*(1), 69–94.

Massey, D. S. (2009). The political economy of migration in an era of globalization. In S. Martinez (Ed.), *International migration and human rights: The global repercussions of US policy.* University of California Press.

Natter, Katharina. (2018). *Rethingking immigration policy theory beyond 'western liberal democracies'. Comparative Migration Studies, 6*(4), 1–21.

Nguyen, D. T. (2018). *Assessing the policy on state administrative decentralization and assignment of powers in Vietnam.* The Communist Review No. 914.

Nguyen, T. T. H., & Nguyen, T. B. T. (2015). *Lao động nước ngoài ở việt nam thực trạng và những vấn đề đặt ra.* http://ilssa.org.vn/vi/news/lao-dong-nuoc-ngoai-o-viet-nam-thuc-trang-va-nhung-van-de-dat-ra-131.

Nguyen, Van Chinh. (2013). *Recent Chinese migration to Vietnam. Asian and Pacific Migration Journal, 22*(1), 6–30.

Papademetriou, D., Somerville, W., & Tanaka, H. (2008). *Hybrid immigrant-selection system: The next generation of economic migration schemes.* Washington, DC: Migration Policy Institute.

Pham, M. H. (2011, August). *Lao động nước ngoài tại Việt Nam – Góc nhìn khác.* http://vov.vn/vov-binh-luan/lao-dong-nuoc-ngoai-tai-viet-nam-goc-nhin-khac-183387.vov.

Stallings, Barbara, & Kim, Eun Mee. (2017). *Promoting development: The political economy of east asian foreign aid.* London: Palgrave Macmillan.

Thayer, Carlyle A. (2016). *Weak states and strong societies in Southeast Asia.* In Amin Saikal (Ed.), *Weak states, strong societies: Power and authority in the New world order.* I.B.Tauris: London and New York, NY.

Trinh, L. K. (2016). *Work related rights of foreign migrant workers in Vietnam. Journal of Asian Development, 2*(2), 1–20.

Vietnam News. (2019, August). *Ministries call for enhanced management of foreign workers in Việt Nam.* http://vietnamnews.vn/society/524495/ministries-call-for-enhanced-management-of-foreign-workers-in-viet-nam.html#wChQxYOqhtsziss2.99.

Wang, Hong-zen, & Tsai, Cheng-hung. (2007). *Ethnic glass ceiling: Ethnic division of labor and position attainment in Taiwanese-owned factories in Vietnam. Taiwan Journal of Southeast Asian Studies, 4*(2), 53–74.

World Bank. (2013). *Vietnam development report 2014: Skilling up Vietnam: Preparing the workforce for a modern market economy.*

World Bank. (2019). *Doing business 2019: Training for reform.* http://www.worldbank.org/content/dam/doingBusiness/media/Annual-Reports/English/DB2019-report_web-version.pdf. Accessed 15 January 2019.

Zolberg, A. R. (1989). *The next waves: Migration theory for a changing world. International Migration Review, 23*(3), 403–430.

Part II
Immigration Policy in Europe

Masses of Immigrants to Europe and Political Reactions: Influence on African Migration

Dieter Eißel

Abstract It was an act of humanity to support refugees fleeing their countries of war and hunger. In the first stage of refugees arriving in Germany they were warmly welcomed by thousands of people willing to help, without whom the German administration could not have managed the so-called "refugee crisis." Over time however, this attitude has changed. In view of a growing number of migrants, more and more people turned against the "tide" incited by right-wing populists. In addition, the increasing criminality of the mostly young men from North-Africa contributed to changing the welcome-culture to rising xenophobia. This is, in part pushed by some politicians of the far right. Nevertheless, the German constitution guarantees the right of asylum and is therefore obliged to help. The problem is that in this respect Germany faces a lack of solidarity in the European Union when it wants other member states to accept a certain quota of refugees, too.

1 The Background of Fleeing

The war in Syria and the Taliban bombings in Afghanistan and Pakistan led to hundred thousands of refugees fearing for their life and trying to find a safer place to live. Aside from the threat of war endangered "human security" is an important reason for flight. Endangered human security concerns people who are in situations of extreme vulnerability, whether due to social, political or economic marginalization. From the perspective of human security, what matters in terms of security is not so much that states and societies should be involved in guaranteeing peace from external threat, but rather that they should guarantee the minimum conditions for people to be and feel secure in their societies by ensuring social peace. "The guarantor of national security is no longer military power, but favourable social, political and economic

Originally this paper was published in the journal of in *Journal of Global and Area Studies* 2020. Vol. 4 (1) pp. 1–28. The authors updated and revised the content for the book chapter.

D. Eißel (✉)
Institute of Political Science, University of Giessen, Giessen, Germany
e-mail: eissel@sowi.uni-giessen.de

© The Author(s), under exclusive license to Springer Nature Singapore Pte Ltd. 2021
C.-P. Chu and S.-C. Park (eds.), *Immigration Policy and Crisis in the Regional Context*,
https://doi.org/10.1007/978-981-33-6823-1_8

conditions, promotion of human development, human rights and inclusive policies" (UNDP 2004, p. 141). Extreme poverty with demoralising outlook of finding a well-paid job in the future, hunger and a lack of medical support drove many African migrants to flee the violence and hunger and make perilous desert crossings on foot to reach lawless Libya, where they wait to cross the Mediterranean on dilapidated boats that have carried thousands upon thousands before them to their deaths.

Even if there are fewer war activities in the future, there will still be the additional threat of climate change and extreme weather conditions with heavy floods in one part of the world and extreme drought in other parts. Together with rising sea levels, the negative impact of climate change on the supply of food will lead to increasing numbers of refugees seeking a sustainable life in better regions. African countries are among the poorest in the world, and it should not be a surprise that the desperate young generation seeks a better future, mainly in Europe. On average, Africans had a GDP per capita of €1895 per year in 2016, which is 15 times less than the EU average of €29,000. In addition, in contrast to Europeans who saw an increase of 12% from 2011, Africans lost 7%. But this average does not tell the truth when looking at the worst living condition for instance in the Sahel zone with extremely poor countries like Niger and Mali.

2 The Increasing Number of Immigrants and Unfair Distribution

The number of asylum seekers has fallen to a relatively low level since its height in 2014/15 when more than a million "flooded" Europe (as right-wing parties say) (Fig. 1). Stricter control has been "successful". From 2014 to June 2018, 3,831,455 asylum seekers entered the EU. Most of came from Syria (938,770), followed by Algeria (451,650), Iraq (321,695), Pakistan (150,805), Nigeria (142,200) and Albania (137,985). More recently, however, rescue vessels with hundreds of Africans have been prevented from arriving in European harbours, while the rescue ships of private NGOs, as well as the search plane "Moonbird", are now impounded in Malta and Italy.

Furthermore, some search and rescue teams from these ships have been accused of cooperating with smuggler gangs which send desperate refugees on unsuitable rubber dinghies on this risky trip. The idea of hardliners in Europe is to prevent Africans from starting their risky trip across the Mediterranean Sea because there will be no more private rescue teams. Control of the sea should only be in the hands of military guards like Frontex or the Libyan coast guard. The latter will take survivors back to detention camps in Libya, which are places of rape and torture. Of 32 awful camps, only seven are controlled by the Libyan state; the others are run by private organizations. The result of the new agenda of "protecting" European borders is that in June 2018 we faced 629 deaths—the highest number in 2018. The number of people who died on their trip through the Sahara is unknown. Because the EU has

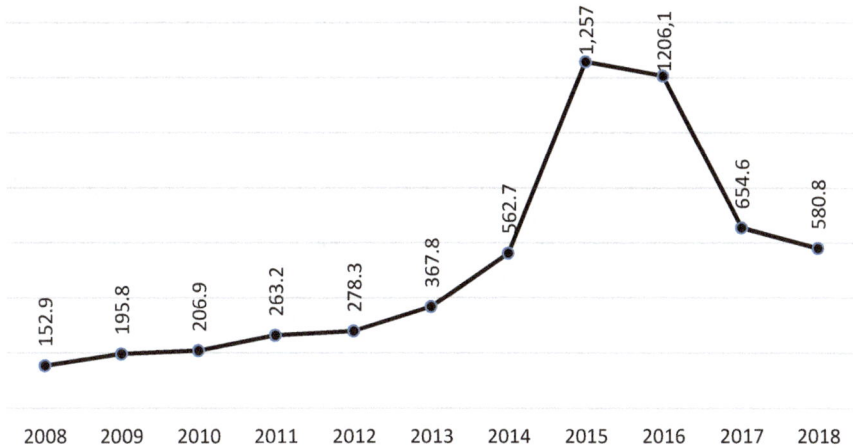

Fig. 1 Development of asylum seekers in thousands in the EU (*Source* https://ec.europa.eu/eur ostat/statistics-explained/index.php?title=Asylum_statistics)

financed a transit camp in the Sahara town of Agadez (Niger), where currently about 600 African people are registered and because the military forces of Niger intensified their control on the normal transit routes through the Sahara, attempt to reach Libya through the Sahara now take riskier routes. That is why the numbers of dead on this riskier route through the Sahara are not known. Thanks to the camp in Agadez, we must now realize that Europe's border now extends into Africa.[1]

Despite the fact that the number of asylum seekers is falling dramatically, countries like Italy, which was ruled by a right-wing coalition, and Malta, where many boatpeople first entered Europe, are no longer willing to allow refugees to enter their harbours. Despite the fact that the reduction of asylum seekers would create minor problems, several EU countries are still unwilling to receive an appropriate quota of asylum applicants, indicating at the same time a lack of solidarity in the EU with those countries that have a relatively high number of refugees like Germany, which hosts 41.3% of all asylum seekers.

However, the declining number of refugees to Europe in no way gives hope that another large wave of refugees like in 2015 could not to be repeated. The cause has mainly to be seen in the war in Syria, where Russian fighter jets are helping the Syrian ruler to destroy the resistance groups in Syria. The Russian bombing of the civilian population is largely responsible for the flow of nearly one million refugees towards Europe. This has led to unsustainable conditions in Turkey. In Turkey there are already 3,700,000 refugees, mostly from Syria (in Germany: 1,100,000). The other countries in Europe have felt secure that they will not face another wave of refugees, because the European Union paid Turkey to close the borders to Europe. The European Union has promised Turkey a total of €6 billion that should be used to

---

[1] See the TV-report of the German "Monitor" of 5.7.2018; http://mediathek.daserste.de/Monitor/Monitor-vom-05-07-2018/Video?bcastId=438224&documentId=53840900.

care for the refugees. However, Turkish President Erdogan unilaterally overruled the agreement concluded in March 2016 by opening the borders. That has led to chaotic conditions in the Greek border area. The overwhelmed Greek state was no longer able to accommodate the refugees at least reasonably. In the end, tear gas was even fired to keep the refugees away from the Greek islands (Fig. 2).

Poland, in particular, with only 29,650 asylum applicants, Czechia with 4,770 and Slovakia with a mere 810 belonged to the group of unsupportive objectors. Aside from the escalation of right-wing parties, which want people to believe that getting rid of refugees will solve nearly all social and economic problems, it seems that those countries with a low quota of foreigners are strong opponents to accepting asylum seekers, perhaps because they lack experience of a multi-cultural society (Fig. 3).

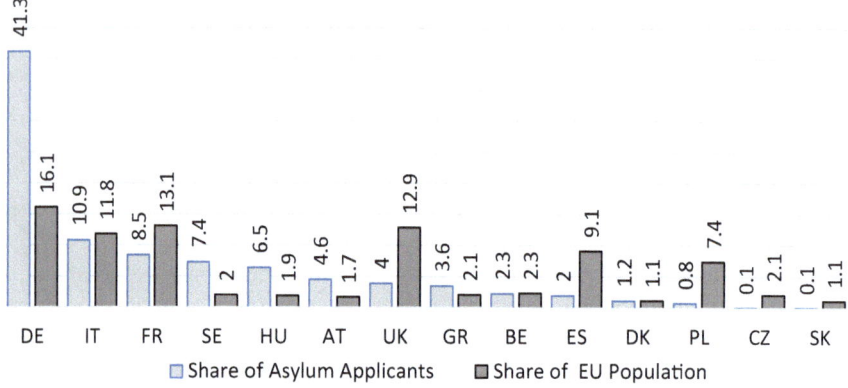

Fig. 2 Share of asylum applicants in relation to share of EU population 2014–6/2018 (*Source* Frontex, Eurostat, UNHCR, German BaMF)

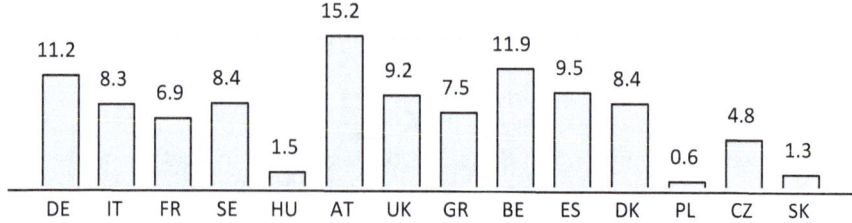

Fig. 3 Percentage of foreigners in EU countries (*Source* Eurostat 2018)

3 Germany's Chancellor Merkel as the Scapegoat

In 2015, when German chancellor, Angela Merkel, decided to open Germany's borders to war refugees, in particular, from Syria and Afghanistan, the situation was tragic. "Tragedy" here means that in a catastrophe of this kind, every choice was seen as wrong. In this emergency, facing the catastrophic situation of masses of refugees in Hungary and Austria, the German government was asked to welcome more asylum seekers. Merkel reacted at once but without the backing of her coalition partners. Nevertheless, she behaved in a humanitarian way and did not chose to use barbed wire, water guns, machine guns or tanks to chase away thousands of desperate refugees on the German border, nor to chase them back to Austria, Hungary, Greece, or Turkey and possibly back to the war in Syria or Afghanistan. Initially, a majority of Germans were welcoming, providing the refugees with clothing and food. This humanitarian behaviour raised Germany's prestige around the world. Nevertheless, soon, this attitude in Germany changed. Reports on crimes committed mainly by young male refugees, turned the formerly welcoming culture to just the opposite. Meanwhile, a majority in Germany perceive the open-door policy as a mistake, ignoring that Merkel has acted in a humanitarian way. The attacks against Merkel following the opening of the border in 2015 sometimes escalated to hysterical heights. Populists like the German AfD (Alternative für Deutschland) and even now the Bavarian CSU, as well as the governments in the Visegrad countries and in Austria show an increasing xenophobia.

Meanwhile, within Germany, the diverging views of East and West Germans almost model the difference between Eastern and Western states in the European Union. Here, too, we see that the effect of a dictatorship does not end with its downfall. The countries of the former Eastern Bloc, where there are hardly any foreigners and where very few refugees were accepted, have the greatest fear of them.

Despite increasing pressure to act on a national level, Merkel is trying to find a European solution to the immigration challenge. Most German parties support her insistence on finding a European solution to the refugee crisis, but they have great doubts that a European solution could be implemented because of nationalist interests of some member states. The question of how to distribute refugees fairly is a huge challenge given the traditions of the EU. The question on the agenda during a meeting of the European Union's leaders, therefore, is: How can the European states come to an agreement on securing their external borders without abandoning the notion of a humane asylum policy? There is still a majority of those who insist on EU regulations. Nevertheless, there are heavy doubts about whether fair EU regulation can be put into practice (Fig. 4).

Overall, across the EU the results are nearly the same: immigration from outside the EU is perceived as the biggest challenge for the EU (40%), followed by the threat of terrorism (20%) (Table 1).

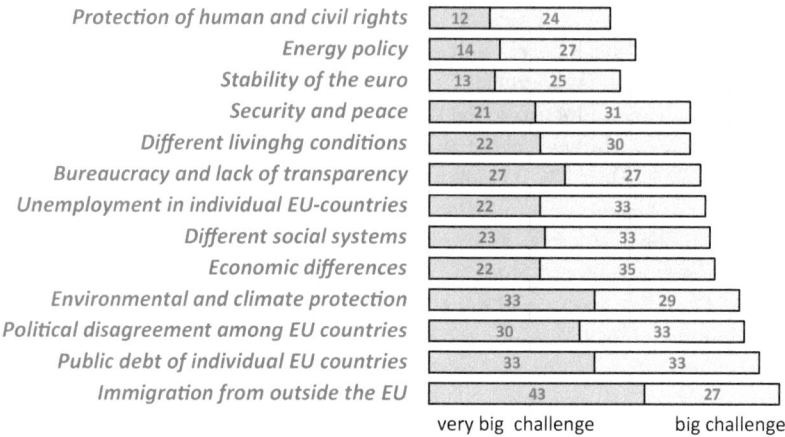

To what extent - if any - are the following issues a challenge for the the future of the EU?

	very big challenge	big challenge
Protection of human and civil rights	12	24
Energy policy	14	27
Stability of the euro	13	25
Security and peace	21	31
Different livinghg conditions	22	30
Bureaucracy and lack of transparency	27	27
Unemployment in individual EU-countries	22	33
Different social systems	23	33
Economic differences	22	35
Environmental and climate protection	33	29
Political disagreement among EU countries	30	33
Public debt of individual EU countries	33	33
Immigration from outside the EU	43	27

Fig. 4 To what extent are the following issues a challenge for the future of the EU?—Survey in Germany, 2018 (*Source* Eurobarometer 89)

Table 1 Aspirations of German parties

Where to solve the refugee crisis: at the EU or the national level?			Chance of realization	
	EU	National	Yes	No
Green party	90	10	50	47
SPD	85	13	44	52
Left	85	13	43	53
CDU/CSU	81	27	38	54
Liberals	77	22	31	68
AfD	32	67	11	87

Source Infratest, Dimap, 2017

4 Cause of the Emergence of Populist Right-Wing Parties

We can see the emergence of right-wing nationalism as a political force worldwide and even in Europe, which has prompted fears that liberal democracy is at risk of sliding towards illiberal and authoritarian forms of government. As this nationalism strengthens, it poses a threat to socially inclusive democracy and solidarity in Europe. The cause of this emergence of nationalist and right-wing parties is related to the ruling neo-liberal belief that markets and the withdrawal of the states would better help to overcome an economic crisis and would be supportive for higher growth rates. Causes of the current crisis go back to the world-wide deregulation of the financial markets, which was accompanied by a massive increase in financial assets in fewer hands. This rapidly increased the amount of speculative investment. More and more capital was invested in the financial markets and correspondingly, less in industrial capital, i.e., in production and services and in jobs. Globalization, digitization, and demographic and cultural change led to uncertainty among people. Large parts of the population did not benefit from the growing prosperity and the positive aspects of the changing economic world. That creates winners and losers. In regions, which economically are in danger of being decoupled, people lose confidence in politics and in the democratic institutions. The fear of descent and exclusion grows. Frustration and insecurity are spreading. The increasing inequality of working and life situations is one cause of the growing right-wing populism (Giebler and Regel 2017).

Furthermore, in a more and more globalized world, big companies can compel governments to support their competitive forces by reducing the tax load and protective labour regulations. In consequence, states started a tax race to the bottom, favouring the rich and capital. The political class in Europe pursued its new neo-liberal preferences, reflecting the demands of employers, and reducing taxes on income from capital while helping to build an extensive low wage sector. At the same time, it neglected the problem of a weak domestic market, which stemmed from wages that had stagnated for more than a decade. Alongside deregulation the new economic dogma concerned the reduction of the tax load on the rich, which would then lead them to invest in working places.

The wealth gains of recent years are almost entirely on account of the super-rich. The super-rich are mostly entrepreneurs; very often their wealth is based on tax avoidance and wage-squeezing at the expense of the community. Not only are the assets very unevenly distributed, but so are the incomes. A textile worker in Bangladesh earns as much in her entire life as the chairman of the board of a leading company in four days (Euro-Memogroup 01/2018). While the masses lost their income position and public and private poverty increased, the rich intensified their search for alternative investments, creating what Susan Strange (Strange 1986) called "casino capitalism."

Moreover, greater inequality makes a greater proportion of the population vulnerable to poverty. Finally, rising inequality if not addressed, can also lead to a backlash against economic liberalization and protectionist pressures (Jaumotte 2008). In industrialized countries, the low-wage sector and precarious employment have been promoted for decades, while the number of employees protected by collective agreements fell. Taxes for rich people lead to fewer state resources. The state as a balancing actor is thus becoming more and more exhausted. Welfare states were at risk of continuing their social protection of the poor and unemployed (Eißel et al. 2014). The already disadvantaged are particularly affected. Rising inequality fuels social tension, is economically harmful and it harms democracy—money creates power. Furthermore, in this situation immigrants are perceived as competitors for rare working places, and they are considered additional entrants in the welfare system.

Apart from increasing xenophobia and attacks on refugees, many European citizens are deeply disappointed with the EU and the "bureaucracy" in Brussels. A failed anti-social crisis policy has supported the rise of new right-wing populist parties. The background to this attitude can be seen in the example of the Brexit decision, although there are similar feelings in other parts of the EU.

Neglected by the welfare state and increasingly disappointed with the traditional ruling parties, many people turned to the populist parties. These right-wing parties concentrate on three goals: (1) stopping immigration and send the refugees back, (2) insisting on national solutions to the misery without the ("helpless or even blocking") EU and (3) getting rid of the ruling elites. The widening gap between rich and poor, the decline of the middle classes, and the new phenomenon of the working poor then became the key factor for a profound crisis of political representation. Within the "neglected masses" a deep distrust in the traditional parties and in the rule of the political elites created the basis for emerging populist parties and the steady rise of right-wing nationalism. Furthermore, right-wing and nationalist parties attack the EU as being an institution that is inadequate to overcome the social crisis. The slogans are the same almost everywhere: "We want our country back" (UKIP), or "We will bring back our country and our people!" from the leader of the German AfD Gauland. The dangers are seen in migration and failing policies by the elite in the own country and the EU. European scepticism is widespread not only in the United Kingdom, the Netherlands, Poland and Hungary but also in Germany. Most complains that Germany has been abandoned by the other EU states in the refugee crisis.

Even in the EU institutions sceptical and right-wing populist parties are present. In the last EU-Parliament these groups numbered 110 members—a share of 16%. This increase in votes was lower than predicted, and is made up by right-wing parties from four countries:

France with the "Rassemblement National" renamed "Front National", Great Britain with the "United Kingdom Independence Party" (UKIP), Denmark with the "Danish People's Party" and Germany with "Alternative for Germany." Not included are the national-conservative and Euro sceptical parties in Eastern Europe, mainly PiS from Poland and Fidesz from Hungary. If we count all these groups together, they make up almost 30%. With regard to the new elections in 2019 the outlook is even darker. While the Social Democrats, and even the Greens and the Conservatives are predicted to lose, the nationalist and populist parties could double their seats.

Last but not least, immigration was addressed as the main obstacle to regaining general and social security. Among unemployed Europeans, 43% believed that immigrants take jobs away from local workers; the European average was 35%. Those whose financial situation deteriorated in 2010 saw immigrants as a greater threat to the labour market than the average of 56%. The majority in all countries expect immigrants to take advantage of health care and social benefits more than the native population, while they themselves bear the tax burden (Table 2).

We must be aware that the states' neoliberal strategies in reacting to increased competition in a more globalized world have led to an increase of xenophobia in many countries. As UNESCO has pointed out: "Two causes are put forward, to explain the resurgence of xenophobic and racist movements towards the end of the

Table 2 European parliaments with right-wing populist

Year of election	Seats in parliament	Radical right right-wing populist seats	Participation in government
Hungary 2018	199	Fidesz 134; Jobbik 26	Absolute majority
Poland 2015	460	PiS 235	Absolute majority
Germany 2017	631	AfD 94	
Denmark 2015	179	DF 37	
Austria 2017	183	FPÖ 51	
Finland 2015	200	True Fins PERUS 38	
Latvia 2014	100	National Alliance 17	Participation in government
France 2017	577	FN 8	
Italy 2018	630	Lega 125	Participation in government
Netherlands 2017	150	Freedom Party 20	
Belgium 2014	150	New Flemish Alliance 33	
Sweden 2014	349	Sweden Democrats 49	
Greece 2015	300	Golden Dawn 18	
Slovakia 2016	150	Slov. National Party 14	Participation in government

Source https://en.wikipedia.org/wiki/List_of_active_nationalist_parties_in_Europe

twentieth century". The first cause is new migration patterns that have developed as an effect of the gradual internationalization of the labour market during the postcolonial era. In the receiving countries, social groups in dis-favourable positions considered the newcomers as competitors for jobs and public services. This cultivated a social and political climate that generated xenophobia and racism (i.e. defensive reactions against migrants), as well as nationalism (i.e. demands that the state provide better protection against foreigners for its own population).

The second cause believed to reinforce xenophobia and racism is globalization. Increased competition between states has led states to reduce their services in areas of social welfare, education and healthcare. These reductions particularly hit the segments of the population living on the margins of society. These groups are often in direct competition with migrants for welfare services, and they are the main breeding ground for xenophobic and racist ideologies. Research has shown that severe economic inequalities and hindering access to basic economic and social conditions give rise to tensions and manifestations of racism and xenophobia. Those perceived to be outsiders or foreigners are the main targets.[2]

Like almost no other topic, "refugees" has been central in last years and gave impetus to right-wing populism. The media disproportionately reported on the "flood

---

[2]Xenophobia   (http://www.unesco.org/new/en/social-and-human-sciences/themes/international-migration/glossary/xenophobia/).

of refugees" coming to Europe, while some politicians put it on their agendas, sometimes because they thought it could help win back support. Of course, it was a huge challenge when over a million refugees entered the country in such a short time, and it caused many problems. Nevertheless, there was mostly a welcoming culture in countries like Germany. However, pictures of crowds of people entering the country, then being herded into shelters, with the corresponding conflicts and being hopelessly doomed to doing nothing, increased fears and rejection. This is in part due to the reports in the media and by describing the immigration as a "refugee tsunami" (like Germany's Federal Minister for Interior Affairs Horst Seehofer). In particular, the reports on (sexualized) violence and murders, mobilized ancient, deep-seated stereotypes of cultural history that the strange man from the Orient always has a knife behind his back and robs women (Küpper 2017) (Table 3).

Given the numerous losers in the global economy and the simultaneous dismantling of the welfare state in the wake of market dogmatism or neoliberal doctrine, it is easy to find support for right-wing populism, with a mix of lies and truths against the political elite or the establishment. In addition, these parties denigrate the press ("the lying press") and despise people with attitudes in solidarity as "good hearted people". The promise of salvation, to restore the good old times, to create jobs for the "forgotten," relies on the simple strategy: "foreigners out" (in Germany that would be about one-fifth with a migration background). However, this attempt to find a scapegoat for its own predicament in immigration policy excludes the causes of misery, namely neo-liberal politics with tax donations to the rich, rescue of the banks, the dismantling of workers' rights and welfare cuts in the face of growing inequality. However, many citizens communicated their disappointment by teaching the government a lesson. Facing the increasing number of citizens in the Member

Table 3 Immigration is more of a problem

Country	%	Country	%
Hungary	63%	Belgium	36%
Greece	63%	Germany	35%
Malta	63%	Netherlands	34%
Bulgaria	52%	Romania	33%
Italy	51%	UK	31%
Cyprus	50%	Lithuania	28%
Czechia	49%	Ireland	26%
Latvia	41%	Portugal	26%
Croatia	39%	Spain	26%
France	38%	Denmark	24%
Slovenia	38%	Finland	22%
Poland	37%	Sweden	19%
Austria	37%	Luxembourg	17%
Estonia	37%	EU 28	38%

Special Eurobarometer 469: Integration of immigrants in the European Union, Fieldwork Oct. 2017, publ. April 2018

States who perceive immigration from outside the EU as a problem, it became the main topic in election campaigns.

5   EU's Harmful Influence on African Migration

5.1   Humane Alternatives to "Fortress Europe" via Fair Trade with Africa

The main regulation on how to manage migration to the EU is inscribed in the Dublin Regulation. This convention as a European Union (EU) law determines the EU Member State responsible for examining an application for asylum seekers seeking international protection within the EU under the Geneva Convention and the EU Qualification Directive. It is the cornerstone of the Dublin System, which consists of the Dublin Regulation and the EURODAC Regulation, which establishes a Europe-wide fingerprinting database for unauthorised entrants to the EU. The Dublin Regulation aims to "determine rapidly the Member State responsible [for an asylum claim]" and provides for the transfer of an asylum seeker to that Member State. Usually, the responsible Member State will be the state through which the asylum seeker first entered the EU.

The problem now is that the refugees do not care about staying in the country of the EU they entered (Italy, Greece, Spain), but they try to reach mainly Germany in secondary migration.

The Bavarian sister party of the Christian Democrats the CSU, through their federal minister for internal affairs threatened to turn back at the border these secondary migrants, who had already been registered in the other countries. This nationalist concept was opposed by German chancellor Merkel, who insisted on a European solution. Even after reaching some compromises at the EU meeting, the CSU remained opposed to Merkel threatening to ending their partnership in the government. In the end, the wish of both conservative sister parties to remain in power meant that a deal was struck. Camps would be created at the Austrian border, making it possible to send back those refugees to Austria which had already been registered there or who had no chance of getting asylum. This would be done by an agreement with Austria. The SPD, as a junior partner in the government agreed to this strange compromise as long as these camps are not run like prisons. The welcoming culture of Germany, which earned so much admiration around the globe, has ended. Even Merkel, a former exponent of humanitarian politics, is forced or even willing (?) to move to the right side of "fortress" Germany to remain in power.

Furthermore, the EU member states have found only a poor compromise: they want to strengthen Frontex, to create detention camps on the EU's external borders or even in neighbouring countries, and leave nearly all other policies, in particular, the fair distribution of refugees to the individual member states. There is a threat that the EU as a union of solidarity is at risk. The great idea and its development are in danger. The minimal agreement found by the heads of the EU Member States is approaching the concept of "fortress Europe" neglecting humanitarian aspects.

Respecting the socio-economic background of the distrust in the political elites, Slavoj Žižek, a Slovenian psychoanalyst, a Marxist, and one of the most exciting contemporary European philosophers, concluded that it is not that the refugees endanger our society, but global capital is a threat to the entire world order. "The 'rich world' urgently needs to address the reasons behind mass migration, rather than its symptoms."[3] Therefore, he demands to fight the economic reasons for flight and terror. It is clear that we need a global and national poverty reduction strategy, a policy that distributes wealth equitably. We need more progressive taxation of high incomes, assets and inheritances, more public investment in education, health and infrastructure, and an end to the tax race to the bottom.

This policy has undermined the ability of national governments to effectively address social concerns, with subsequent negative effects on the legitimacy of democratic rule. What the EU should do instead is to fight unfair trade mainly with the poorest continent, Africa. In his book "The Chances of Globalization" (Stiglitz 2019), Joseph Stiglitz, a former employee of the World Bank and Nobel laureate, said that unlike the euphoric promises of free trade theorists, the corresponding deregulation and opening of markets in globalization have not led to greater prosperity for all. Only a few developing countries have succeeded in using globalization, in particular, China and some countries in East Asia. However, in his view, what is necessary, above all, is fair conditions around the globe. The North, in particular, the US and the EU, must finally adopt a subsidy policy to end the detriment of the South and implement fair trade (Stiglitz 2002).

The fight against poverty requires other ways than market and free-trade theories. The trade between the EU and Africa continues an imperialistic strategy of exploiting its raw materials while at the same time exporting highly subsidized food from EU farmers that African farmers cannot compete with. The independence that African countries gained seems only to be political independence. However, commercial and financial colonialism, in the form of neo-colonialism or Commercial Colonialism, continues as strongly as ever. The group "Trade Unionists against the EU" complain that the EU practises "a brutal neo-colonial relationship with the third world, particularly Africa".[4]

The most obvious and damaging example is, of course, the European Union's Common Agricultural Policy (CAP) which takes up half the EU budget and lavishes subsidies onto the EU's biggest landowners at the expense of millions of the poorest farmers in Africa.

The subsidy regime allows the EU to dump thousands of tons of heavily-subsidized food into Africa every year. This effectively blocks African producers from exporting their own products because they cannot compete with the lower prices made possible by the CAP (Independent 16.5.2006).

---

[3]https://www.rt.com/op-ed/442485-migrants-poverty-rich-zizek/.

[4]http://www.tuaeu.co.uk/how-the-eu-starves-africa/.

As a result, it is now estimated that Africa imports over 80% of its food when, not so long ago, Africa was totally self-sufficient in food production (The Zimbabwean 25.9.2017).

Here are some examples, published by the British newspaper The Independent and Trade Union against the EU: *"European farmers are guaranteed a price for their sugar three times higher than the world price and there are restrictions on foreign imports - backed up by import tariffs of 324 per cent. Export subsidies, meanwhile, allow surplus EU sugar to be dumped at bargain prices in African countries. (...) Mozambique loses more than £70 m a year - equivalent to its entire national budget for agriculture and rural development - because of restrictions on importing into Europe coupled with the dumping of cheap exports at its door, while 12,000 workers in Swaziland have lost their jobs because the local industry cannot compete; and South Africa also loses £31 m a year. (...) While chicken producers in Europe do not receive direct payments, the grain that feeds the birds is subsidised, substantially reducing the cost of farming."* (Independent 16.5.2006). *"Kenya, Nigeria and Senegal have been hit by cheap, subsidised imports from Europe while the £30 paid to British farmers for every tonne of wheat they produce inflates the price of breakfast cereals, bread and other goods in Britain.*

Thousands of tonnes of surplus powdered milk from the EU are dumped in West African countries such as Mali at a cheaper price than local cattle owners can sell at, devastating the economy and driving them out of business."[5]

"Unwanted EU chicken thighs and wings are often frozen and exported to Africa where they are sold for rock-bottom prices. Chicken farmers in Senegal and Ghana used to supply most of the country's demand – now their market share has virtually disappeared because subsidised imports are 50 per cent cheaper" (The Zimbabwean 25.9.2017).

As Claire Godfrey, trade policy adviser for Oxfam, said: "Not only does the Common Agricultural Policy hit European shoppers in their pockets but (it) strikes a blow against the heart of development in places like Africa."[6]

It shows that flight to Europe and the huge number of African refugees are in most cases economically motivated. Those who exclude huge groups of the population from welfare and social participation, and those who undermine governments should not be surprised when societies collapse and people become extremists or try to reach wealthier countries.

The European Commission is now attempting to impose a 'free trade' deal, which African trade unionists have described as the latest 'colonialist scramble' for the continent.

TUC-Africa general secretary Kwasi Adu-Amankwah said that the proposed Economic Partnership Agreements (EPA) would allow the continued exploitation of the continent by European big business. The colonial economic structure, which is set up to export raw materials and import manufactures remained. "Structural

---

[5]Ibid.

[6]Quoted in the Independent, 16.5.2006, https://www.independent.co.uk/news/world/politics/eu-sub sidies-deny-africas-farmers-of-their-livelihood-478419.html.

adjustment foisted on Africa with the active involvement of the European Union has killed off the little industrial capabilities countries mastered immediately after independence." He warned that the terms of the agreements would only make it harder for Africa to achieve the 2030 Sustainable Development Goals. The alleged market access offered under this and previous trade agreements, was "contrived." "As the tariffs came down on African raw materials, they went up for manufactures. "It is highly disingenuous to conceive of free trade between the poorest continent on Earth and the world's most powerful trading bloc as the solution" (Morning Star, June 16, 2016).

Therefore, it is clear that these EPA's are designed to open up the markets of all African, Caribbean and Pacific countries for EU exports, exposing third world producers to overwhelming competition from the world's most powerful and rapacious transnationals."[7]

Summing up, the trade balance of the EU with Africa was negative until 2015, when it became positive for the first time. In 2016, imports from Africa amounted to €116.9 bn, and exports from the EU to Africa were €143.9 bn, mainly concerning machinery and vehicles.[8] In his book "The New Harvest: Agricultural Innovation in Africa", Calestous Juma (2011) argues that there are at least three ways in which EU policies affect Africa's ability to feed itself: tariff escalation, a lack of innovation and food export preferences. "African agriculture is currently at a crossroad, at which persistent food shortages are compounded by threats from climate change. But, as this book argues, Africa can feed itself in a generation and help contribute to global food security. To achieve this Africa has to define agriculture as a force in economic growth by: advancing scientific and technological research; investing in infrastructure; fostering higher technical training; and creating regional markets. To govern the transformation Africa must foster the emergence of a new crop of entrepreneurial leaders dedicated to the continent's economic improvement.

This new edition of "The New Harvest" by Juma provides ideas on how to implement a series of high-level decisions adopted by African leaders to place agriculture at the centre of the continent's long-term economic transformation. It puts agriculture in the context of the Science, Technology and Innovation Strategy (STISA-24) adopted by African presidents in 2014. More importantly, this edition provides a policy framework that could be adopted for other sectors such as health, industry and green innovation. Incorporating research from academia, government, civil society, and private industry, the book suggests multiple ways that individual "African countries can work together at the regional level to develop local knowledge and resources, harness technological innovation, encourage entrepreneurship, increase agricultural output, create markets, and improve overall economic performance."[9]

---

[7]http://www.tuaeu.co.uk/how-the-eu-starves-africa/.

[8]http://ec.europa.eu/eurostat/statistics-explained/index.php/Africa-EU_-key_statistical_indica tors#Main_tables.

[9]https://ouidabooks.com/product/the-new-harvest-agricultural-innovation-in-africa.

5.2 Stopping Ruthless People Smugglers

Of course, the EU is right to aim at stopping criminal tug gangs and widespread bribery and corruption within state structures that support ongoing dangerous migrations. Tug allegiances are often ruthless and brutal—yet their business is booming: The tug industry is experiencing a global boom. The risk of the smugglers is small; their profits are high. Waves of desperate people are slipping across international borders every year and smugglers are making billions from an industry built on human misery. The secretive nature of this dark and deadly trade means experts can provide only an educated estimate of the profits it generates for the criminals involved. But the International Organization for Migration's (IOM) best assessment is that it's worth a staggering US$10 billion a year. "It could even be more. We do not have reliable figures," says Frank Laczko, the director of the IOM's Global Migration Data Analysis Centre in Berlin. Laczko is a global leader in migration research and despairs about what the world still doesn't know: how many people are engaged in smuggling, how many people are smuggled each year, and how many migrants are dying during their journeys. The several thousand deaths in the IOM documents each year is presumed to be just a fraction of the true figure.[10]

It is a business in which the networks are becoming more professional, as security experts report. At the same time, smugglers are acting more ruthlessly. Experts in Africa and the EU border agency Frontex complain about this. The smugglers accept that their "transport commodity" dies of thirst or drowns, or that the women are raped. The IOM has calculated that since 2000, at least 60,000 migrants have died or gone missing while fleeing. Since January 2014 alone, the number of victims is 20,000.[11]

The migrants often know what they are risking. They accept that they depend on greedy profiteers of misery. They know the stories of people coerced into forced labour or prostitution. This is well-known from the detention camps in Libya. However, the refugees want to use their chance for a better life. But even if the desperate people are able to do it again, they are far from safe. The Mediterranean is considered the deadliest escape route in the world. During the dangerous route across the Mediterranean Sea 16,607 had died or gone missed by April 2018. Although the number of crossings has fallen sharply compared to 2016, the risk has increased: in the previous year, there was one death for every 88 people who managed to reach the coast of Italy, Malta, Greece, Spain or Cyprus.

---

[10]https://publications.iom.int/books/migrant-smuggling-data-and-research-global-review-eme rging-evidence-base, see also: https://coconuts.co/yangon/features/the-10-billion-industry-built-on-human-misery/ (7.7.2017).

[11]https://www.focus.de/politik/praxistipps/schlepperbanden-so-funktioniert-das-milliardengesch aeft-mit-menschenschmuggel_id_7243249.html.

5.3   Stop Arms Export to African Crisis States

"Global security has deteriorated markedly in the past decade. The number, complexity and lethality of armed conflicts have increased, and there has been prolonged and shocking violence in large parts of the Middle East, Africa and South Asia. The world total of forcibly displaced people is over 65 million and has been climbing sharply in recent years. Further layers of complexity exacerbating human insecurity are the internationalization of what often start as purely internal conflicts, the nexus of criminal violence and the activities of a multitude of armed groups, and the impact of climate change. (…) There were seven active armed conflicts in sub-Saharan Africa in 2017: in Mali, Nigeria, the CAR, the DRC, Ethiopia, Somalia, and South Sudan. A number of other countries experienced post-war conflict and tension or were flash points for potential armed conflict, including Burundi, Cameroon, Gambia, Kenya, Lesotho, Sudan and Zimbabwe.[12]

Following the publication of the Stockholm International Peace Research Institute (SIPRI) fact sheet, the three largest importers in Africa between 2013 and 2017 were Algeria (52% of African arms imports), Morocco (12%) and Nigeria (5.1%). The top five arms importers in sub-Saharan Africa were Nigeria, Sudan, Angola, Cameroon and Ethiopia. Together, they accounted for 56% of arms imports to the sub-region. In particular, Nigeria had an enormous increase in arms imports by 42% between 2008 and 2017.[13]

All states in sub-Saharan Africa received 32% of total African imports between 2013 and 2017. Russia, China and the USA were by far the major exporters to Africa. However, EU member states were among the exporters, too. Among the 25 largest world arms exporters in the period 2013–2017 were France (with a share of 6.7%), Germany (5.8%), and the UK (4.8%), with Spain, Italy, Netherlands, Sweden, Finland, and Portugal together making 8.8%. France, in particular, which is the third-largest arms exporter in the world behind the United States and Russia, according to SIPRI- is engaged in increasing arms exports worldwide, and to Africa (by more than 20% of its exports),[14] even though it has taken the lead in several initiatives aimed at preventing and countering illicit flows of conventional weapons.[15] While Algeria's major arms supplier is Russia, its neighbour and rival Morocco is France's best weapons client (€8,554 million between 2011 and 2015).[16] However, currently about 60% of French sales go to the Middle East. They are facing criticism from lawmakers and rights groups for selling arms that are being used in the conflict

---

[12]Dan Smith's introduction, in the SIPRI yearbook 2018, summary; see https://www.sipri.org/sites/default/files/2018-06/yb_18_summary_en_0.pdf.

[13]Ibid., p. 7.

[14]https://www.defensenews.com/global/europe/2017/05/18/france-sees-14-percent-increase-in-foreign-arms-exports/.

[15]https://www.defense.gouv.fr/content/download/453467/7156832/file/2016-FranceControlArmTrade.pdf.

[16]https://bigthink.com/strange-maps/mapping-the-worlds-biggest-weapons-exporters-nil-and-their-best-customers.

Table 4 Value of arms exports from Germany from 2000 to 2017 (according to the SIPRI Trend Indicator Value (TIV) * in millions)

	2000	2001	2002	2003	2004	2005	2006	2007	2008
TIV	1610	895	902	1660	1126	2068	2764	3310	2380
year	2009	2010	2011	2012	2013	2014	2015	2016	2017
TIV	2521	2725	1351	847	738	1774	1764	2535	1653

*The statistics show the value of armaments exports from Germany in the years between 2000 and 2017 according to the SIPRI Trend Indicator Value (TIV) in millions
https://de.statista.com/statistik/daten/studie/152204/umfrage/entwicklung-der-ruestungsexporte-aus-deutschland-seit-dem-jahr-2000/

in Yemen.[17] Unlike in many other Western countries, no parliamentary approval is required for arms sales in France. Only a committee headed by the prime minister and a handful of other cabinet officials must agree to any sales. Once approved, the details are rarely reviewed or made public.

Even the German government, which has decided to reduce arms export, is engaged in African conflict regions. This stands in stark contrast with its development aid policy. German companies sold about €4.2 billion worth of armaments in 2015 (excluding small arms and ammunition). The most important customers were countries in the crisis zone in the Middle East and North Africa, in particular, Saudi Arabia, followed by Algeria, Egypt and Qatar. Between January and April, 54.3% of all arms export licenses went to states that were not members of the EU or NATO. The export of small arms to third countries multiplied in the period from January to April 2017 compared to the same period of the previous year: from €51,597 to €7,831,969.[18] Based on the SIPRI data there has been a boom in arms exports in recent years, but with a small reduction in German exports (Handelsblatt 23.7.2018).

At the same time the international arms trade has become more and more confusing. Despite strict restrictions, rifles, including German-made ones, reach dictators and crisis states. SIPRI found that the US, Russia, France, Germany and the UK are the largest arms exporters in the world. These five states produce 75 percent of all weapons sold. But what is particularly frightening is that none of the five supply only democratic states (Table 4).

"These facts are scary. As early as 2008, the news magazine Spiegel asked a question that today has lost none of its relevance: How far is Germany jointly responsible for the slaughter in African countries."[19]

---

[17]https://www.alaraby.co.uk/english/news/2018/7/4/france-arms-sales-to-middle-east-double-fueling-conflict.

[18]https://africa-alliance.org/deutsche-waffen-fuer-afrika.

[19]Ibid.

6 Peaceful Multiculturalism at Risk and Rising Xenophobia Against Muslims

The rising xenophobia in many European countries is aimed at Muslims due to a number of specific reasons. One reason for the change from initially welcoming culture to the rising rejection of refugees is due to jihadist terror attacks and obviously the relatively high number of crimes committed mainly by young male refugees. The jihadist terror attack in Paris 2015 with 93 deaths and the attack one year later using a car in Nice with 87 deaths are extreme events. Nevertheless, terrorist attacks (included unsuccessful ones) in 2017 were experienced in the UK with 107 attacks, followed by France with 54 attacks, Spain with 16, Italy with 14, Greece with 8, Germany and Belgium with 2 and Finland and Sweden with 1. Together with the nearly daily TV-reports on the war crimes of the so-called Islamic State in Iraq, Afghanistan and Syria, Nigeria etc. people increasingly believe that the threat is arriving with jihadists. Despite these awful reports, the fact is that between 2007 and 2017 most terror attacks in the European Union were committed by separatist and ethno-nationalist movements accounting for about two-thirds of all attacks that happened during these ten years. The share of religious motivated terror attacks was 16.1%, while right and left-wing anarchist attacks was about 14% (Handelsblatt 27.5.2020). Jihadist attacks, unlike separatist attacks, can happen anywhere, and they may lead to greater awareness of the uncertainty of a threat. Furthermore, they have led to more deaths than the other attacks. "But guaranteeing and strengthening security must necessarily go hand in hand with the respect of fundamental rights. In a European Union founded on the respect of human dignity, democracy, the rule of law and Human Rights, the protection and promotion of citizens' security and the respect fundamental rights are complementary and must mutually strengthen each other" (Mascagna 2019). Populist right movements ignore this mutual side of protection.

Another reason for people rejecting Muslims is due to the suppressive and arrogant behaviour that the men have toward women. Europeans have learned and developed a gender attitude that increasingly respects women—even if they are still disadvantaged in many areas, like equal pay. Against this friendlier gender attitude, Europeans see that Islamic women are heavily suppressed by the very traditional understanding of their role. The headscarf, or even the total concealment of the face by a burka, is seen by Europeans as a symbol of this suppression. Additionally, as a prominently visible symbol of Islam, it ignites debates about the acceptance of Muslim ways of life. There is a widespread demand for the headscarf to be banned for teachers, educators and judges. Only a minority see it as an expression of religious self-determination in a pluralistic society. This different culture, together with the fear of jihadist terrorists, is one reason to reject Muslims coming to "Christian Europe".

The level of rejection reflects the social structure. Less educated, older and poorer people show a more negative attitude towards Muslims than young and better-off people. Is related to the perception of incoming refugees as competitors in the social security system, among others.

Table 5 Percentage of people willing to accept Muslims or Jews as members of their family

	Muslim	Jews		Muslim	Jews
Netherlands	88	96	Austria	54	65
Denmark	81	92	UK	53	69
Sweden	80	92	Slovakia	47	73
Belgium	77	89	Italy	43	57
Spain	74	79	Poland	33	57
Portugal	70	73	Bulgaria	32	55
France	66	76	Greece	31	35
Finland	66	82	Romania	29	39
Ireland	60	70	Hungary	21	57
Germany	55	69	Czech Republic	12	51

Source PEW research centre (2018)
https://www.pewforum.org/2018/10/29/eastern-and-western-europeans-differ-on-importance-of-
religion-views-of-minorities-and-key-social-issues/pf-10-29-18_east-west_-00-15/

Compared with Western Europeans, people in Central and Eastern Europe are less accepting Muslims. Their national identity excludes people born outside the country. According to a survey conducted by the Pew Research Centre, between 2015 and 2017 in 34 Western, Central, and Eastern European countries,[20] Western Europeans are more likely than Central and Eastern Europeans to say they would accept Jews or Muslims into their family. "The continental divide in attitudes and values can be extreme in some cases. For example, in nearly every Central and Eastern European country polled, fewer than half of adults say they would be willing to accept Muslims into their family; in nearly every Western European country surveyed, more than half say they would accept a Muslim into their family. A similar divide emerges between Central/Eastern Europe and Western Europe with regard to accepting Jews into one's family."[21] Again, Western societies show, on average, a greater acceptance. "Anti-Semitism is getting worse and Jews are increasingly worried about the risk of harassment, according to a major survey of 12 EU countries. Hundreds of Jews questioned by the EU's Fundamental Rights Agency said they had experienced a physical, anti-Semitic attack in the past year, while 28% said they had been harassed."[22] France is identified as having the biggest problem with anti-Semitism. Germany, the UK, Belgium, Sweden and the Netherlands also saw incidents. According to a 2019 article in The Guardian "Antisemitism is rising sharply across Europe, as France reported a 74% increase in the number of offenses against Jews in 2018 and Germany said the number of violent antisemitic attacks had surged by more than 60%. The figures confirm the results of three recent Europe-wide surveys showing Jewish people feel

---

[20] https://www.pewforum.org/2018/10/29/eastern-and-western-europeans-differ-on-importance-of-religion-views-of-minorities-and-key-social-issues/pf-10-29-18_east-west_-00-15/.
[21] Ibid.
[22] https://www.bbc.com/news/world-europe-46439194.

Table 6 Religious affiliation in Germany	Non-religious	36.2%
	Catholics	28.5%
	Protestants	26.5%
	Muslims	4.9%
	Other affiliation	3.9%

https://www.deutschland.de/en/topic/life/religious-faith-in-ger many%3Amany-germans-are-leaving-the-church

at greater risk, and are experiencing markedly more aggression, amid a generalized increase in racist hate speech and violence in a significantly coarser, more polarised political environment" (Table 5).[23]

The PEW survey went on to say, "In a separate question, Western Europeans also are much more likely than their Central and Eastern European counterparts to say they would accept Muslims in their neighbourhoods. For example, 83% of Finns say they would be willing to accept Muslims as neighbours, compared with 55% of Ukrainians. And although the divide is less stark, Western Europeans are more likely to express acceptance toward Jews in their neighbourhoods as well."

In the case of Germany, the first immigration wave was related to the booming economy in the 1960s and a shortage of labour. The Federal Republic solved this problem with the help of "guest workers" with many coming from Turkey. Because the political and economic situation in their homelands worsened in the 1970s, many Turkish families remained. Today they are German citizens. Many more Muslims fled civil wars (as in Syria), violence in disintegrating states (the former Yugoslavia), terror in their own country (Afghanistan) or state repression (Iran).

How widespread Islam really is in Germany cannot be determined exactly. The state does not cover all religions. Researchers estimate that about 4.5 million Muslims live there, meaning that bone in twenty people in Germany is Muslim. However, the average German perceives the situation quite differently: they estimate the proportion of Muslims in the population to be four times higher.

The number of Muslims varies greatly in the sixteen federal states. One-third of all Muslims live in North Rhine-Westphalia, while Baden-Wurttemberg, Bavaria and Hesse also have large Muslim populations. Muslims live mainly in cities, less in the countryside. Very few of them live in the new federal states. When, before the 1990s, many of them immigrated, Germany was still divided into two parts, so the GDR was not an emigration destination for them. According to a 2017 study by the Bertelsmann Foundation, Muslims feel extremely connected to Germany. Accordingly, the majority of Muslims often interact with people outside their own sphere of religion and are actively involved in working life. Only five percent of all Muslims in Germany are unemployed, for non-Muslims, there are seven percent. More than half of all Muslims are involved in German clubs, mostly in sports (Table 6).

---

[23] Ibid.

Table 7 Different perception of religions

	A threat (%)	Enriching (%)
Islam	51	29
Judaism	19	53
Atheism	18	48
Christianity	10	73
Buddhism	10	60

Source Bertelsmann Stiftung—Religionsmonitor 2013

Nevertheless, many Muslims encounter rejection. More than one in three Muslims said they felt discriminated against during the year prior to questioning. In the case of immigrant Muslims, as many as one in two felt that they were excluded from German society because of their origin. Anti-Muslim attacks have steadily increased in the past few years worldwide. The Federal Criminal Police Office counted such attacks on mosques between 2001 and 2016. The number of unreported cases is likely to be much higher. Many cases are not reported to the police or they are classified differently in the statistics. German authorities registered at least 950 attacks on Muslims and Muslim institutions such as mosques in 2017 with 33 people injured in these attacks (Table 7).[24]

If we consider the current situation in Germany, we have to face the fact there is ongoing rejection, despite the fact that Germans (in the West!) had a long period of peaceful multicultural living together. The majority of Muslims, coming from Turkey as workers and from Iran as intellectuals, fleeing during the Shah Reza regime, are now in the third-generation Germans, integrated into society as workers or even entrepreneurs. However, this peaceful multicultural society is now at risk. A representative survey of the Protestant church from August 2018 indicates that 53.7% of Germans disagree with the statement "the Islam is compatible to Germany." Only one-third said yes, they belong to Germany, while 13.1% were undecided. In East Germany the rejection of Muslims was even higher, at 61%.[25]

As the extreme-right party of AfD focus on criticizing immigration, it should not be a surprise that this party has relatively high support among the electorate of the former GDR. As the head of the AfD Alexander Gauland, put it during the election campaign: "We will get our country and our people back."[26] However, this xenophobia, is not only seen in Germany but also in many other countries of the EU.

---

[24]https://www.theguardian.com/news/2019/feb/15/antisemitism-rising-sharply-across-europe-latest-figures-show.

[25]https://www.ekd.de.

[26]https://www.br.de/bundestagswahl/afd-politiker-gauland-ueber-merkel-wir-werden-sie-jagen-100.html.

7   Conclusion: Christianity as Part of National Identity and as Exclusion of Muslims? Implications for Western Value

According to the Pew Research Centre, "Attitudes toward religious minorities in Central and Eastern Europe go hand in hand with differing conceptions of national identity." They go on to say "In Western Europe, by contrast, most people don't feel that religion is a major part of their national identity. In France and the United Kingdom, for example, most say it is not important to be Christian to be truly French or truly British."[27]

In contrast, for most people in Central and Eastern Europe being Christian (whether Catholic or Orthodox) is a key component of national identity, at the same time perceiving Christianity as a European value, connoting the exclusion of others. This attitude disregards the "Charter of Fundamental Rights of the European Union" which includes respect for cultural and religious diversity; prohibitions against discrimination based on religion and sexual orientation; the right to asylum for refugees; and guarantees of freedom of movement within the EU. However, since the enlargement of the EU in 2004, when it welcomed Central and Eastern states, the understanding of "Western" values has changed towards being less receptive to religious and cultural pluralism than they are in Western Europe. Since masses of immigrants entered Europe from predominantly Muslim countries, articulations of opposition to the EU's conception of European values have not only become stronger in Central and Eastern Europe, but they have infiltrated the West, too. This is clearly seen by the rise of extreme right-wing parties in nearly all EU member states demanding the right to reject the ideology of multiculturalism. Nevertheless, there is more openness toward multiculturalism in the West than in the East. We could reduce harmful migration by ending the disastrous impacts of European trade policy, mainly on Africa and by stopping arms export to conflicting regions. Nevertheless, we are unable to stop migration which is caused by hunger due to the impacts of ongoing climate change. Therefore it is necessary to support basic attitudes towards multiculturalism and peaceful living together. Among others, this needs a functioning welfare state and a good education system, which provides the view that immigrants are no competitors in the labour market and in the social security system, but an enrichment of social, economic and cultural life. However, this will take time.

References

Eißel, D., Rokicka, E., & Leaman, J. (2014). *Welfare state at risk*. Heidelberg, N.Y., London et al.: Springer.

---

[27] https://www.pewforum.org/2018/10/29/eastern-and-western-europeans-differ-on-importance-of-religion-views-of-minorities-and-key-social-issues/pf-10-29-18_east-west_-00-15/.

Eurobarometer 89. *European citizenship* (Report). http://ec.europa.eu/commfrontoffice/publicopi nion.

Euro-Memogroup. (2018). *EuroMemorandum 2018*. http://www.euromemo.eu/euromemorandum/ euromemorandum_2018/index.html.

Eurostat. (2018). The European Union and the African Union, a statistical portrait 2018.

Giebler, H., & Regel, S. (2017). Wer wählt rechtspopulistisch, in Friedrich-Ebert-Stiftung, Wiso Diskurs.

Jaumotte, F., et al. (2008). *Rising income inequality: Technology, or trade and financial globalization?* (IMF Working paper WP, 08(185)).

Juma, C. (2011). *New harvest: Agricultural innovation in Africa*. https://ouidabooks.com/product/ the-new-harvest-agricultural-innovation-in-africa.

Küpper, B. (2017). *Rechtspopulistische Einstellungen in Ost- und Westdeutschland, in: Institut für Demokratie und Zivilgesellschaft (IDZ)*. https://www.idz-jena.de/wsddet/rechtspopulistische-ein stellungen-in-ost-und-westdeutschland/.

Mascagna, S. (2019). Protecting European citizens in an ultra-connected world. In Foundation Robert Schumann/European Issue Nr. 511, 16(4).

PEW Research Centre. (2018). https://www.pewforum.org/2018/10/29/eastern-and-western-eur opeans-differ-on-importanceof-religion-views-of-minorities-and-key-social-issues/pf-10-29- 18_east-west_-00-15/.

Stiglitz, J. (2002). *Globalization and its discontents*. London: Penguin Books.

Stiglitz, J. (2019). *The end of neoliberalism and the rebirth of history on 26th November 2019*. https://www.socialeurope.eu/the-end-of-neoliberalism-and-the-rebirth-of-history.

Strange, S. (1986). *Casino capitalism*. Oxford: Blackwell.

The New Harvest: Agricultural Innovation in Africa. (2016, May). https://ouidabooks.com/product/ the-new-harvest-agricultural-innovation-in-africa/.

UNDP. (2004). *Human Development Report 2004: Cultural Liberty in Today's Diverse World*. New York. http://hdr.undp.org/en/content/human-development-report-2004.

Implications of the EU's Immigration Governance to Normative Power Europe (NPE) in the Case of Refugee Crisis

Yun-Chen Lai

Abstract In recent years, it has become widely accepted that the EU acts as a "normative power" in defining its uniqueness, which has made it different from other traditional international actors. This paper uses immigration policy as a metric to examine the EU's realization of so-called normative power. First, the EU's development of immigration policy is briefly reviewed. To make the discussion more focused, the refugee policy is examined, especially after the refugee crisis of 2015, to test whether the policies of the EU are consistent with the character of normative power, i.e., the respect for and promotion of norms. Subsequently, the concept of normative power is investigated, corresponding to the achievements and difficulties of the development of immigration policy. The reasons for these achievements/difficulties are also explored.

Keywords EU · Normative power · Immigration · Governance · Asylum

1 Introduction

The EU is a unique entity in global politics, as it is neither a traditional state nor an international organization, and because the competence of the supranational institution of the EU is far more than that of a normal international body. To elucidate the EU's unique role in global politics, scholars have devoted themselves to exploring the EU's behavior and aims. With the development of the rhetoric of an 'area of freedom, security and justice', an important change has occurred in the character of the EU, i.e., a gradual transformation from being an organization that is primarily concerned with economics into a political one, which possesses its own foreign policies and political agendas (Lavenex 2001, p. 870). Consequently, in recent years, it has been widely accepted that the EU acts as a "normative power" in defining its uniqueness, which makes it different from traditional international actors. In other words, the idea is gaining acceptance that the EU is not a potential conventional great power,

Y.-C. Lai (✉)
Department of Public Administration, National Dong Hwa University, Hualien, Taiwan
e-mail: yunchen.lai@gms.ndhu.edu.tw

© The Author(s), under exclusive license to Springer Nature Singapore Pte Ltd. 2021   147
C.-P. Chu and S.-C. Park (eds.), *Immigration Policy and Crisis in the Regional Context*,
https://doi.org/10.1007/978-981-33-6823-1_9

but rather a normative power that acts primarily through ideas and values, and not military or economic force to exert its influence in global politics (Falkner 2006, p. 2).

The notion of normative power comes from the argument of Ian Manners, who states that the EU has the ability to influence the behavior of others by exporting its values, rendering it a distinct kind of actor in global politics (Noureddine 2016, p. 1). Manners argues that the EU represents a new and distinct kind of actor within the international system, and transcends the anarchic and self-interested behavior of states (Manners 2002, p. 240). The EU's constitution, as an "elite-driven, treaty based, legal order," means that its identity and behavior are fundamentally based upon a set of common values (Manners 2002, p. 241; Noureddine 2016, p. 2). According to Manners' often-quoted definition, normative powers are only those actors that can "shape what can be 'normal' in international life" by changing the norms, standards, and prescriptions of world politics (Manners 2002, p. 239). He goes on to assert that "the ability to define what passes for 'normal' in world politics is, ultimately, the greatest power of all" (Kavalski 2013, p. 248; Manners 2002, p. 253).

After the concept of normative power was proposed, it has become widely accepted that the unique role of the EU in global politics could be observed from the perspective of spreading norms and values. For this reason, the debate about the nature of the EU's power should move away from traditional concerns over whether the EU should be a civilian or military power, and should focus more on the ideational impact of the EU's international identity as representing normative power with the ability to shape conceptions of normality (Lightfoot and Burchell 2005, p. 79; Manners 2002, pp. 238–239).

According to Manners, the normative role of the EU can be observed from the historical evolution of a normative basis to the EU, through the development of treaties, declarations, policies, etc., providing key information for understanding its actions (Lightfoot and Burchell 2005, p. 79). This paper, therefore, aims to explore the EU's normative role through empirical observation.

The promotion of norms and values is sensitive, as it involves the core identity and ideas of people. As one of the prevailing definitions of power, the ability to influence others to do what they do not want to do, or not to do what they want to do, has been broadly accepted, with the action to promote such norms and values thus not consisting of so-called "power." In other words, it is the ability to ask others to respect the values that they originally neglected, which could be considered as normative power. For this reason, observation of the operation of normative power can be considered to be a sensitive issue.

Among various issue areas, immigration policy is a complicated one. On the one hand, it is involved with national security, the core interest of nations in which nations tend to be conservative; whereas, on the other hand, it is concerned with human rights, which is the most basic idea of the promotion of so-called normative power. As a consequence, there are tensions underlying EU's asylum and migration policies because the policy stems from the values of security and community, which derives from the particularism of state sovereignty, emphasizing the need to control and limit immigration. It is also critical, however, to acknowledge that the core tenets of freedom and human rights come from a liberal universalism in which openness is mandated (Lavenex 2019). Herein, the EU faces what scholars have termed the "liberal paradox" (Hollifield 1992).

From the effects perspective, immigration is also a crucial political issue in the EU due to its electoral impact, which has led to the rise of new parties and challenges to existing party systems (Givens and Luedtke 2004, p. 145). European immigration policies affect state sovereignty from both within and from without. Internally, the abolition of internal migration policies, developed from the idea of freedom of movement, deprives member states of their sovereignty over the admission of EU citizens and long-term resident third-country nationals. Externally, the development of shared European policies regarding third-country nationals has augmented this decline of state sovereignty and reflects the EU's adoption of quasi-statist features (Lavenex 2019). Furthermore, immigration policy is involved with a variety of processes that consider numerous factors, including international stability, security, border-free areas, labor migration, the human rights of migrants, etc. However, among EU member states, consensus has often been difficult to reach (Van Klingeren et al. 2017, p. 544). Overall, the immigration issue has attracted great attention from the public, and the "harmonization" of immigration policy has faced political blockages, despite being regarded by most observers as necessary (Givens and Luedtke 2004, p. 145).

Even though immigration policy is sensitive to national states due to its linkage to national security, it cannot only be justified on the basis of material interests, but is strictly normative in character. Refugee protection in liberal democracies is a "republican" notion derived from universal human rights. Therefore, the degree to which a common European refugee policy is likely to be realized indicates more than the extent of the realization of the "Community Method". Indeed, it also comprises the EU's ability to establish a "community of values", as well as the extent to which novel normative paradigms, such as the Charter of Fundamental Rights, have become a reference for the courts and political entities (Lavenex 2001, p. 852).

Based on the importance of immigration mentioned above and its implications for both national security and normative power, this paper utilizes immigration policy as a metric to examine the EU's realization of normative power. Immigration policy has been developed since the 1950s from the structure of the Treaty of Rome. In the following sections, the EU's development of immigration policy will be briefly reviewed. To make the discussion more focused, this paper addresses individual parts of the refugee policy, especially after the refugee crisis of 2015, to test whether the policies of the EU are consistent with the character of normative power, i.e., the respect and promotion of norms. The concept of normative power will then be examined, corresponding to the achievements and difficulties of the development of immigration policy. The reasons for these achievements/difficulties are also explored.

2 Development of the EU's Immigration Policy

The cooperation of immigration stems from the Treaty of Rome in 1957. The Treaty of Rome, which constituted the initiation of European integration, aimed to establish the common market to eliminate barriers obstructing the movement of goods, people, services, and capital between Member States. As a consequence, issues brought by the common market, such as the free movement of goods, capital, and even labor were also addressed in the Treaty of Rome. However, regarding the issue of labor, the regulation only applies to labor forces moving from one Member State to another. As for illegal immigrants, visas and asylum, there was no clear regulation. Immigrants entitled to move freely inside of Europe did not include citizens of third countries. Therefore, the external immigration issue was not handled at the beginning of European integration.

In the 1970s, due to the energy crisis and economic recession, Western countries introduced a huge number of workers from developing countries, and thus faced the pressure of immigration and, at the same time, recognized the importance of transnational cooperation. In 1976, the Council of Ministers passed a resolution calling for the European Community to address immigration, including third-country nationals. The issue of immigrants of non-Member States has been prominent since then, and no practical cooperation has been achieved. Member States would have needed governmental cooperation to coordinate immigration policy; however, due to the differences of geographical position, various sources of immigrants, as well as the different traditions in approaching immigration, no single immigration policy was produced at that time. The most important development of immigration cooperation in Europe during that period was the establishment of the TREVI group, an intergovernmental network of national officials from different ministries of justice and the interior. TREVI dealt with public security problems, such as combating international terrorism, extremism and violence, which are all parts of immigration issues. Concerning the free movement of people, no significant progress was made. In other words, before the Single European Act in 1985, there was no EC policy for third-country nationals. Indeed, cooperation in visa recognition and border controls remained ad hoc and voluntary (Kostakopoulou 2000, p. 498; Caviedes 2004, pp. 292–293).

Significant cooperation in immigration occurred in the 1980s. In 1985, there were two significant developments. The establishment of the single European market was confirmed under the Single European Act in 1985. In Art. 8a of the Single European Act, it is stated that Europe would establish a single internal market to cancel borders, allowing the free movement of goods, people, services, and capital. The major objective was similar to that of the Treaty of Rome, in focusing on economic development to remove internal borders among the 12 member states by 1992 in order to achieve integration as a single European market. With the construction of the European single market, the free movement of people was officially included in the regulations of the European Community (Art. 13). Issues involving border regulations and the treatment of third-country nationals, such as the free movement of people, illegal immigration regulations, refugee asylum, etc., have become increasingly urgent, bringing further cooperation among member states. In this way, cooperation within internal borders expanded into external border cooperation during this period. In 1985, Germany, France, the Netherlands, Belgium, and Luxemburg signed the Schengen Agreement to form the Schengen Zone in order to remove border controls among members, create a common immigration and refugee policy, allow free movement of their citizens, and coordinate border controls outside of the zone. This has become the foundation of the current Schengen Zone. In 1988, the Rhodes Summit suggested establishing a cooperation organization to deal with the movement of people (Philip 1994). In the summit, it was discussed how to organize the Group of Coordinators to oversee all work in EU bodies on asylum, immigration, customs, as well as judicial and security policies. Furthermore, in the 1990 Dublin Summit, a convention on political asylum was produced. Even though the rights and the integration of third-country nationals were addressed in those discussions, they have since been downgraded to very long-term objectives (Ireland 1996, p. 134).

The Treaty of Maastricht expanded the EU's competence to juridical and internal affairs. Immigration issues are regulated commonly under the first pillar and the third pillar of the EU. Member states should take asylum policy and movement of persons between borders as a common interest (K1). In the meanwhile, this regulation does not affect Member States' responsibility to maintain law, order, and the safeguarding of internal security. In other words, the cooperation of judicial and internal issues under Art. K emphasizes governmental cooperation, which refers to Member States still enjoying autonomy in issues of immigration.

The idea of European citizenship was mentioned in the Treaty of Maastricht in Article 8, Chapter II, providing citizens of Member States with the rights to move and reside freely within the territory of the Member States (8a), to vote and to stand as a candidate in municipal elections in the Member State in which he or she resides, under the same condition of that State (8b), and to be entitled to enjoy diplomatic or consular protection of any Member State (8c). These articles provide citizens of Member States with the capability to move, reside, and immigrate freely inside of European borders. Since then, the subject of enjoying the right of free movement has been augmented. Prior to the Treaty of Maastricht, only economic immigrants were allowed to move to other Member States; after the implementation of the Maastricht treaty, however, all European citizens have been entitled to move freely inside of the so-called "European fortress". Therefore, the Treaty of Maastricht is an important landmark for common internal immigration law of the EU. Cooperation under the Treaty of Maastricht is limited, however, in the areas of asylum and reciprocal recognition of transit visas, which are located in the third pillar of Justice and Home Affairs. This is because, in the third pillar, cooperation remains voluntary, as decisions require the unanimity of Member States, while the European Court of Justice could not rule on the validity of provisions or act to enforce them (Caviedes 2004, p. 293). Even though the Treaty of Maastricht established common immigration policy, it still required a major consensus among all Member States. The Maastricht Treaty handled the treatment of European citizens, realizing internal liberalization; however, it did not deal with external immigration policy. For immigrants from third countries, those regulations put larger constraints on their rights, while their position and treatment deteriorated.

The Treaty of Amsterdam in 1997 introduced Title IV on "Visas, Asylum, Immigration and Other Policies Related to the Free Movement of Persons" to the first pillar, providing a robust foundation for EU institutions. The issues originally regulated under the third pillar, including visas, asylum, immigration, external border controls, the free movement of persons and the rights of third-country nationals, were moved to the first pillar of the European Community for common regulation. In other words, those issues were categorized into the competence of supranational organizations, and required EU Member States to build common immigration and visa regulations. Overall, immigration cooperation was dealt with by governmental cooperation in the third pillar in the early years. Since the Treaty of Amsterdam, it has been upgraded to the EU level in order to achieve common methods, bringing the communitarisation of immigration issues. However, for the transition period of the first five years, Member States still ensured a joint power initiative together with the European Commission, whereupon final decisions by the European Council had to be taken unanimously. Member States were to decide after the transition period whether any of the areas in Title IV would be further "Europeanized" by means of a qualified majority voting procedure (Caviedes 2004, p. 293). Therefore, under the Treaty of Amsterdam, Member States still retained their power to decide in the future whether to authorize greater supranationalization of immigration policy (Stetter 2000, p. 294). For that reason, there has not yet been a major critical juncture from the previous EU immigration paradigm (Kostakopoulou 2000, p. 514).

The next development was the Tampere European Council in 1999, which is widely considered as an important landmark of EU immigration policy, as it mapped out the future course of the EU's external immigration policy. In the Tampere Council, the Presidency announced that, due to the creation of the EU's new "union of freedom, security and justice," common asylum and immigration policy should become more urgent. Furthermore, the EU's external immigration policy should include four separate elements, including partnership with countries of origin, a common European asylum system, fair treatment of third-country nationals, and management of migration flows (Caviedes 2004, p. 294).

The newest treaty of the EU, the Treaty of Lisbon, included the objective of a "common immigration policy" (Art. 17), reaffirming that external immigration policy operates in conjunction with internal immigration regulations. In other words, to protect the freedom of free movement of people in internal areas, external border controls, asylum, and immigration measures were necessary. Consequently, issues of criminal justice and police cooperation, which had been under the third pillar, were now moved to the first pillar to be regulated by the European Court of Justice. Preparation to communitarise the external immigration policy had thus been formed. However, there were still no comprehensive and common regulations regarding the entry of third-country national labor immigration. Only students, researchers, high-tech workers, and shifts of internal workers of companies were regulated. In 2009, after implementation of the Lisbon Treaty, even though Member States still possessed the power to restrict the number of immigrants, the European Parliament's power of co-decision in negotiations was augmented (Lavenex 2016).

The attempt to communitarize the EU's external immigration policy encountered challenges after the refugee crisis in 2015. Since the Arab Spring in the early 2010s, increasingly numbers of refugees have fled into Europe due to warfare. Although the EU adjusted its neighborhood policy and the structure of the Mediterranean Union to respond to it, minor changes were not sufficient to deal with the deteriorating situation that accompanied the Syrian Civil War in 2014. As a result, the Commission initiated the "European immigration agenda," "European common asylum system," "Common external border," and "European border and coast guard." Those proposals caused controversies and debate among Member States. Through news reports and social media, the public became more empathic on the refugee issue. After the European Parliament agreed on the allocation plan of refugees in Member States, the European Commission started to enforce the plan to allocate the refugees. The common policy, however, caused disagreement in Central and East European Member States. As a result, several Member States raised disputes against the Commission in the European Court of Justice in an effort to disallow the refugee allocation plan. Even though Member States lost the case in the ECJ, the Member States' action of accusing EU institutions frustrated the EU's attempt to communitarise an external immigration policy. Moreover, the refugee issue cultivated the development of populism inside of Europe. Indeed, traditional parties have faced enormous challenges from populism. Populist parties have achieved major success in Poland, Hungry, Austria and Italy, obstructing the comminitarisation of EU policy. The failure of an external immigration policy has even challenged the existing results of other common policies, and obstructed the EU's attempt to move towards further communitarisation.

3   Normative Power and Immigration Policy

Human rights are the most prevailing values that the EU promotes around the world, and have earned the EU the reputation of a normative power. There are several foundations to the EU's normative role in promoting human rights, including the European Convention on Human Rights, the EU Charter on Human Rights, and the Treaty on European Union. In Article 2 of the Treaty on the European Union, it is stated that the EU is founded on the values of human dignity, freedom, democracy, equality, the rule of law and respect for human rights, including the rights of persons belonging to minorities. These values are common to the Member States in a society in which pluralism, non-discrimination, tolerance, justice, solidarity, and equality between women and men prevail.

The general definition of human rights are the rights inherent to all human beings, regardless of race, sex, nationality, ethnicity, language, religion or any other status, including the right to life and liberty, freedom from slavery and torture, freedom of opinion and expression, work and education, etc. (United Nations 2020). To protect the rights mentioned above, many underprivileged subjects receive special attention, such as women, children, minority groups, ethnic groups, etc. As such, migrants are one of the groups of focus because they are vulnerable to human rights violations and tend to face situations of discrimination, exploitation and marginalization, often living and working in the informal economy, afraid to complain, and are denied human rights and fundamental freedoms (OHCHR 2020). Therefore, to observe the EU's role as a normative power and protect human rights, not only should the EU's export of the right to urge other international actors to protect human rights, such as dignity and freedom, be regarded, but also the EU's own behavior in dealing with migrants should be considered.

The concept of normative power has become the policy basis of the EU to define its unique role in global politics. In the area of immigration, scholars have considered that the most concrete policy output from the idea of normative power was the Commission's proposals for directives on family reunification in 1999 and on the status of long-term resident third-country nationals in 2001. Another important aspect to observe normative power is the EU's asylum policy.

The directive on family reunification in 1999 establishes common minimum standards for legal residents of third-country nationals who join members of their family. Those rights are under the protection of the European Convention on Human Rights and the EU Charter on Human Rights. However, even though those policies are supported by Convention and Charter, the Commission still faced strong resistance from the Council. As a consequence, the Commission amended the proposal twice before a much diminished directive was adopted four years after its first initiation. The final version was widely criticized, because it barely advanced the rights of third-country nationals. Indeed, its minimum standards were under those of existing national legislation, and it was largely remiss in considering legal obligations (Lavenex 2019). In 2003, the Commission proposed The Long-Term Directive, also called the Tampere Conclusion. Faced with the same problems as the previous directive, the Council diluted the principle of equal treatment with EU nationals by allowing Member States to limit mobility rights for third-country nationals by means of national labor market preferences, set quotas on the administration of third-country nationals, and establish requirements to comply with certain integration measures (Carrera 2006).

Regarding asylum policy, the Tampere European Council Conclusion in 1999 affirmed the EU's commitment to universal liberal values on asylum and a firm objective to promote these values externally globally. It is stated in the conclusion that "the European integration has been firmly rooted in a shared commitment to freedom based on human rights, democratic institutions and the rule of law…, This freedom should not be regarded as the exclusive preserve of the Union's own citizens.., This in turn requires the Union to develop common policies on asylum and immigration" (European Council 1999).

The statements above reflected the EU's efforts to preserve and promote their values, as well as to establish the scope of those values. In other words, we can find the normative power ambition and the EU's normative identity from the policy above. This intention was also reaffirmed by the European Council, when it asserted the importance of the Union and its Member States to respect rights while dealing with the asylum issue. It is also declared that the Union will work towards establishing a Common European Asylum System, based on application of the Geneva Convention. In addition, the Tampere Conclusions state that "The European Union must ensure fair treatment of the third country nationals who reside legally on the territory of its Member States. A more vigorous integration policy should aim at granting them rights and obligations comparable to those of EU citizens. It should also enhance non-discrimination in economic, social and cultural life and develop measures against racism and xenophobia" (European Council 1999). This demonstrates that EU level institutions also strove to expand their power of normative power to legally resident non-EU nationals, by elevating the legal status of third country nationals to that of Member States' nationals' rights concerning the issue of freedom of movement (Lavenex 2019). The Treaty of Amsterdam further established the need to establish the national asylum system as a precondition for realization of the 1990 Dublin Convention, and subsequent regulations which introduced the principle of mutual recognition of the examination of asylum claims.

The asylum issue gained the attention of the European Convention while discussing the European Charter of Fundamental Rights. International standards, such as those in the Geneva Convention and other human rights treaties, were taken into consideration while initiating the European Charter of Fundamental Rights. Consequently, the Charter included the right of asylum (Lavenex 2019).

The Lisbon Treaty further supported the concept of normative power by recognizing the Charter of Human Rights as legally binding. Consequently, the Commission advanced revised directives present in the Amsterdam Treaty to limit discretion possessed by Member States through restricting common standards (Lavenex 2019).

Even though the attempts above provided the basis for the EU's asylum policy, the empirical development of policy realization encountered challenges, especially after the refugee crisis in 2015. Refugees had flown into Europe after the Arab Spring in the early 2010s, and this had gained momentum after the Syrian Civil War in 2014. In 2015, after the tragic photograph of a dead, small Syrian boy on a Turkish beach was widely published, European civil society was shocked, and many people urged the government to deal with the issue and accept the refugees. In particular, they insisted that humanitarian concerns be addressed, which was a fundamental value of the Union. In response, the Commission initiated plans, including the "European immigration agenda," the "European common asylum system," a "common external border," and the "European border and coast guard." The plans sparked major controversy and debate among EU Member States. The frontiers of the refugee trend, i.e., the Central and East European States, strongly disagreed with the asylum system and refused to fulfill the obligations set by the Union. This resistance from Member States greatly frustrated the EU's ambition to act as a normative power, as these controversies showed that the call for normativity was not a comprehensively-accepted behavior rule for all Member States. Furthermore, the supervision system legislation did not require Member States to propose concrete plans for the rescue of refugees. In this way, rescue still depended on Member States' willingness and actions, rather than on common legislation at the EU level. As a result, the EU's asylum governance was not able to fulfill its expectation to save the lives of refugees. Indeed, the tragedies of shipwrecks and the death of refugees still occur.

4 Interaction Between the Supranational and Intergovernmental Levels in Immigration Governance

The European Union's governance, as a new type of political regime, is decided at both a supranational level and an intergovernmental level. Institutions at the supranational level include the European Commission, the European Parliament and the European Court of Justice, representing the integrated interests of the Union as a whole. To balance the power of the supranational level, the European Council and the Council of Ministers tend to advocate for the interests of each Member State. Regarding immigration governance, it is also found that bargaining between the two levels occurs, as the integrated interests and positions of Member States can diverge greatly in the area of immigration. In this section, the positions of the various actors are explained, and the reasons causing challenges in immigration governance are explored.

4.1 Positions of Actors

Cooperation in asylum and immigration policies of the EU has gradually attained communitisization. Prior to the 1990s, intergovernmental decisions held the dominant position in immigration policy with representatives of the Council of Ministers, i.e., the Ministers of Justice and Internal Affairs, possessing the core decision-making power of the common policies. With the development of the Maastricht Treaty bringing communitization of decision-making, supranational institutions now shared core decision-making and responsibility with Member States. After the Treaty of Amsterdam, supranational institutions in the EU level started to have priority in decision-making. Immigration policy is regulated in the Treaty of Amsterdam as the EU's supranational competence. Prior to the Treaty of Lisbon in 2009, the decision of the Council required unanimity. The Treaty of Lisbon expanded Qualified Majority Voting (QMV) to policy areas that required unanimity according to the Nice Treaty, including immigration and asylum. Moreover, the competence of Parliament was increased.

In the current design, the Commission enjoys exclusive initiation power, and the European Parliament has the power to take part in decision-making under the "co-decision legislative procedure." In other words, in the current legislative process, it is important to obtain agreement from the European Parliament. In addition, the

QMV design means that no single Member State holds veto power. As a result, immigration governance depends highly on the consensus of the majority of all of the participants. Overall, all participants enjoy (partial) decision-making power regarding immigration policy. In negotiations, however, Member States still possess the right to control the number of the entry of immigrants.

In the decision process, it is well-accepted that the supranational level holds more liberal preferences (Kaunert and Léonard 2012). The Commission and the Court take a more "rights-oriented" role in strengthening the rights of immigrants and reducing pertinent restrictions (Bonjour et al. 2018, p. 413). For example, scholars observe that the Commission, the Parliament, and the Court are more refugee-friendly than interior ministers (Thielemann and Zaun 2013, p. 1406). The Commission and the Court consider themselves to be protectors of family migration rights (Block and Bonjour 2013, p. 223). EU law limits national deterrence measures, curtails free-riding opportunities, and establishes standards for refugee protection in Member States (El-Enany and Thielemann 2011; Kaunert and Léonard 2012; Thielemann and El-Enany 2010; Thielemann and Zaun 2013). Furthermore, the EU's rule of law in the area of immigration was upheld by the Court and limits the ability of Member States to adopt excessive rules (Bonjour and Vink 2013; El-Enany and Thielemann 2011; Kaunert and Léonard 2012). In other words, the EU level of supranational institutions is characterized as a venue in which migrants' rights are protected from Member States' restrictions (Bonjour et al. 2018, p. 413).

The EU level is also considered to uphold normative power most consistently regarding asylum and migration issues. The Parliament, in particular, is considered as the agency that promotes values the most. For example, in the "Committee on Civil Liberties and Internal Affairs (LIBE)" established in 1992, the Council referred to the human rights issue as Justice and Home Affairs, making it a domestic issue under Member States' competence. However, the European Parliament distinguishes it as relating to "human rights problems in the Community" from legal affairs, symbolizing its detachment from the statist community-building frame of the Council. This normative power approach is employed by the European Parliament to set itself apart from other EU institutions (Lavenex 2019).

Even under the efforts of supranational institutions, the immigration governance of the EU is still encountering major obstacles, as the policy considerations of immigration involve not only the economy, but also security (Caviedes 2004, p. 293). Ever since the 911 terrorist attack in the U.S., along with other terrorist actions, such as the Madrid train explosion in 2004, and the underground and bus explosions in London in 2004, the immigration issue has escalated to high levels of politics involving national security from original economic and societal low politics (Kicinger 2004), with investigations ratifying those issues relating to immigrants and/or their descendants. Furthermore, terrorists have used the free borders of the Schengen Area to move within the area and cause public panic. The spread of terrorism has made Member States, on the one hand, realize the limitations of a single country, creating the incentive to strengthen cooperation in the security area; on the other hand, the situation also has made Member States tend to tighten their borders to constrain the entry of immigrants and strengthen the regulations. The above concerns have created room for supranational cooperation, which has brought the possibility for supranational institutions to augment their competence. However, for Member States, cooperation, which they desired, aimed to tighten control, which differs from the intention of supranational institutions. As a result, the contradiction between the supranational level and the intergovernmental is revealed in immigration governance.

The Europeanization of common immigration policy does not solely influence the allocation of competence-sharing between Member States and the EU. Indeed, it also obliges the domestic national laws and constitutions of Member States to express the human rights' basis of refugee policy (Lavenex 2001, p. 870). However, Member States have different opinions regarding the stance of the Commission. For instance, to set common minimum procedural standards for the examination of asylum claims, the Commission announced the Asylum Procedures Directive. However, its adoption was delayed several times for more than a year beyond the Amsterdam Treaty deadline in 2005. In exchange for cooperation from Member States, the directive made a compromise in the end, providing several exception clauses and used weak legal language. Consequently, fierce criticism of the directive occurred from the European Parliament, as well as other refugee organizations (Lavenex 2019).

The complexity of the situation is further increased, as several incidents have shown that Member States differ from each other in making their own constraining policies. For example, Denmark introduced custom controls on illegal immigration in 2011, which were opposed to the 1995 Schengen Agreement; a Member of Parliament in the Netherlands proposed to close all EU borders and abandon its refugee policy; and Italy operated against EU regulations by providing temporary Schengen-visas to immigrants on the island of Lampedusa (Van Klingeren et al. 2017, p. 544). These various stances of Member States show that the harmonization attempt of the supranational level faces political obstruction from the intergovernmental level (Givens and Luedtke 2004, p. 145).

Many scholars consider that the EU tends to take a more liberal stance, while Member States are more conservative. However, different opinions also exist. For example, Bonjour and colleagues point out that the interests of the Member States are various, so that not all countries tend to be constraining. Furthermore, even at the supranational level, not all policies are liberal (Bonjour et al. 2018, p. 413). Kaunert and Leonard agree with the above opinion, and contend that the general analysis is over-simplified. They state that the preference formation analysis should be viewed as endogenous to institutionalized cooperation and may evolve (Kaunert and Léonard 2012, p. 1340).

Besides the possible various policy stances among Member States, the contention that supranational EU institutions pursue liberal policies has also been questioned. For example, some academics hold the opinion that the Commission wants to present itself as siding with Member States by supporting tougher border controls and immigration enforcement (Lahav and Luedtke 2013, p. 111). Moreover, in different policy fields, the position of the Commission may be varied. Concerning the asylum issue, the Commission tends to support the restrictive preferences of the Council in visa and border issues (Scipioni 2015). There are also scholars that have observed that the Parliament has tended to adopt much less liberal positions since it has been granted greater legislative power (Bonjour et al. 2018; Servent 2015; Trauner and Ripoll Servent 2016). As a consequence, the EU asylum policy in the 2010s was slightly more harmonized and less restrictive than the original legislation in the early 2000s.

In reality, it is much easier to make progress in restrictive policies of immigration governance. Since immigration is involved with national sovereignty and national identity, it is understandable that Member States take a conservative position. Even though EU's competence and obligations have been increased, its policy relies on coordination with its Member States. Furthermore, many issues could only be dealt with by Member States. As a result, cooperation could only be obtained in areas in which Member States share common interests, such as tightening controls on migrants and borders, combating illegal migrants, and the avoidance of asylum abuse. Regarding entry policy, progress has been much more difficult to achieve (Lavenex 2001, p. 1).

4.2 Difficulties in Conducting Immigration Governance

From the analysis above, it can be seen that the supranational level and the inter-governmental level have different positions in terms of immigration governance. Supranational organizations, such as the Commission and the Court, want to defend immigrant rights (Den Boer 1995; Guiraudon 2003); whereas, state actors aim to maximize their sovereignty in immigration control (Givens and Luedtke 2004, p. 148). The supranational level attempts to fulfill the so-called normative role to exert normative power. However, Member States tend to be conservative in order to constrain the entry and rights of migrants, which essentially contradicts the normative power concept. The reason for Member States' non-compliance can be observed from several perspectives.

The fundamental reason for the various policy stances of the EU members is that EU Member States have different immigration situations, including the time of immigration waves, the origin of major migrants, the types and proportion of the migrants in the total population, etc. For example, some countries have received migrants since the nineteenth century, while some have only faced the issue after the Second World War. Regarding type, some countries have received a large number of labor migrants, who could contribute to their economy; whereas, other countries have faced a serious situation with asylum-seekers.

The various domestic situations of Member States have made them assume different standards in recognizing the status of refugees or immigrants. Furthermore, each Member State holds the power to decide on the entry of migrants and refugees. As a consequence, the approval rates of asylum-seekers with the same nationality in different Member States can differ greatly. For instance, Afghanistan refugees in Romania and Bulgaria were recognized at a rate 19%, while 80% were recognized in Italy, Finland, and France (Lavenex 2001).

The domestic atmosphere towards refugees in EU members is also varied. In Germany and Sweden, for example, governments established an open refugee policy, which caused major criticism from the public. In the Southern Member States, governments have tended to adopt a constraining refugee policy, while some citizens have provided humanitarian assistance to the refugees. In Central and Eastern Europe, both the government and the public are largely against refugees. In Germany and Sweden, who both face the problem of an aging population, the governments believe that the refugees could be turned into a work force to make up for the labor shortage; however, a part of the citizenry is concerned about the social impact brought by the new migrants. For the religious Southern Europe, such as Italy and Spain, under appeals from the Pope, the public has provided assistance by receiving refugees. As for Central and Eastern Europe, including Hungary, Poland, Romania, Slovakia and the Czech Republic, they argue that an excess of Islamic refugees will influence their societies, which are based on Christian beliefs, and cause a serious unemployment problem and a weak economic structure.

Overall, due to different histories and experiences, EU members have various considerations toward refugees. For Germany and Sweden, who benefitted from immigrants in the 1970s and 1980s, they consider that refugees could become a labor force in reserve; the Southern states have taken a humanitarian angle by taking care of the poor; Central and Eastern Europe have considered the issue from the society and identity perspective, including economic competition, regarding refugees as competitors. Consequently, the allocation system faces strong resistance from several members. Hungary and Slovakia have even launched a lawsuit in the Courts against the allocation. Moreover, a political space for the extreme right-wing has been created around the issue of immigration, which has caused challenges for Member States to coordinate actions (Lavenex 2001).

The differences between states has also resulted in an inefficiency problem, leading to massive distortions in the European labor markets. This has created incentives for refugees to seek asylum in specific countries (Bordignon and Moriconi 2017), causing Member States to worry that liberal domestic asylum legislation would become a magnet for refugees and paralyze their domestic societies. For example, Germany, which has assumed a more liberal position, is concerned about attracting refugees who have been rejected elsewhere, in effect becoming a refugee sanctuary of Europe, or "Reserveasylland" of asylum-seekers (Lavenex 2001, p. 862; Niemann and Lauter 2011, p. 146). In addition, France has suspended Schengen several times due to terrorist attacks, such as after the terrorist bombs exploded in the Paris subway in 1995 (Bort 2005, p. 66) and the Charlie Hebdo shooting in 2015. Moreover, after they predicted a large influx of refugees as a result of the Dublin Convention, The Netherlands attempted to obstruct the common approach of the EU by enacting the Aliens Act (Lavenex 2001, p. 863).

To deal with the refugee crisis in 2015, the Commission initiated the Relocation Scheme under the support of the major Member State, i.e., Germany. The allocation quota was set based on the capacity of Member States to take care of applicants for international protection, including population size, total GDP, average number of asylum applications per one million inhabitants, and unemployment rate. Even though the Relocation Scheme was a quick response to deal with the issue, the program possessed inherent problems. First, in terms of the nature of the policy, the relocation system only applied to refugees from Syria, Eritrea, and Iraq. Moreover, it offered a temporary corrective mechanism in the Dublin regulation framework, making it address the symptoms only, instead of the actual causes. In addition, some have claimed that the Commission's plan was only a temporary program, rather than an institutional long-term common policy for dealing with the general immigration and asylum issue. Second, from the implementation perspective, the program presumed that all Member States could fully and effectively implement the Reception Conditions Directive (2013/33EU) to offer adequate and identical reception conditions. However, this is unrealistic. In reality, many Member States have not, or have only partially, fulfilled the obligations of the Commission's directive.

Due to the various considerations, the promise made by supranational institutions regarding the refugee relocation program is not being kept, making the first-entry countries carry a disproportionate burden. The Dublin Regulations oblige the first-entry country to examine asylum applications. However, Member States are very different in their cultural attitudes towards immigration, so that reaching a common solution has become untenable (Bordignon and Moriconi 2017).

5 Conclusion

From the analysis above, it can be seen that the Europeanization of the EU's immigration policy is not yet advanced (Caviedes 2004, p. 289). Various actors operating within the Union have different considerations. As a result, normative performance seems to be weak in terms of immigration governance. In the 2015–2016 refugee crisis, even though the supranational institutions wanted to create a common policy, the legal and political issues made the Member States resist the directives from the supranational level, who eventually left the management of the crisis mostly in the hands of Member States. This has made the management incompatible with an integrated economic area that has largely abolished internal borders (Massimo Bordignon and Moriconi 2017). It is also incompatible with the founding European Union principles, e.g., the free mobility of people, which constitutes the normative basis of the EU in the world.

These reasons have created the problem that the EU is still struggling with itself between several concepts. The integration process started with a market concern. After the successful integration of the market, the EU has attempted to build itself as an integral statist power. By differentiating itself from other traditional political entities, the EU has now tried to employ a "normative basis" to distinguish itself among existing world powers (Lavenex 2019).

In recent years, the EU has promoted certain norms globally, such as human rights, democracy, and sustainable development. However, concerning its internal governance, major controversy remains, as consensus among various actors is yet strong. When the issue relates to the core issues of national security, sovereignty and identity, Member States tend to be hesitant and conservative in protecting their own interests and ethnic identity. The driving point of the EU's asylum policy is towards internal market safety, rather than universal human rights. Furthermore, as the policy is led by major refugee-receiving Member States, e.g., Germany, it is not surprising that cooperation would focus on reducing the number of asylum-seekers in Europe, rather than on the pursuit and protection of human rights. Therefore, most EU measures that have been implemented in the context of a legally binding intergovernmental agreement indicate elements that are limiting, instead of policies that reflect openness (Lavenex 2001, p. 860).

EU immigration can be divided into two policy areas. One is the internal policy to advance the integral European market, while the other is the external policy to protect the so-called "European fortress." In this situation, the two policy areas cause contradiction. To establish a free zone inside of the fortress, the EU needs a more liberal policy to deepen integration. However, the free zone inside of the fortress makes Member States more cautious about external migrants, which will result in social pressure and problems of societal security. Consequently, national sovereignty, interest, identity and even nationalism are being revived, obstructing the development of a common external immigration policy. Essentially, EU immigration faces a reality dilemma coming from the need to have a common policy for the process of integration versus the diversified demands of national sovereignty states.

From the normative perspective, the EU has yet to accede to the European Convention for the Protection of Human Rights and Fundamental Freedoms, even though it is required to do so under Art. 6 of TEU. In addition, the participation of EU Member States in protecting migrants' rights is rare. For example, no Member States have signed or ratified the International Convention on the Protection of the Rights of All Migrant Workers and Members of Their Families. Regarding the Convention on Action against Trafficking in Human Beings, although many Member States have ratified the Convention, they still maintained several reservations.[1] The poor participation of Member States has undermined the EU's human rights policies and its stated commitment to protect these rights.

The failure in practice of the normative dimension has undermined the EU's consistency. Indeed, it has placed the concept of Europe's normative power into question. The securitization of migration has emphasized governmentality and territorial demarcation. The EU's response to the refugee crisis is reflected in the EU's difficulties in the interests versus values debate. The promotion of values has created the EU's unique role in global politics; however, leaders in Member States have put their interests ahead of values. The asylum and migration policy of the supranational level's version does not coincide with the interests of Member States and, as a result, major resistance has appeared.

To be a credible and effective normative power, the EU needs to reach a consensus over norms within its region first. However, the diversified interests and internal divisions concerning the immigration issue have made consensus fragile or even impossible. The lack of consensus assumes the asylum system's interchangeability,

---

[1] https://www.coe.int/en/web/conventions/full-list/-/conventions/treaty/197/declarations?p_auth= RIZvsK1m.

as well as impedes the implementation of a shared European asylum system (Lavenex, 2001, p. 861). If the EU continues to fail in finding a consensus in its policy-making and implementation, not only will it harm the EU's distinct role in global politics, but it will also diminish the prospects for deeper integration.

References

Block, L., & Bonjour, S. (2013). Fortress Europe or Europe of rights? The Europeanisation of family migration policies in France, Germany and the Netherlands. *European Journal of Migration and Law, 15*(2), 203–224.

Bonjour, S., Ripoll Servent, A., & Thielemann, E. (2018). Beyond venue shopping and liberal constraint: A new research agenda for EU migration policies and politics. *Journal of European Public Policy, 25*(3), 409–421.

Bonjour, S., & Vink, M. (2013). When Europeanization backfires: The normalization of European migration politics. *Acta Politica, 48*(4), 389–407.

Bordignon, M., & Moriconi, S. (2017). *The case for a common European refugee policy.*

Bort, E. (2005). European borders in transition: The internal and external frontiers of the European Union*Borders in a global world: Holding the line* (pp. 63–89).

Carrera, S. (2006). A comparison of integration programmes in the EU. *Challenge papers, 1.*

Caviedes, A. (2004). The open method of co-ordination in immigration policy: A tool for prying open Fortress Europe? *Journal of European Public Policy, 11*(2), 289–310.

Den Boer, M. (1995). Moving between bogus and bona fide: The policing of inclusion and exclusion in Europe. *Migration and European integration: The dynamics of inclusion and exclusion* (pp. 92–111).

El-Enany, N., & Thielemann, E. R. (2011). *The impact of EU asylum policy on national asylum regimes.*

European Council. (1999). *Tampere European Council 15–16.10.1999: Conclusions of the presidency—European Council tampere 15–16.10.1999: Conclusions of the presidency.* https://www.europarl.europa.eu/summits/tam_en.htm.

Falkner, R. (2006). *The European Union as a" green normative power"?: EU Leadership in international biotechnology regulation.* Minda de Gunzburg Center for European Studies: Harvard University.

Givens, T., & Luedtke, A. (2004). The politics of European Union immigration policy: Institutions, salience, and harmonization. *Policy Studies Journal, 32*(1), 145–165.

Guiraudon, V. (2003). The constitution of a European immigration policy domain: A political sociology approach. *Journal of European Public Policy, 10*(2), 263–282.

Hollifield, J. F. (1992). *Immigrants, markets, and states: The political economy of postwar Europe.* Harvard University Press.

Ireland, P. R. (1996). Asking for the moon: The political participation of immigrants in the European Union'. In *The impact of European integration* (pp. 131–150). Praeger.

Kaunert, C., & Léonard, S. (2012). The development of the EU asylum policy: Venue-shopping in perspective. *Journal of European Public Policy, 19*(9), 1396–1413.

Kavalski, E. (2013). The struggle for recognition of normative powers: Normative power Europe and normative power China in context. *Cooperation and Conflict, 48*(2), 247–267.

Kicinger, A. (2004). *International migration as a non-traditional security threat and the EU responses to this phenomenon.*

Kostakopoulou, T. (2000). The 'Protective union'; change and continuity in migration law and policy in Post-Amsterdam Europe. *JCMS: Journal of Common Market Studies, 38*(3), 497–518.

Lahav, G., & Luedtke, A. (2013). Immigration policy. In *The Europeanization of European politics* (pp. 109–122). Springer.

Lavenex, S. (2001). The European refugee crisis in the context of EU migration and asylum policies. *Journal of Common Market Studies, 39*(5), 851–874.

Lavenex, S. (2016). Multilevelling EU external governance: The role of international organizations in the diffusion of EU migration policies. *Journal of Ethnic and Migration Studies, 42*(4), 554–570.

Lavenex, S. (2019). Common market, normative power or super-state? Conflicting political identities in EU asylum and immigration policy. *Comparative European Politics, 17*(4), 567–584.

Lightfoot, S., & Burchell, J. (2005). The European Union and the world summit on sustainable development: Normative power Europe in action? *JCMS: Journal of Common Market Studies, 43*(1), 75–95.

Manners, I. (2002). Normative power Europe: A contradiction in terms? *JCMS: Journal of Common Market Studies, 40*(2), 235–258.

Niemann, A., & Lauter, D. (2011). Playing two-level games in Berlin and Brussels: Maintaining control of asylum policies? In *The Europeanization of control: Venues and outcomes of EU justice and home affairs cooperation* (Vol. 10). LIT Verlag Münster.

Noureddine, R. (2016). *Critically assess and analyse the notion that the EU is a normative power. 2016* CESAA essay competition. https://eeas.europa.eu/sites/eeas/files/cesaa_essay_com petition_raja_noureddine_.docx.

OHCHR. (2020). *OHCHR | Migration and Human Rights.* https://www.ohchr.org/en/issues/migrat ion/pages/migrationandhumanrightsindex.aspx.

Philip, A. B. (1994). European Union immigration policy: Phantom, fantasy or fact? *West European Politics, 17*(2), 168–191.

Scipioni, M. (2015). *Delegation to the European Commission in EU migration policy: Expertise, credibility, and efficiency.* Ph.D. thesis, University of London, Birkbeck.

Servent, A. R. (2015). *Institutional and policy change in the European Parliament: Deciding on freedom, security and justice.* Springer.

Stetter, S. (2000). Regulating migration: Authority delegation in justice and home affairs. *Journal of European Public Policy, 7*(1), 80–103.

Thielemann, E., & El-Enany, N. (2010). Refugee protection as a collective action problem: Is the EU shirking its responsibilities? *European Security, 19*(2), 209–229.

Thielemann, E., & Zaun, N. (2013). *Escaping populism–safeguarding human rights: The European Union as a venue for non-majoritarian policy-making in the area of refugee protection.* ECPR General Conference.

Trauner, F., & Ripoll Servent, A. (2016). The communitarization of the area of freedom, security and justice: Why institutional change does not translate into policy change. *JCMS: Journal of Common Market Studies, 54*(6), 1417–1432.

United Nations. (2020). *Human Rights.* https://www.un.org/en/sections/issues-depth/human-rig hts/.

Van Klingeren, M., Boomgaarden, H. G., & De Vreese, C. H. (2017). Will conflict tear us apart? The effects of conflict and balanced media messages on polarizing attitudes toward EU immigration and border control. *Public Opinion Quarterly, 81*(2), 543–563.

The German Parties' Reaction to the 2015 Refugee Crisis—A Long-Term Analysis of Party Positioning Dynamics

Eike-Christian Hornig

1 Introduction

In 2015, more than one million refugees arrived in Germany in what was broadly called the refugee crisis. In the weeks following the refugees' arrival, an unprecedented wave of support swept across the country that came to be known as "Willkommenskultur," a culture of welcoming (Laubenthal 2019, p. 418). The perception of broad German approval of refugees' arrival in the country was intensified by media coverage (Haller 2017; Dostal 2017). Migration quickly became the most dominant political issue in the country, reaching its peak in the second half of 2015 when in some polls, almost 90% of respondents identified migration as the number one political problem (Forschungsgruppe Wahlen 2019). Although the attitudes of the German population did not profoundly change between 2015 and 2017, polarization on the issue increased (Kober and Kösemen 2019, p. 21; Ademmer and Stöhr 2018, p. 5). While many people welcomed refugees almost with euphoria in the early days, more critical positions emerged later on, especially voiced by the rightwing party Alternative for Germany (AfD) (Geiges 2018). It is, thus, no surprise that migration dominated the discussions surrounding the 2017 federal elections (Franzmann et al. 2019; Liesching and Hooffacker 2019).

The decision of the German government on September 4, 2015 not to close the borders and allow refugees to come into the country was closely connected with Chancellor Angela Merkel of the Christian Democrats (CDU) (Mushaben 2017; Laubenthal 2019). She justified this decision with humanitarian reasons and has repeatedly pointed to the benefits and opportunities of migration symbolized by her iconic refrain, "Wir schaffen das" (We can do it). Both developments, a CDU chancellor allowing a million refugees into the country and the parallel rise of anti-immigration, right-wing populists, are widely seen as having a causal relationship.

E.-C. Hornig (✉)
University of Erfurt, Erfurt, Germany
e-mail: Eike-Christian.Hornig@uni-erfurt.de

© The Author(s), under exclusive license to Springer Nature Singapore Pte Ltd. 2021
C.-P. Chu and S.-C. Park (eds.), *Immigration Policy and Crisis in the Regional Context*,
https://doi.org/10.1007/978-981-33-6823-1_10

Accordingly, the CDU gave way to the rise of the AfD and the 2015 refugee crisis "fundamentally changed the country's party landscape" (Kurbjuweit 2016). Based on polls, Mader and Schoen make a crucial observation in this context: *"During the refugee crisis, German citizens witnessed a shift in the immigration position of the major centre-right party – Chancellor Merkel's CDU. While the CDU had been reluctant to accept foreigners to Germany previously, Chancellor Merkel now decided to allow refugees to enter Germany. […]. Despite this internal dissent, Merkel outwardly kept the CDU/CSU on an immigration-friendly course that resonated with segments of German society that welcomed the refugees to the country"* (Mader and Schoen 2019, p. 71). The authors conclude that Chancellor Merkel's decision to keep borders open for refugees "led to an alienation of immigration-sceptical CDU supporters" (Mader and Schoen 2019, p. 83). The perception of the public and voters seems to be very clear: Merkel, and the CDU alongside her, changed positions and thus gave way to the anti-immigration Alternative for Germany (AfD).

However, doubts remain regarding this nexus of the refugee crisis and the party system, especially in the case of the CDU. In 2015, Merkel had led and dominated the party for over fifteen years as chairwoman and for over ten years as chancellor. The party's major win in the 2013 Bundestag-elections gave her an undisputable position in the party, even stronger than that of Helmut Kohl after reunification. Had signs of a turn in immigration policy appeared before this point? Was this critical juncture in migration history also a critical juncture in the party's policies or part of a longer gradual development? The border decision may also have been a singular decision, whereas the party position on immigration in general could have been different. Against this background, the objective of this research is to analyze the positions of German political parties regarding migration policy and place the events of 2015 into a larger temporal context. My leading research questions are: What are the dynamics of party positioning in the field of migration? Were there any deviations from these longtime patterns after 2015, which potentially opened up the space for the rise of the AfD? Despite the large amount of research that has been conducted on migration and party positions (Lehmann and Zobel 2018; Vranceanu 2019), there is still an absence of a long-term account of the nexus between refugee numbers and party positions in Germany. To answer the research questions, I analyze the positions of the CDU/CSU and four other German parties on migration by examining the parties' electoral manifestos from 1990 to the recent elections in 2017.

The analysis builds on concepts on party positioning, which help provide an understanding of the conditions under which parties are guided either by policy or responsiveness. The concept of path dependence focuses on continuity (in party positions), whereas the responsiveness concept explains changes (of party positions) due to external factors. In the third section, I introduce these concepts and develop hypotheses about the saliency of the migration issue and the parties' respective position changes. After reporting the applied methods in Sect. 4, the empirical results are displayed in Sect. 5 and discussed in Sect. 6. The results show that the main German parties reacted to the 2015 refugee crisis in a very predictable manner instead of making abrupt position changes.

2 Migration Policy and Politics in Germany

According to Amnesty International, migration refers to the temporary or permanent movement of people from place A to place B without an indication of reasons. Migration can occur within the same region or country or beyond national borders and may be motivated by many reasons. In contrast, people seeking asylum move to another country because they fear oppression in their own country. This also describes refugees, who have no choice fleeing from war, either within their country or beyond its borders.[1] Thus, migrants may or may not be refugees and may or may not seek asylum. Furthermore, immigration refers to migration that involves coming to a place, whereas emigration refers to leaving a place. In German public debate, the term of "people with migration backgrounds" (in German: "Menschen mit Migrationshintergrund") is very present. However, this term is not a legal category; it refers to people who have moved to Germany after 1949, people born in Germany without German citizenship, and people who possess German citizenship, were born in Germany, and have at least one parent who is not from Germany (Hoesch 2018, p. 287). To not overstress the complexity of the notion, I generally use the term migration in this paper to refer to the movement of people from one country to another.

Migration policy (and with it citizenship policy) is marked by four major characteristics, as Green points out (2006, p. 113). First, migration is a field where traditional state sovereignty is demonstrated. The question is: who is allowed access to the state territory and who is allowed to become part of the nation. Second, migration has a domestic and foreign politics dimension. Third, migration is an issue that is politically highly charged and symbolic. According to Green, this makes migration policy suitable for exploitation by party politics and electoral campaigns. Fourth, migration and citizenship are issues in which the people directly affected by decisions have no ability to change the policy to their advantage because they are not eligible to vote in the first place (Green 2006, p. 113).

The governance of migration in Germany has changed profoundly over recent decades, from being a classic nation state competency to becoming highly entangled with the European level and institutions. Member states and the European Union share competences regarding migration, yet the treaties at the European level have come to establish the major framework for the governance of migration and asylum in the member states (Hofmann 2017). According to Wessels (2017, pp. 3–6), authority over migration began to move from the national to the European level starting in the 1970s with the so-called TREVI-Group and continued with the Treaty of Maastricht and its intergovernmental order. The treaties of Schengen of 1985 and 1990 led to the free passage of persons and goods in a Europe without borders. The Treaty of Amsterdam of 1999 introduced the area of freedom, security, and justice, but still had limited impacts. In the course of further integration, competences and resources were continuously allocated and shared in this framework (Tekin 2017), and the area

---

[1] Source: www.amnesty.ch/de/themen/asyl-und-migration/zahlen-fakten-und-hintergruende/grundl agen-und-begriffe.

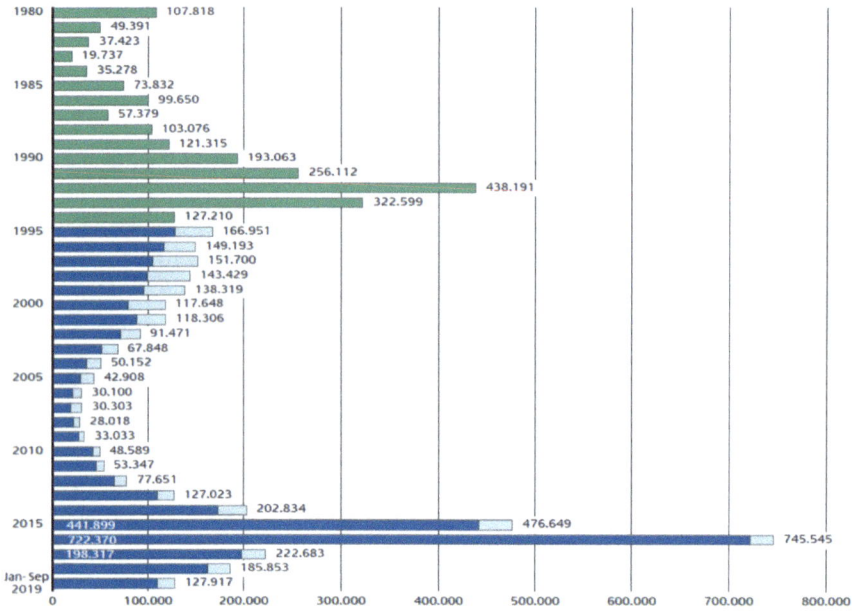

Fig. 1 Number of applications for asylum in Germany per annum (*Source* BAMF 2019, p. 5)

now comprises asylum, immigration, external borders, judicial cooperation in civil and criminal matters, police cooperation, and personal data protection.[2]

Germany has seen different waves of migration, which Hess and Green relate to three major critical junctures since 1949 (Hess and Green 2016, pp. 317–321). In the first years after World War II, around 12 million expellees from the former German parts of Central and Eastern Europe arrived in both parts of Germany. Furthermore 2.7 million people moved from East to West Germany until this was prohibited by the Wall in 1961. At the same time, the first wave of migration of non-German people to Germany unfolded: "*West Germany's flourishing economy in the 1950s soon created strong demand for additional labour, which was met through active recruitment programmes in Southern European and Mediterranean countries, notably Turkey. Especially during the 1960s, millions of so-called guestworkers (Gastarbeiter) were employed in West German factories up and down the land; although the majority also returned home in accordance with the temporary nature of this programme, around 3 million remained in the country by the time of the first turning point in late 1973*" (Hess and Green 2016, p. 317). The recruitment ban of 1973 was the first turning point in migration policy ending this first wave.

A second major wave of migration started in the late 1980s, shortly before German reunification. Figure 1 shows the numbers of applications for asylum in Germany for each year since 1980. The first peak occurred in 1993, with around 438,000

---

[2]See: www.europarl.europa.eu/factsheets/en/section/202/raum-der-freiheit-der-sicherheit-und-des-rechts.

applications. These were predominantly people from the former Yugoslavia and the Balkans. Additionally, "more than 1.4 million ethnic Germans from Central and Eastern Europe and the former Soviet Union arrived in (West) Germany between 1989 and 1993" (Hess and Green 2016, p. 318). At the same time, right-wing extremist parties gained ground in local and regional elections, accompanied by repeated riots against foreigners. The federal government reacted by restricting asylum right and curtailing ethnic German migration, which marked the second turning point in the history of migration (Hess and Green 2016, p. 318). The third turning point was marked by changes in migration policy in 1998 by the then-new government of the SPD and Greens, through which it was acknowledged that Germany is a country of immigration. This led to a new Citizenship Law in 1999 and the opening of the country to highly skilled migrants in 2004. This track was also not abandoned after the government changed to a Grand Coalition led by the CDU in 2005 (Hess and Green 2016, p. 319). Meanwhile, the number of asylum seekers continued to drop until it reached the lowest point in twenty-five years. After the turning point in 2008, the number of asylum seekers constantly increased again and suddenly exploded, surpassing the threshold of 476,000 in 2015 and reaching three-quarters of a million people in 2016 (BAMF 2019, p. 5). This so-called "refugee crisis" was the most dramatic wave of migration to Germany in recent decades. It was primarily caused by the war in Syria, but also by many other conflicts around the world. Initially, public discourse was dominated by an almost euphoric welcome extended to the refugees, termed as "Willkommenskultur." Media coverage intensified the perception of a very broad approval of the refugees' arrival in the country, neglecting to highlight the potential difficulties and challenges it would cause (Haller 2017) (Fig. 2).

Question asked: In your opinion, what is currently the most important problem in Germany? (Translation ECH).

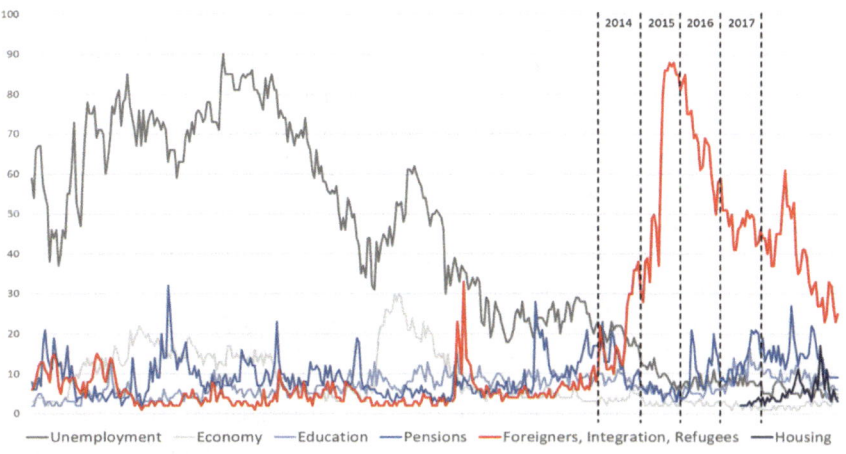

Fig. 2 Most important political problems for German public from 1/2000 to 9/2019 (*Source of data* Forschungsgruppe Wahlen 2019; own figure)

Migration quickly became the most dominant political issue (Forschungsgruppe Wahlen 2019). It reached its peak in the second half of 2015 when almost 90% of all respondents to polls identified migration as the number one political problem in Germany. This was also the peak of the refugee crisis in the country. Since 2015, the importance of migration has fallen, but it remained the dominant issue in 2019. Media coverage and debates between the two candidates for chancellery prior to the federal elections in 2017 were still dominated by the issue of migration (Liesching and Hooffacker 2019). Studies and polls show that the attitudes of the German population did not profoundly change between 2015 and 2017, but polarization occurred (Kober and Kösemen 2019, p. 21; Ademmer and Stöhr 2018, p. 5).

3   Change or Continuity in Party Positions

Political parties pursue certain policies, which are often the reasons the parties were founded in the first place. In Western Europe, we find a strong continuity of traditional party families, like Christian or Social Democrats, Liberals, and Greens. On the other hand, parties cannot ignore the wishes of the electorate if they want to be successful. Responsiveness to the wishes of the electorate is the basic idea of democracy. How parties position themselves between change and continuity depends on their dominant party goal (Harmel and Janda 1994, pp. 272–273). Whereas advocating policy and implementing party democracy point to continuity, the goal of winning votes/elections and gaining executive office refer to change and responsiveness. Both perspectives are the basis to understand the development of the German party system in the context of migration policy.

Over the decades, the evolution and nature of the national party systems in Western Europe have been the product of political cleavages on the macro level, producing stable policy positions (Lipset and Rokkan 1967). *"It is fairly accurate to talk about an association between left parties and issues related to the welfare state such as health, education, social security, unemployment and the environment. Right parties are associated with issues related to national interests such as law and order, asylum/immigration, the EU and to some extent also the size of the state, such as taxes"* (Seeberg 2016, p. 488). From this perspective, parties possess one or more core issues in which they enjoy a *"reputation for policy and program interest, produced by a history of attention, initiative and innovation toward problems, which leads voters to believe that one of the parties is more sincere and committed to do something"* (Petrocik 1996, p. 826). However, an issue can be owned by one or no party or be contested between parties, especially in a multiparty system (Wagner and Meyer 2014; Bos et al. 2017).

The mechanism assuring continuity here is path dependence. I follow Pierson's understanding of the concept that *"the key mechanism at work in these path-dependent sequences is some form of self-reinforcement or positive feedback loop. Initial steps in a particular direction may encourage further movement along the same path"*

(Pierson 2004, p. 64). The increasing return that keeps the path alive is the positive feedback from voters and members over time. With that, the concept of path dependence is especially helpful in explaining continuity (Capoccia and Kelemen 2007). As consequence, a party's specific mix of issues limits major policy changes by setting boundaries on the room the party has to maneuver regarding a certain policy. As long as the path prevails, current policy positions are determined by past decisions. Parties cannot pursue 180-degree changes without the risk of losing their credibility. Rather, they move over time within a certain corridor of positions in which no other party is present. This also has implications for how parties treat the saliency of issues. Parties have "their" issues that they emphasize, and voters acknowledge this by attributing competences to the parties. Here, parties are agenda-setters trying to increase the saliency of "their" issues (Klüver and Sagarzazu 2016, p. 384).

The second explanation of party positioning claims that political actors—either parties or single candidates—are responsive to voters' preferences. Responding elites change policies in reaction to public pressure. Responsiveness *typically analyzes the effect of public opinion or preferences on policy outputs*" (Beyer and Hänni 2018, p. 18). Beyer and Hänni point to upcoming elections as a major force leading to responsive behavior (Beyer and Hänni 2018, p. 20). In the work of Ansolabehere and Iyengar (1994), candidates address issues that are salient in the news and integrate them into their electoral communications. Klüver and Sagarzazu (2016) showed that German parties take cues from voters in their everyday political communication via press releases. According to Spoon and Klüver (2016), parties emphasize those issues in their manifestos, which are also important to voters. With this strategy of responsiveness, "a party can show that it is responsive to public concerns" and avoid the accusation that it is out of touch with the people (Wagner and Meyer 2014, p. 1020). This relates to the classic democratic idea of responsive government.

The probability that parties will act responsively to public opinion and "ride the wave" seems to follow general changes seen in parties in the past 150 years. Since the institutionalization of democratic party competition, parties have gradually opened up to voters' preferences with each new stage of party change indicating a clear trend toward the voter-orientation (Katz and Mair 1995). Recently, political and economic crises in Europe have further accentuated the question of parties' responsiveness (Vranceanu 2019; Bremer 2018; Clements et al. 2018). This interest in party responsiveness has also been fueled by what Mudde has called the "Populist Zeitgeist"—the demand for more responsive government (Mudde 2004, p. 558). From this perspective, the rise of populism may be interpreted as a reaction to self-referential (and therefore non-responsive) political elites (Fig. 3).

On the basis of these two concepts of party positioning, it is possible to formulate a hypothesis on the expected behavior of the German parties in terms of issue saliency and political positions. The independent variables here are Party Issue Ownership (PIO) and outside pressure. I expect **rising saliency** under the condition of high outside pressure and both variants of party issue ownership. Parties emphasize their issues. When the public pays high attention to these issues, parties elevate their saliency further. Parties may feel obligated to be responsive to public debates and stress issues for which the voters attribute them with competence. In the case of low

Fig. 3 Expected dynamics of saliency

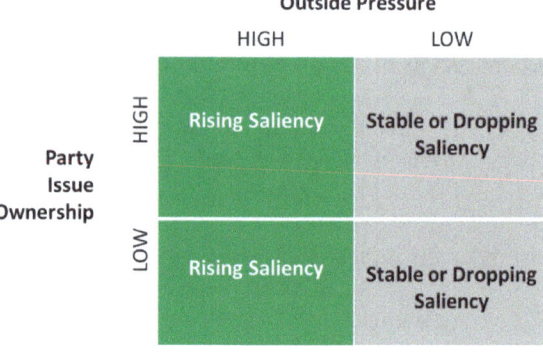

Fig. 4 Expected dynamics of political positioning

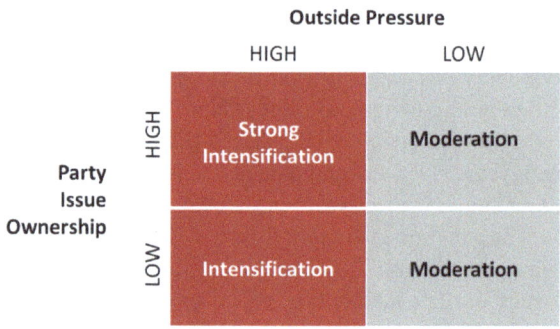

PIO and high outside pressure, parties also jump on the train and try to highlight their positions, even though the rise of saliency may unfold at a lower level. In contrast, I expect a **stable or dropping saliency** in the case of low outside pressure and both variants of PIO. Parties with a high and low PIO do not give up the issues but can adapt their saliency in times of low outside pressure (Fig. 4).

The second set of assumptions focuses on parties' political positions as the core of the argumentation. How do parties position themselves in relation to migration policy under certain conditions? First, I expect an **intensification** of a party's position in the case of high PIO and high outside pressure. In this highly political situation, the parties that own the respective issues are confronted with a high public pressure and issue saliency. The parties try to defend and benefit from their ownership of the issue. Due to path dependence, however, these parties do not change their position by 180 degrees. Instead, they stay on-message and put significant effort into being recognized with a clear and distinguishable position from their competitors. Therefore, they intensify their traditional position. A strong intensification of parties' positions leads to polarization concerning the issue; parties with a positive position become more positive and critical parties become more critical. Further, also parties with a lower PIO try to become recognizable with a clear position. Thus, here I also expect an intensification, albeit a less strong intensification. In contrast, **moderation** applies for the two combinations with low outside pressure. The pressure to act and to sharpen the party's profile concerning the issue is lower and the issue is not so much in focus. Under these conditions, parties with high and low issue ownership can tone down their rhetoric and may also seek compromise.

4 Method

In this section, I detail the measurement of the variables. I start with the dependent variables—issue saliency and political position. Three major approaches to measure the positions of political parties may be referred to. "[P]*arty manifesto data reports the self-ascribed position of the party, media data shows which parts of this position are brought into the public debate, and expert data shows how the position is perceived*" (Lehmann and Zobel 2018, p. 1057). For Lehmann and Zobel, manifesto data is clearly superior to other data types: "*Manifesto data […] measures the unified position a party ascribes to itself, which has not been mediated by a third actor*" (Lehmann and Zobel 2018, p. 1060). Given these advantages and the accessibility of respective data in the Party Manifesto Dataset, I chose to use manifesto data to measure the positions of the German parties on migration.

In the Party Manifesto Project (Volkens et al. 2019a), the issue of migration has attracted major attention within the last years. The regular Party Manifesto Dataset offers data of the issue of immigration for German parties[3] only from the year 2017 on. In 2018, a specific dataset was introduced that explicitly covers the development of party positions concerning migration policy between 1998 and 2013 (Lehmann and Zobel 2018). To cover a larger temporal range, I combine six different proxy variables from the Party Manifesto Data set that are related to the migration issue. The use of proxy variables is a widely applied strategy in research on party positions (for example, Akkerman 2015). The question, therefore, is which indicators to choose. Alonso and Fonseca (2011, p. 871) combine three negatively connoted indicators from the Party Manifesto Dataset (*multiculturalism negative, national way of life positive,* and *law and order*[4]) with two positively connoted indicators (*multiculturalism positive* and *underprivileged minority group*). This set of indicators covers one of the two major frames in the political discourse on migration: the ethno-pluralist doctrine, "*according to which the mixing of different ethnicities poses a threat to national culture; ethnicities have to be kept separate in order to prevent cultural extinction*" (Alonso and Fonseca 2011, p. 871). The other main frame in the

---

[3]Indicators "immigration positive" (number 602.2) and "immigration negative" (number 601.2).

[4]According to Alonso and Fonseca, the law and order indicator in particular comes with some tradeoffs: "The problem with this issue category is that some of the matters it covers have little or nothing to do with immigration, such as the organization and funding of police forces. Including 'law and order' in our issue dimension may thus inflate the relevance of immigration in manifestos. Excluding it, however, may have the opposite effect of not capturing immigration in one of its fundamental framings by the parties, namely law and order. We rather take the risk of inflating the saliency score of immigration for some parties than of not fully grasping their takes on the issue" (Alonso and Fonseca 2011, p. 871).

discourse is the welfare chauvinist doctrine, which cannot be reflected on the basis of the Party Manifesto Dataset (Alonso and Fonseca 2011, p. 871). Alonso and Fonseca also offer methods for calculating the saliency of issues and the positions of parties. Accordingly, the saliency of the migration issue in party manifestos is the sum of the percentages of sentences related to the mentioned categories. Furthermore, they construct an indicator for party position by subtracting the anti-immigration share from the pro-immigration share in each manifesto (Alonso and Fonseca 2011, p. 872).

I follow Alonso and Fonseca in their selection of indicators and the construction of the scores for saliency and political position on the basis of the Party Manifesto Dataset. In the German case, it seems especially reasonable to also include the law and order criterion after the events of New Year's Eve 2016 in Cologne.[5] Furthermore, I also include "*national way of life negative*" from the Party Manifesto Dataset as a further indicator for a positive position on migration. This is because with reference to German history, the opposition to patriotism and nationalism may also play a strong role in advocating for the importance of asylum as a political principle. Thus, I include three indicators for immigration-skeptical positions and three indicators for supportive positions. Table 1 shows an overview of the indicators and the calculation methods.

In order to measure the path dependence of former policy positions, I refer to the level of Party Issue Ownership (PIO) of the five parties for the years in which election manifestos were published. The numbers were taken from polls by the Forschungs-gruppe Wahlen.[6] The question asked was "Which party is the most competent to solve problems in a certain policy?" (Berger et al. 1999, 2003). In 1990 and 1994, the polls asked a slightly different question—whether a government led by the CSU/CSU or SPD would be most capable of solving the problems related to migration or foreigners (Forschungsgruppe Wahlen 1991). Thus, the Greens and Liberals are not included in 1990 and 1994. The Left Party/PDS could not be included in 1990 since the party was not yet part of the party system. In the numbers of Fig. 5, we see that competences regarding migration were mainly assigned to the CDU/CSU, but the SPD also played an important role. In the years 1998 and 2002, both parties had similar scores. The gap between both the SPD-line and the CDU/CSU-line only starts to grow after 2002. From then on, the Christian Democrats dominate more clearly. From 2013 to 2017, the gap between both parties reaches its maximum. The percentage of people who assign the migration issue to the CDU/CSU more than doubles that of people who assign it to the SPD. Thus, it looks like the SPD has lost its former strong position concerning the issue and the CDU/CSU has recently had exclusive ownership of the

---

[5] A series of sexual assaults occurred during the New Year's celebration in Cologne in 2015/2016. The assaults were mainly conducted by male refugees. Given the sheer number of incidents, law enforcement was not capable of controlling the situation for hours. In the aftermath, 1222 criminal offenses were reported, 513 of which cited sexual violence (Werthschulte 2017). The German Interior Minister at that time, Thomas de Maiziere (CDU), described the events as the turning point in the debate on migration and refugees, after which a different approach would be necessary. See online: www.spiegel.de/panorama/gesellschaft/thomas-de-maiziere-nennt-koelner-silves ternacht-wendepunkt-a-1118162.html.

[6] See online at: https://dbk.gesis.org/dbksearch/index.asp?db=e.

Table 1 Selected indicators, definitions, and methods for constructing the saliency and direction of party positions

Indicators positively related to migration	Definition in PMP Codebook (Volkens et al. 2019b)
Multiculturalism positive	"Favourable mentions of cultural diversity and cultural plurality within domestic societies. May include the preservation of autonomy of religious, linguistic heritages within the country including special educational provisions" (p. 20)
National way of life negative	"Unfavourable mentions of the manifesto country's nation and history. May include: Opposition to patriotism; opposition to nationalism; opposition to the existing national state, national pride, and national ideas" (p. 27)
Underprivileged minority groups	"Very general favourable references to underprivileged minorities who are defined neither in economic nor in demographic terms (e.g. the handicapped, homosexuals, immigrants, indigenous). Only includes favourable statements that cannot be classified in other categories" (p. 21)
Indicators negatively related to migration	**Definition in PMP Codebook**
Multiculturalism negative	"The enforcement or encouragement of cultural integration. Appeals for cultural homogeneity in society" (p. 20)
National way of life positive	"Favorable mentions of the manifesto country's nation, history, and general appeals. May include: Support for established national ideas; general appeals to pride of citizenship; appeals to patriotism; appeals to nationalism; suspension of some freedoms in order to protect the state against subversion" (p. 18)
Law and order	"Favourable mentions of strict law enforcement, and tougher actions against domestic crime. Only refers to the enforcement of the status quo of the manifesto country's law code. May include: Increasing support and resources for the police; Tougher attitudes in courts; Importance of internal security" (p. 19)
Calculation methods	
Saliency of migration issue	Addition of all percentages
Political position	Sum of positive indicators' percentages minus sum of negative indicators' percentages

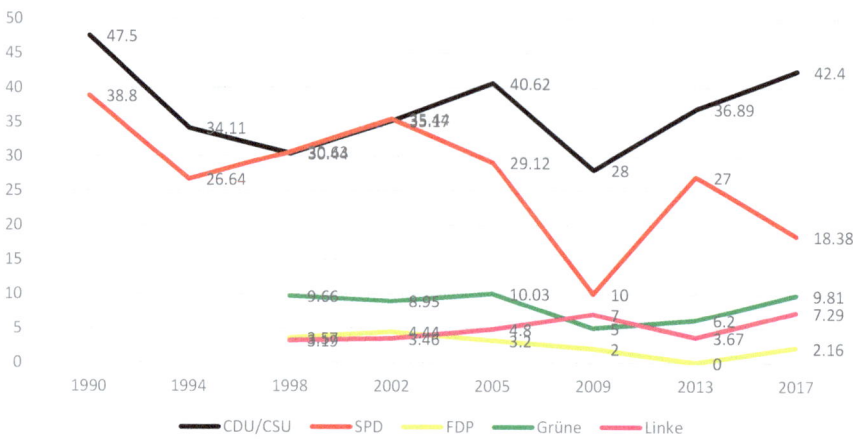

Fig. 5 Party issue ownership of migration from 1990 to 2017 in % of respondents in polls

issue. Of the other parties, the Liberals do not play a role in the issue, whereas the share of the Greens moves between 5 and 10%. Further, the Left Party experienced a small growth in numbers between 2013 and 2017.

The measurement of outside pressure on parties to act builds on four aspects. The first two are the number of asylum seekers in Germany per year[7] and the saliency of the migration issue among voters. For the latter, I turn to polls on the most urgent problems in Germany (Berger et al. 1994, 1998).[8] Since election manifestos are written in advance of the actual elections, I refer for both indicators to the year before the respective election. Both indicators are combined by addition and division by two.[9] In the next step, this general saliency score and is adapted; I assume that the degree of pressure on parties to engage in the policy of migration may also depend on whether a party is carrying responsibility in government. Here, the options are either yes or no. For government parties, the general saliency score is unchanged. In case of opposition parties, I assume the pressure to be less intense. Opposition parties are not assigned direct responsibility for certain developments and obviously lack the ability to significantly influence policy decisions. Therefore, the general saliency score is multiplied by 0.75. Finally, the degree of pressure on parties to engage in migration policy may also depend on whether a party is leading the responsible ministry. In case a party representative is the responsible Minister of the Interior, the score from the previous step remains unchanged. Otherwise, the score is again multiplied by 0.75 in order to further reduce it. The final result is the external pressure score (Fig. 6).

---

[7]See online at: http://www.bamf.de/EN/Startseite/startseite-node.html.

[8]The scores for the years 2001–2017 are taken from the longtime measurement of the Forschungs-gruppe Wahlen (2019) available at: http://www.forschungsgruppe.de/Umfragen/Politbarometer/Langzeitentwicklung_-_Themen_im_Ueberblick/Politik_II/#Probl1.

[9]To reduce imbalances between both scores, the score for the number of asylum seekers is reported in the thousands. For example, this will change the original number of 743,000 in 2016 to 743.

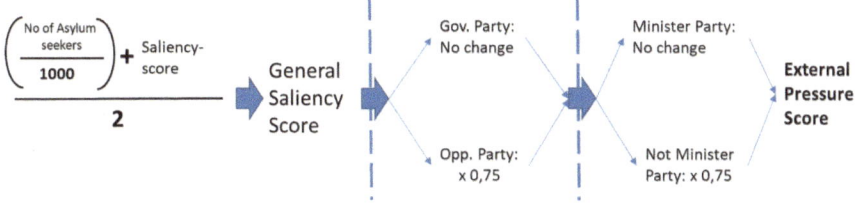

Fig. 6 Calculation method for external pressure on political parties

In the analysis, I focus on the five main parties of the German party system since reunification in 1990. These are the Christian Democrats of the CDU/CSU, the Social Democrats of the SPD, the Liberals (FDP), the Greens, and the Left Party, the former PDS. Since the 1990 elections, only these five parties have been represented in the Bundestag, though not always continuously. The AfD only joined the Bundestag in 2017 and therefore is not appropriate for a long-term comparison. This is also because the research questions deal with the reaction of the other parties to the refugee crisis. The overall time span of analysis is from 1990 to 2017. This long time span offers the chance to include the context of the high refugee numbers in the early 1990s as a comparison for the 2015 situation.

5 Results

I start with the question of saliency. As expected, the CDU/CSU as the party with the highest PIO raises the saliency of the migration issue simultaneously to the two peaks of general issue saliency. As the pressure from migration drops until 2005, the saliency of the issue also drops in the party manifesto of the Christian Democrats. The parties with a lower PIO also show at least some reaction to the two peaks of outside pressure. Concerning the latest refugee crisis in 2015, the saliency of migration rises from 2013 to 2017 in all five parties; all parties pay more attention to the issue. The main German parties, especially the CDU/CSU, did not neglect the issue of migration in their manifestos—in fact, the opposite is true. On the other hand, in the year 2005, all saliency scores were very close, in a range between 3 and 5%. In other words, in this year, migration was equally unimportant for the five parties, even the CDU/CSU. Thus, the expected dynamics of saliency become visible. We see a considerable amount of adaption by raising saliency in times of political tension and a downgrade of the issue in times of less outside pressure. Importantly, the development between 2013 and 2017 shows no deviant behavior from the parties. Thus, we can determine that it was not the neglect of the migration issue by the established parties that led to the establishment of the AfD in the party system. As proof for the optical patterns, there is also a statically significant positive correlation of 0.268 (on the significance level of 0.05) between saliency and external pressure. This is despite the visible up and downs in some parties' numbers, which seem to follow no clear

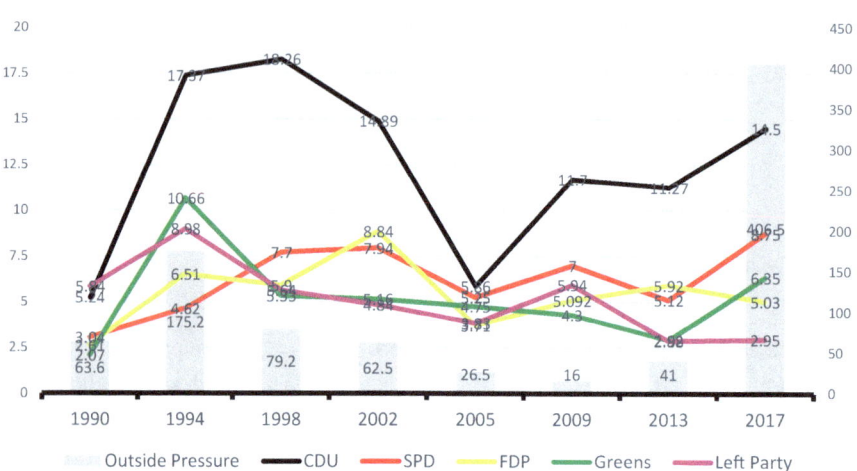

Fig. 7 Saliency of migration issue in party manifestos from 1990 to 2017 in % of all sentences in the party manifestos and outside pressure scores

pattern. In 2009, outside pressure from migration dropped to its lowest score, but for example, the SPD score increases. Finally, in line with the theoretical expectations, we find no linear relationship between party issue ownership and saliency because parties with high and low PIO-numbers raised the saliency of the migration issue in times of growing external pressure (Fig. 7).

Next, I turn to the political positions as the core of the argumentation. Also here, the results present clear proof of the theoretical assumptions, showing a dynamic of intensification and moderation. We see that times of polarization seem to occur in parallel to times of high external pressure. In contrast, in times of low external pressure, the polarization diminishes. In 2005, the five parties were rather close to each other's positions, whereas the order from supportive to critical is kept intact. Thus, once party competition intensifies with a rising general saliency of the issue, the parties return to their more traditional positions, increasing polarization on the issue. This shows that the policy spectrum of the German parties contracts and expands in alignment with the circumstances. The parties undergo very similar up-and-down dynamics since 2002, only on different levels of the spectrum. The scores of all five parties increase up until the 2009 manifestos and drop after that until 2017. In other words, three of the five parties became more migration-skeptical after 2015, and the other two became more migration-friendly. Between 1990 and 1998, the CDU/CSU, SPD, and FDP experience a rather similar development as well, again only on different levels. The scores of the Greens and the Left Party/PDS become more negative between 1994 and 1998, leading to 2002 when the Greens, FDP, and the Left Party shared the almost exact same balanced position on migration. Thus, the long-term positioning of all five parties concerning migration displays changes similar to that of waves moving up and down. The party systems therefore offers the necessary polarization in times of high external pressure, which also provides

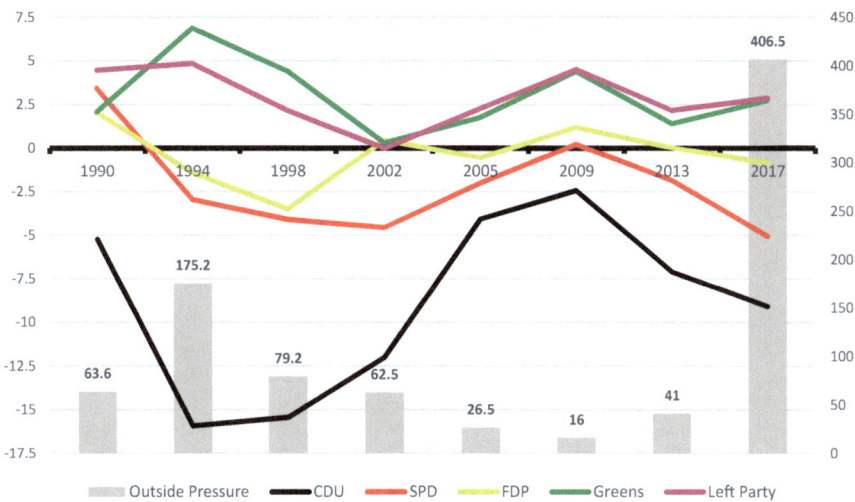

Fig. 8 Political positions on migration between 1990 and 2017

evidence against the perception of a common migration-friendly position among the five parties that gave way to the AfD (Fig. 8).

As expected, the CDU/CSU as the party owning the issue, shows the strongest intensification. The intensification of the party's position from 2009 on contradicts the common perception that the party's position on migration changed in the course of the 2015/2016 refugee crisis. The party was already on a more critical course before the events of 2015/2016, which intensified in the 2017 program. The correlation of the variables confirms the visual result. The correlation between the party's PIO and political position is at −0.651 with a significance on the 0.001 level. The higher the PIO, the more negative the position on migration. However, there is also a negative correlation of −0.281 (at the significance level of 0.05) between the degree of external pressure and the political positions of the parties. Despite the polarization in times of political tensions, the overall tendency of the parties leans more strongly to the critical position on migration. These numbers speak against the perception that the CDU/CSU has moved into the political center in terms of the migration issue giving way to the rise of the AfD. Instead, both parties of the governing Grand Coalition took on more critical positions than those of a decade ago, and this started before the refugee crisis of 2015/2016. There is no overwhelming trend of more positive positions toward migration in 2017—the opposite is true. Interestingly, the range of positions between the five parties has reduced over the course of time. Whereas the Greens and Christian Democrats were almost 22 points apart in 1994, this range has decreased to about 6 points. In 2017, we find again the CDU/CSU and the Greens at both ends of the spectrum, raising doubts about their ability to form a coalition, which has been discussed lately (Table 2).

Table 2 Correlations of variables

		Saliency	Political Position
External Pressure	Pearson Correlation	**.268***	−.281*
	Sig. (1-tailed)	.047	.040
	N	40	40
Issue Ownership	Pearson Correlation	.243	−.651***
	Sig. (1-tailed)	.065	.000
	N	40	40

*= Correlation is significant at the 0.05 level (1-tailed)
***= Correlation is significant at the 0.001 level (1-tailed)

6 Discussion of Results and Conclusion

Migration is a complex political issue with various dimensions and perspectives. Since the major refugee crisis in Europe in 2015/2016, the issue has not only dominated the political discourse, it has also changed the political landscape in many ways. On the European level, the refugee question has become a major force of division among member countries. European regulations and systems for asylum and refugee distribution have more or less collapsed, and member states have become the central actors again. Within European countries, the political landscapes have also changed since 2015/2016. Although these changes have not occurred everywhere in the same manner, right-wing populist parties or actors are on the rise in almost every European country fueled by the refugee crisis. This applies also for Germany, where politics have become a roller coaster. Since the refugee crisis, the major people's parties CDU/CSU and SPD have been caught in internal turmoil and the Alternative for Germany (AfD) is celebrating one electoral success after the other. In summary, the refugee crisis of 2015/2016 served as a turning point and critical juncture in many ways. This study examined whether the refugee crisis was also a turning point in German parties' handling of the migration issue. Did especially the Christian Democrats contribute to the rise of the AfD by moving toward the center in response to the migration question?

The results presented here raise doubts on the prevalent interpretation of these parties' responses to the 2015 refugee crisis. In contrast, we see a strong continuity and predictability in party positions on migration. The parties' post-2015 positions do not represent a deviation from the long-standing patterns of party behavior. There is no evidence of abrupt moves that could sustain the interpretation of the established parties giving room for the anti-migration AfD. The numbers instead show that the parties reacted to the 2015 crisis in a very predictable manner, especially the CDU/CSU as the party owning the issue almost exclusively since 2005. Accordingly, we see a strong reaction from almost all parties to the 2015 situation by raising the saliency of the issue in their 2017 manifestos. There is no sign of a neglect of the migration situation in 2017. All parties, and especially the Christian Democrats, were responsive. When they are exerted to high pressure, parties raise the saliency of the migration issue, and in times of low pressure they are less determined. The numbers under scrutiny here were only over a time span of 27 years, and further research should expand the temporal scope. Over these 27 years of migration policy, however, I identified a dynamic of contraction and expansion, of the polarization and moderation of positions. The numbers do not fully explain the reasons behind the parties' movements on their positions, but highlight developments. There seems to be a repeating pattern that in times of growing policy pressure, polarization intensifies, and vice versa. With that, the development of the positions in the turn from 2013 to 2017 was also very predictable. The parties sharpened their positions on migration. In particular, the CDU/CSU's political position became more immigration-skeptical, but this process had begun way earlier. Therefore, we do not see a big turn in migration policy in the CDU/CSU positions, which allegedly gave room for the establishment of the anti-immigration AfD. The opposite is true. The last time the CDU/CSU's position was a s negative on migration was in 2002.

How does this relate to the 2015 Merkel government's decision to let one million refugees into the country and the perceived swing of the CDU/CSU in migration policy? The answer is that these are different strands of action. The decision of the government to not close the border has to be seen as an isolated act that was not mirrored by the party manifesto of the CDU/CSU nor of the SPD, the other government party. It was rather a single occasion born out of the context (Alexander 2017) and not representative of the party's positions as laid out in the electoral program. Due to the impact of this action, however, the widespread perception was that of a change of the CDU, which in fact is misleading and is a simplification of the complex situation. The Christian Democrats did not change their (official) position on migration, and the AfD did not come in and take that position. The AfD was and is far more anti-immigration in its positions than the other parties. Therefore, it did not require a shift of the CDU/CSU. The presented results have limitations that must also be mentioned. First, the documents to which the Party Manifesto Dataset refers are in the German case actually "only" electoral manifestos. These may be rather vague, and parties do not always feel necessarily obliged to follow them in day-to-day politics.

Finally, the results of this study offer some hints for future party positions on migration and the saliency of the issue, particularly concerning the identified wave dynamic. Hypothetically, we will see a further decrease of the saliency of the migration issue in Germany in the coming years accompanied by a change of the major parties toward more immigration-friendly positions. This decrease of the polarization of the issue may also bring the CDU/CSU and Greens again closer together and open the door for a potential coalition—until the next polarization.

References

Ademmer, E., & Stöhr, T. (2018). *Europeans are more accepting of immigrants today than 15 years ago: Evidence from eight waves of the European Social Survey*, Mercator Dialogue on Asylum and Migration, POLICY BRIEF 2018/1.

Akkerman, T. (2015). Immigration policy and electoral competition in Western Europe: A fine-grained analysis of party positions over the past two decades. *Party Politics, 21*(1), 54–67.

Alexander, R. (2017). *Die Getriebenen: Merkel und die Flüchtlingspolitik: Report aus dem Innern der Macht*. Siedler.

Alonso, S., & Fonseca, S. C. (2011). Immigration, left and right. *Party Politics, 18*(6), 865–884.

Ansolabehere, S., & Iyengar, S. (1994). Riding the wave and claiming ownership over issues: The joint effects of advertising and news coverage in campaigns. *Public Opinion Quarterly, 58*(3), 335–357.

BAMF (Bundesamt für Migration und Flüchtlinge, Federal Office for Migration and Refugees). (2019). *Aktuelle Zahlen September 2019*, online available at: www.bamf.de/SharedDocs/Anl agen/DE/Downloads/Infothek/Statistik/Asyl/aktuelle-zahlen-zu-asyl-september-2019.html;jse ssionid=99474586371F8B96AFF4F5308108E3A2.2_cid368?nn=7952222.

Berger, M., Jung, M., & Roth, D. (1994). *Politbarometer West 1993 (Kumulierter Datensatz)*. GESIS Datenarchiv, Köln. ZA2378 Datenfile Version 1.0.0. https://doi.org/10.4232/1.2378.

Berger, M., Jung, M., & Roth, D. (1998). *Politbarometer 1997 (Kumulierter Datensatz)*. GESIS Datenarchiv, Köln. ZA3045 Datenfile Version 1.0.0. https://doi.org/10.4232/1.3045.

Berger, M., Jung, M., & Roth, D. (1999). *Wahlstudie 1998 (Politbarometer)*. GESIS Datenarchiv, Köln. ZA3160 Datenfile Version 1.0.0. https://doi.org/10.4232/1.3160.

Berger, M., Jung, M., & Roth, D. (2003). *Politbarometer Kurzbefragung 2002* (Kumulierter Datensatz). GESIS Datenarchiv, Köln. ZA3851 Datenfile Version 1.0.0. https://doi.org/10.4232/1. 3851.

Beyer, D., & Hänni, M. (2018). Two sides of the same coin? Congruence and responsiveness as representative democracy's currencies. *Policy Studies Journal, 46*(S1), S13–S47.

Bos, L., Lefevere, J. M., Thijssen, R., & Sheets, P. (2017). The impact of mediated party issue strategies on electoral support. *Party Politics, 23*(6), 760–771.

Bremer, B. (2018). The missing left? Economic crisis and the programmatic response of social democratic parties in Europe. *Party Politics, 24*(1), 23–38.

Capoccia, G., & Kelemen, D. R. (2007). The study of critical junctures: Theory, narrative, and counterfactuals in historical institutionalism. *World Politics, 59*(3), 341–369.

Clements, B., Nanou, K., & Real-Dato, J. (2018). Economic crisis and party responsiveness on the left–right dimension in the European Union. *Party Politics, 24*(1), 52–64.

Dostal, J. M. (2017). The German Federal Election of 2017: How the wedge issue of refugees and migration took the shine off Chancellor Merkel and transformed the party system. *The Political Quarterly, 88*(4), 589–602.

Forschungsgruppe Wahlen. (1991). *Wahlstudie 1990 (Trenduntersuchungen)*. GESIS Datenarchiv, Köln. ZA1920 Datenfile Version 1.0.0. https://doi.org/10.4232/1.1920.

Forschungsgruppe Wahlen. (2019). *Politbarometer: Wichtigste Probleme seit 01/2000*, online available at: www.forschungsgruppe.de/Umfragen/Politbarometer/Langzeitentwicklung_-_Themen_ im_Ueberblick/Politik_II/.

Franzmann, S. T., Giebler, H., & Poguntke, T. (2019). It's no longer the economy, stupid! Issue yield at the 2017 German federal election. *West European Politics*, published online 30 Oct 2019.

Geiges, L. (2018). Wie die AfD im Kontext der "Flüchtlingskrise" mobilisierte: Eine empirisch-qualitative Untersuchung der "Herbstoffensive 2015". *Zeitschrift für Politikwissenschaft, 28*(1), 49–69.

Green, S. (2006). Zwischen Kontinuität und Wandel: Migrations- und Staatsangehörigkeitspolitik. In M. G. Schmidt & R. Zohlnhöfer (Eds.), *Regieren in der Bundesrepublik Deutschland: Innen- und Außenpolitik seit 1949* (pp. 113–134). VS Verlag.

Haller, M. (2017). *Die "Flüchtlingskrise" in den Medien: Tagesaktueller Journalismus zwischen Meinung und Information.* Otto-Brenner-Stiftung.

Harmel, R., & Janda, K. (1994). An integrated theory of party goals and party change. *Journal of Theoretical Politics, 6*(3), 259–287.

Hess, C., & Green, S. (2016). Introduction: The changing politics and policies of migration in Germany. *German Politics, 25*(3), 315–328.

Hoesch, K. (2018). *Migration und Integration: Eine Einführung.* Wiesbaden: Springer VS Verlag.

Hofmann, R. (2017). *Flucht, Migration und die neue europäische Sicherheitsarchitektur: Herausforderungen für die EU-Kriminalpolitik.* Springer VS.

Katz, R., & Mair, P. (1995). Changing models of party organization and party democracy: The emergence of the cartel party. *Party Politics, 1*(1), 5–28.

Klüver, H., & Sagarzazu, I. (2016). Setting the agenda or responding to voters? Political parties, voters and issue attention. *West European Politics, 39*(2), 380–398.

Kober, U., & Kösemen, O. (2019). *Willkommenskultur zwischen Skepsis und Pragmatik Deutschland nach der "Fluchtkrise".* Bertelsmann Stiftung.

Kurbjuweit, D. (2016). Germany enters a dangerous new political era: Stability used to define Germany's political system: But the refugee crisis has fundamentally changed the country's party landscape: The rise of the fringe has eroded the traditional centers of power. In *SPIEGEL ONLINE INTERNATIONAL*, online available at: https://www.spiegel.de/international/germany/how-the-refugee-crisis-has-change-german-politics-a-1081023.html. Accessed on 18 October 2019.

Laubenthal, B. (2019). Refugees welcome? Reforms of the German asylum policies between 2013 and 2017 and Germany's transformation into an immigration country. *German Politics, 28*(3), 412–425.

Lehmann, P., & Zobel, M. (2018). Positions and saliency of immigration in party manifestos: A novel datasetusing crowd coding. *European Journal of Political Research, 57,* 1056–1083.

Liesching, M., & Hooffacker, G. (2019). *Agenda-Setting bei ARD und ZDF? Analyse politischer Sendungen vor der Bundestagswahl 2017.* OBS-Arbeitspapier 34.

Lipset, S. M., & Rokkan, S. (1967). Cleavage structures, party systems, and voter alignments: An introduction. In S. M. Lipset & S. Rokkan (Eds.), *Party systems and voter alignments: Cross-national perspectives* (pp. 1–64). New York: The Free Press.

Mader, M., & Schoen, H. (2019). The European refugee crisis, party competition, and voters' responses in Germany. *West European Politics, 42*(1), 67–90.

Mudde, C. (2004). The populist zeitgeist. *Government and Opposition, 39*(4), 542–563.

Mushaben, J. M. (2017). Wir schaffen das! Angela Merkel and the European refugee crisis. *German Politics, 26*(4), 516–533.

Petrocik, J. R. (1996). Issue ownership in presidential elections, with a 1980 case study. *American Journal of Political Science, 40*(3), 825–850.

Pierson, P. (2004). *Politics in time: History, institutions and social analysis.* Princeton, NJ: Princeton University Press.

Seeberg, H. B. (2016). How stable is political parties' issue ownership? A cross-time, cross-national analysis. *Political Studies, 65*(2), 475–492.

Spoon, J.-J., & Klüver, H. (2016). Challenges to multiparty governments: How governing in coalitions affects coalition parties' responsiveness to voters. *Party Politics, 23*(6), 793–803.

Tekin, F. (2017). Differenzierte Integration im Raum der Freiheit, der Sicherheit und des Rechts im Spannungsfeld von Problemlösungsinstinkt und Souveränitätsreflex. *INTEGRATION, 4,* 263–275.

Volkens, A., Krause, W., Lehmann, P., Matthieß, T., Merz, N., & Regel, S., et al. (2019a). *The manifesto data collection.* Manifesto Project (MRG/CMP/MARPOR). Version 2019a.

Wissenschaftszentrum Berlin für Sozialforschung (WZB). https://doi.org/10.25522/manifesto. mpds.2019a.

Volkens, A., Krause, W., Lehmann, P., Matthieß, T., Merz, N., & Regel, S., et al. (2019b). *The manifesto project dataset—Codebook*. Manifesto Project (MRG/CMP/MARPOR). Version 2019a. Wissenschaftszentrum Berlin für Sozialforschung (WZB).

Vranceanu, A. (2019). The impact of contextual factors on party responsiveness regarding immigration issues. *Party Politics*, 25(4), 583–593.

Wagner, M., & Meyer, T. M. (2014). Which issues do parties emphasize? Salience strategies and party organisation in multiparty systems. *West European Politics, 37*(5), 1019–1045.

Werthschulte, C. (2017). "Nach" Köln ist wie "vor" Köln: Die Silvesternacht und ihre Folgen. *Aus Politik und Zeitgeschichte APuZ, 67*(1–3), 10–17.

Wessels, W. (2017). Justiz- und Innenpolitik: Der Raum der Freiheit, der Sicherheit und des Rechts. In W. Wessels (Ed.), *Das Politische System der Europäischen Union*. Springer VS.

Migration Policy in Eastern Europe: The Case of Poland and Hungary

Ewa Rokicka

Abstract This article is an attempt to answer the question of in what spheres the migration policy of the Eastern part of the EU, and more specifically Poland and Hungary, are in conflict with the policy of Western Europe. Based on empirical research conducted in Poland and Hungary, as well as on analysis of newspaper publications, this article discusses Hungarian and Polish migration policies towards refugees, Muslims and asylum seekers. Against a background of "migration crisis" events, the article analyses how the Hungarian and Polish governments responded to the influx of refugees and points to the reasons and consequences of such a reaction.

Keywords Migration policy · Poland · Hungary · European Union

1 Introduction

In 2020, the COVID-19 pandemic, with its severe health, economic, political and social consequences that disorganize the daily lives of billions of people, has relegated the migration crisis and the tensions that caused it, as well as the issues of political persecution, war and poverty to the background. However, it would be naive to expect that as the pandemic subsides, migration pressure on the external borders of the European Union will disappear. The number of people in need of humanitarian aid as well as the number of economic emigrants will remain high.

Interest in migration fell even earlier as the EU had started to implement measures to better control its external borders and the influx of migrants since the climax of the migration crisis in 2015. As a result, unregulated migration has fallen by more than 90%.[1]

---

[1] https://www.consilium.europa.eu/pl/policies/migratory-pressures/.

E. Rokicka (✉)
Professor of Department of Sociology of Social Structure and Social Change,
University of Lodz, Łódź, Poland
e-mail: ewa.rokicka@uni.lodz.pl

© The Author(s), under exclusive license to Springer Nature Singapore Pte Ltd. 2021 185
C.-P. Chu and S.-C. Park (eds.), *Immigration Policy and Crisis in the Regional Context*,
https://doi.org/10.1007/978-981-33-6823-1_11

At the beginning of the migration crisis, the EU did not have a common policy on migration management and border security. At the turn of September 2015, when refugees from Africa and the Middle East gathered in temporary camps in Italy, Greece and Hungary, the EU Council decided to relocate them. The goal of the relocation system was to distribute migrants among member states in proportion to GDP and population. Hungary was the first to withdraw from the relocation mechanism. The Polish government agreed to admit just over 7,000 migrants. By supporting the relocation mechanism, Poland opposed the Visegrad Group countries that voted against such a solution.[2] After the takeover of power by PiS in 2015, the priorities of Polish international policy changed and Poland reneged on its earlier commitment to admit refugees.

In the initial phase of the crisis, the progression of the migration situation forced the Union to take urgent anti-crisis measures. At the extraordinary European Council summit, the heads of state and government called on the European Commission to present a comprehensive EU migration strategy. In response to this call, on May 13, 2015 the European Commission presented the European program on migration. This document sets out, on the one hand, immediate measures to be taken to prevent further accidents involving refugees and to control the migration situation in southern Europe, and on the other, a strategic approach to improving migration management in the Union in the short and medium term. "The tasks that the EU was to undertake immediately included: saving lives at sea, combating people smuggling, receiving people seeking shelter under relocation and resettlement schemes, reviving cooperation with migrants' countries of origin and transit countries, implementing the so-called hotspot approach and financial assistance to the Member States whose asylum systems have been most burdened." (Szymańska 2017, p. 165).

The current migration strategy assumes: first, a departure from conflict-generating forced relocation; and secondly, cooperation with neighboring countries and with African countries in managing migration. The goal of the latter is the need to eliminate the root causes of migration (including through development aid and conflict prevention). The so-called EU Emergency Trust Fund for Africa launched in November 2015 (€4.7 billion) was to help where the source of the problem was; thirdly, to triple the budgetary resources for 2021–27, including supplying Frontex with an external EU border protection service numbering 10,000 people.[3] In addition, work is ongoing to reform the Dublin system, which is the basis of asylum policy, towards fairer sharing of responsibility for migrants.[4]

In March 2016, an agreement was concluded with Turkish President Recep Tayyip Erdogan, who committed to stopping the activities of criminals organizing illegal transport across the Aegean Sea. Under this agreement, all refugees who came to Greece illegally were sent back to Turkey. The Union, meanwhile, committed to admitting 72,000 from this country. In turn, the EU has pledged €3 billion to help

---

[2]The Visegrad Group (V4) is an informal, regional form of cooperation between four Central European countries—Poland, the Czech Republic, Slovakia and Hungary.

[3]https://www.consilium.europa.eu/pl/policies/migratory-pressures/history-migratory-pressures/.

[4]https://www.consilium.europa.eu/pl/policies/migratory-pressures/ceas-reform/.

Syrian refugees in Turkey.[5] As a result of the actions taken, the Eastern Mediterranean route was practically shut down, which largely solved the problem of the rapid influx of migrants.

However, in March 2020, the wave of migration began to swell rapidly. Frontex data shows that during the first three months of this year, 24.5 thousand illegal EU border crossings were recorded, an increase of 26% versus a year ago. The rising wave of migration behind which stood, among other things, Turkey's decisions was interrupted by the epidemic, as evidenced by the fact that in March, the number of detections of illegal border crossings on Europe's main migratory routes fell by nearly half from the previous month to around 4 650.[6]

Fighting the coronavirus pandemic, the EU has suspended receiving refugees and migrants for humanitarian reasons until further notice (UNHCR 2018).[7] As part of humanitarian resettlement, people affected by humanitarian crises were brought to Europe directly from their country of origin. The host countries could thus identify the people they deem in need of protection. During the pandemic, the execution of these programs was suspended due to travel restrictions and problems encountered in operational cooperation with strategic partners. All countries except Ireland have closed their external borders to non-essential travel.[8] In addition, 12 EU countries have restored temporary border controls within Schengen.[9] For now, these restrictions are expected to apply until May 15. The actions taken by European Union countries and the Schengen area to introduce coordinated temporary travel restrictions are typical during a pandemic. Their purpose is obvious; they are to slow down the spread of coronavirus.[10]

To sum up, the last four years of implementing migration policy have shown that the EU is able to respond to unforeseen circumstances, find common solutions and work together to achieve real results. But the massive influx of migrants to Greece has made Europeans aware that not all actions have been completed. The situation is still unstable. The political problem and the question of the limits of European solidarity

---

[5]https://www.consilium.europa.eu/pl/meetings/international-summit/2016/03/07/.

[6]The largest decline occurred on the cross-Mediterranean route from Libya to Italy. The number of irregular migrants crossing the Central Mediterranean in March fell by 88%. Half of the illegal migration cases last month took place in the Eastern Mediterranean, i.e. on the route that leads through Turkey to Greece. However, even there the number of migrants fell by 38% from February to around 2300, despite the spike in detections early in the month.

[7]Like the EU, the International Organization for Migration (IOM) and the Office of the United Nations High Commissioner for Refugees (UNHCR) have officially suspended their refugee reception programs. https://www.unhcr.org/desperatejourneys/?fbclid=IwAR1j3aQ85xlBauA2eiq 8e-YIT4VbeShizwetI-vCq9TlfEpskXXMub8xVgc#.

[8]The situation of Ireland, which is outside Schengen but applies part of its acquis, is different from other EU countries due to the common travel area with Great Britain. Both countries had to agree to introduce restrictions.

[9]These are: Austria, Hungary, the Czech Republic, Denmark, Poland, Lithuania, Germany, Estonia, Portugal, Spain, Finland and Belgium and two associated countries: Switzerland and Norway.

[10]In addition to 22 EU countries, the Schengen area also includes four non-EU countries: Iceland, Norway, Switzerland and Liechtenstein.

imposed by the crisis still remain to be resolved; namely, to what extent are Member States obliged to provide all possible assistance measures to other countries?

Governments, political parties and entire societies have proved to be divided on the admission of asylum seekers into European Member States. This discord is present at various levels but particularly evident between Western European countries and the Visegrad Group. As a result, negotiations on a common EU migration policy are also at an impasse.

The division of Member States on the approach to the migration crisis reveals deeper divisions in the Union resulting from intolerance, xenophobia, Islamophobia and democratic deficits, which undermine the idea of the coexistence of different cultures in Europe and are in conflict with the principles and values upheld by the Union.

This article is an attempt to answer the question of in what spheres the migration policy of the Eastern part of the EU, and more specifically Poland and Hungary, is in conflict with the policy of Western Europe and what are the causes and consequences of this.

2 Poland as a Country of Emigration and Immigration

Traditionally, Poland (just like Hungary) is considered an emigration country. Yet, the significance of immigration to Poland is increasing and, according to demographers' forecasts, the inflow of foreigners will be indispensable to maintaining the stability of the economy and pension system (Report on the state of research on migration in Poland after 1989: 2018).

Nearly 38 million Poles live in Poland. Additionally, approximately 21 million Poles and people of Polish origin live outside of Poland. There are various reasons for emigrating and settling abroad. In the nineteenth century, during the so-called "Great Emigration" period, Poles migrated mainly for political reasons. During the Partitions of Poland, they fled the country mainly in fear of potential repressions by the occupiers.[11] A large portion of people leaving the country have been economic immigrants, migrating in search of work and better living conditions. The 20th-century "El Dorado" for our countrymen was the United States, and to a lesser degree France and Germany, while in the 21st century Great Britain and Ireland have begun to take over this role.[12]

---

[11] The Partitions of Poland were three partitions of the Polish-Lithuanian Commonwealth that took place toward the end of the 18th century and ended the existence of the state, resulting in the elimination of sovereign Poland and Lithuania for 123 years. The partitions were carried out by the Habsburg Monarchy, the Kingdom of Prussia, and the Russian Empire, which divided up the Commonwealth lands among themselves progressively in the process of territorial seizures and annexations. Encyclopedia Britannica online 2008.

[12] Currently, the five countries with the largest Polish communities are: 1. United States (with approximately 10,600,000 people). The largest concentration, in Chicago, is about 1.5 million. New York comes second (700,000), followed by Detroit (400,000). 2. Germany (about 2,100,000

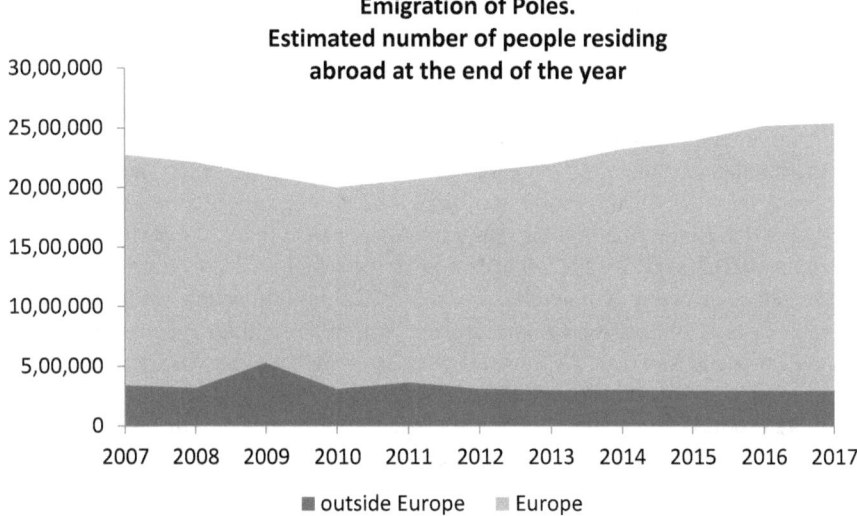

Graph 1. Emigration of Poles. Estimated number of people residing abroad at the end of the year (*Source* GUS Central Statistical Office Poland)

The data presented in the next two graphs illustrates the scale and directions of Poles' migration. They show how many Poles live abroad and which countries they choose most frequently (Graph 1).

Poland belongs to countries with a high level of emigration. It is estimated that in 2107, 2.5 million Poles emigrated, of which 90% remained in Europe (2.121 million going to EU Member States). The number of Poles who decided to leave the country has been growing systematically since 2010—at that time there were 2 million Poles abroad. Recently, we can observe a weakening of the emigration wave, or at least its stabilization, primarily due to the good situation on the labor market in Poland. This mainly diminishes the attractiveness of longer-term temporary economic travel.

These are usually people up to 29 years of age with primary and vocational education, dissatisfied with the wages and working conditions in Poland. Among the people declaring the intention to travel abroad, 4% of respondents want to leave Poland permanently. 10% consider traveling for a fixed period (usually from a few months to several years). The remaining 3/4 of respondents do not want to emigrate. As a negative factor to emigration, they indicate the fear of losing contact with family and friends and not knowing a foreign language. 28% of them are satisfied with their current job and pay.[13] After Brexit, Germany is the most popular destination for Poles,

___

people). The main clusters are those in former West Germany (especially from old emigration and the 1980s). 3. Brazil (approximately 1,900,000 people). 4. France (approximately 1,000,000 people). 5. Canada (approximately 1,000,000 people). In connection with the events of recent history, many Poles also live in Lithuania (Vilnius), Belarus (Grodno) and Ukraine (Lviv). http://archiwum.wsp olnotapolska.org.pl/?id=pwko00.

[13] http://info.randstad.pl/monitor-rynku-pracy-37.

indicated by almost every fourth respondent. The following came respectively: the Netherlands, Great Britain, Norway and Sweden.

The highest number of Polish emigrants resided in Great Britain (720,000), Germany (655,000), the Netherlands (112,000) and Ireland (111,000). In non-EU countries, the largest number of Polish emigrants lived in Norway (approx. 85,000), but the number of Poles also increased in Switzerland and Iceland. The map below illustrates the scale of migration and directions chosen by Polish emigrants from 2004 to 2015. Before the first EU labor markets opened in 2004, less than 800,000 Poles resided abroad. In 2015 (the last year for which official Central Statistical Office data is available) the number was almost 2.2 million people (Map 1).

After Poland's accession to the European Union, labor markets in EU countries gradually opened for Poles. As shown in the map, many Poles have benefited from the opportunity to take up legal work in Western Europe, some of whom will not permanently return to Poland. Their departure caused a noticeable shortage of workers on the Polish labor market. Citizens of other countries, mainly located to the east of Poland, are filling this gap. The next charts illustrate how many immigrants came to Poland and from which countries.

In 2017, the last year for which figures are available, more than 3.1 million people living outside the community were granted visas to EU Member States as part of their first entry (visa for transit through or an intended stay in the territory of the

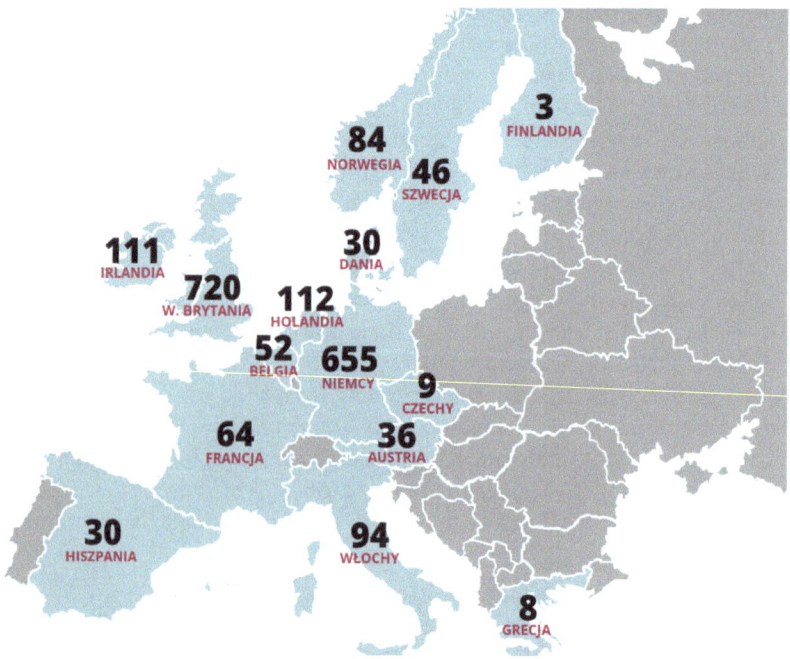

Map 1. Polish emigrants in the European Union (2004–2015) (in thousands) (*Source* tvn24bis.pl, GUS data)

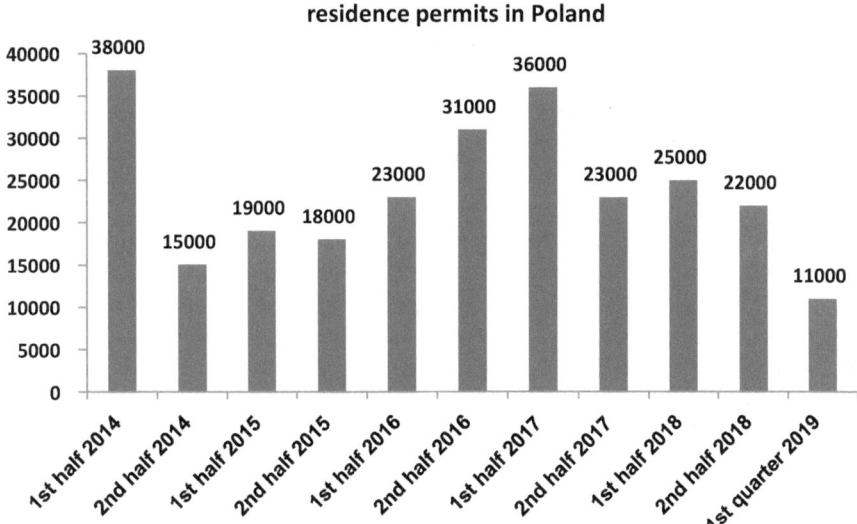

Graph 2. Number of foreigners receiving legal residency in Poland (*Source* Office for foreigners)

Schengen States of no more than three months within a six-month period from the date of first entry—Schengen visa).

The countries most frequently issuing residence permits include Poland 683,000 (22% of all issued documents), Germany 535,446 (17%), Great Britain 517,000 (16%), France 250,175 (8%), Spain 231,153 (7%), Italy 186,786 (6%) and Sweden 129.754 (4%). (OECD 2018)[14] (Graph 2)

Poland issued more visas to foreign workers than any other country in Europe. 85 percent of them went to people from Ukraine. Belarusians are the second largest group, followed by Georgians, Moldavans and Indians. According to data from the Office for Foreigners, the largest number of permits was issued for temporary residence (up to a maximum of 3 years) and permanent residence. The most common reason for foreigners coming to Poland is the desire to work. This concerned almost 72% of cases. Every tenth applicant wanted to stay in Poland for family reasons, and 7% in connection with starting or continuing studies. Many of the newcomers perform unskilled work, replacing Polish nationals who are either rejecting lower-paid jobs after five years of falling unemployment in the booming country or have migrated elsewhere in Europe, chasing higher salaries. A growing number also come to attend Polish universities.

The above data, however, does not include persons temporarily staying in Poland on the basis of private invitations and Schengen tourist visas. From this category of immigrants, a large number of individuals are employed on the 'black' labor

---

[14]https://read.oecd-ilibrary.org/social-issues-migration-health/international-migration-outlook-2018_migr_outlook-2018-en#page19

market, mainly in the so-called care services, cleaning, domestic help, etc. This is a so-called "invisible workforce". This group also includes seasonal construction workers and people working in agriculture and processing. Since the outbreak of the war in Donbass, these are mainly young men, for many of whom this is a way of avoiding military service. There are also those who had previously worked in Russia but now choose Poland. Poland has risen to first place as the economic migration target of Ukrainians, outclassing Russia and the once-dominant Czech Republic and Italy.

Until 2017, the migration balance indicator for Poland was negative. Despite the increase in immigration in recent years, Poland is still among emigration countries, not immigration countries. This means it is classified as a country not directly affected by the migration crisis, which has an impact on the attitude of the Polish government towards the European migration crisis and the way it is addressed. This attitude can be described as Poland's two-faced immigration strategy. With harsh anti-immigrant rhetoric, both internally and on the EU stage, Poland simultaneously accepts a massive influx of foreigners to the country, mainly from Ukraine. The everyday state of affairs, i.e. the lack of hands to work, is at variance with propaganda fueling anti-immigration and xenophobic sentiments.

Poland's massive emigration numbers to EU member states and the largest single economic migration of people from one European country to another in such a short time in all recent history stand in marked opposition to the anti-migrant electoral campaign that helped bring PiS (Law and Justice) to power five years ago. The extreme right party crushed a coalition of opposition parties with 46 percent of the vote in the last European Parliament election, its strongest results ever.

3 The 'Refugee Crisis' and the Polish Government's Migration Policy

During the so-called "refugee crisis," the issue of potential relocation of asylum seekers became politicized and immigration to Poland became constructed as a social problem. Poland's ruling party, PiS, was against the resettlement and relocation of refugees.

The government's objection to immigration appealed to a fear and deep distrust of Muslims. The ruling politicians and right-wing media fueled these fears, making Poles one of the most xenophobic nations in Europe (see Graph 3). The escalation of these negative attitudes was not accidental. It was rooted in fear generated by terrorist attacks in Europe and in the perception of Muslims and terrorists being one and the same. After the attacks in Brussels in March 2016, Prime Minister Beata Szydło said that Poland would not accept any refugees (although the previous government had committed itself to doing so). Such rhetoric was part of the anti-immigration policy of the Polish government—and European right-wing parties—which skillfully fueled the fear of terrorist attacks—and immigrants—building political support on it.

COBS (2019) research shows that almost 90% of Poles do not personally know any Muslims but as many as 45% declare having a negative attitude towards Islam. Most

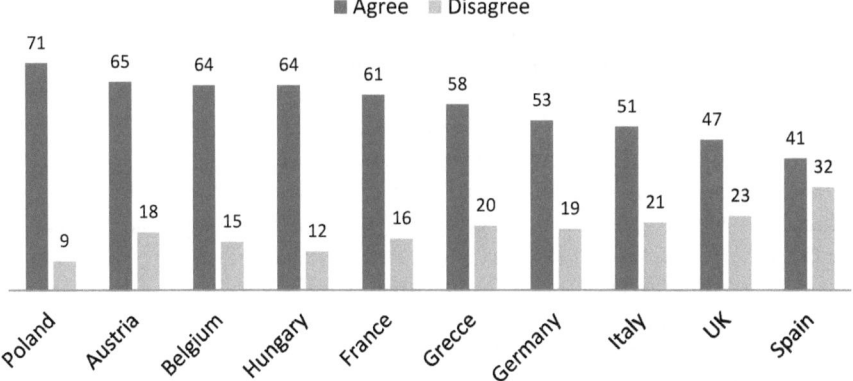

Graph 3. Attitudes towards Muslims (*Source* European Islamophobia report, 2017)

study participants felt that Muslims were not tolerant (63%). 66% of respondents indicated they believed Muslims living in the West disregard Western values, and 61% said that Islam encourages violence more than other religions.[15]

Poles construct their image of Islam and its adherents not on the basis of direct contact but on information flowing from the mass media and on associations with violence or terrorism. Moreover, with the emergence of the organization called the Islamic State, which was accused of the attacks of September 11, 2001, the rhetoric of the clash of civilizations returned to public discourse (Goździak and Márton 2018; Goździak 2019).

The data in Graph 3 and the results of many other comparative studies over time document the growth of populism and xenophobic political and public discourse in many European countries. (Abdelkader 2017) These studies also document Europe's increased polarization on how migration is assessed. In the Scandinavian countries, on the Iberian Peninsula or in Germany, acceptance of migrants is higher, while in the post-communist countries of Eastern Europe, where the level of acceptance of migrants was already lower than in the rest of Europe, it has decreased further.

Referring to the ESS studies, Messing and Ságvári (2019) respond in the following way to the question of what drives anti-migrant attitudes: "The analysis of the data showed that more general societal processes are more likely to shape attitudes: the level of trust in one another and in state institutions, the perception of social cohesion and the feeling of safety in a direct (physical) and indirect (existential) sense. All in all, people who feel politically disempowered, financially insecure and without social support are the most likely to become extremely negative towards migrants. (…) Those countries in which people are more trusting of public institutions, and

---

[15] https://www.cbos.pl/SPISKOM.POL/2019/K_148_19.PDF.

more satisfied with the performance of their governments, democratic institutions and national economies, are the most likely to be more accepting of migrants."[16]

The Polish government's position on immigrants is—as PiS politicians say—dictated by the need to maintain Polish internal security and to protect public order. They argue that the mass reception of refugees by European Union countries has negative effects, citing the examples of countries such as Germany, France, Italy and Greece, which are struggling with very large problems surrounding refugees. Hungary is also pursuing a similar policy on issues of integrated assistance provided by the EU to victims of war in the Middle East or Africa.

The refusal of Poland, the Czech Republic and Hungary to participate in the refugee relocation mechanism was criticized by other EU member states. In 2008, the European Commission lodged a complaint to the Court of Justice (CJEU) against countries refusing to admit refugees. On April 2, 2020, the Court of Justice of the European Union handed down its judgment stating that, by refusing to participate in the temporary mechanism for the relocation of refugees, Poland, the Czech Republic and Hungary violated EU law. The Court ruled that Member States may not, in order to avoid implementing this mechanism, invoke either their obligations regarding the maintenance of public order and the protection of internal security or the alleged malfunctioning of the relocation mechanism.

In the commentary on the judgment, Advocate General of the Court of Justice of the EU Eleanor Sharpston pointed out three important aspects of EU law: the rule of law, the duty of loyal cooperation (between EU countries and institutions) and the principle of solidarity. Failure to comply with legal obligations because they may be poorly adopted or unpopular is a dangerous first step towards the collapse of an orderly and organized society based on the rule of law. Furthermore, she emphasized that the EU's "solidarity principle is sometimes inseparable from accepting burden-sharing."[17]

Though Poland, the Czech Republic and Hungary had broken the law, they were not subject to financial penalties imposed by the CJEU because the dispute with the European Commission was related to relocation provisions for 2015–17 (the relocation was only valid until 2017).

The European Union is currently promoting voluntary relocations. The temporary solution is to relocate children and minors who are left unattended in camps on the Aegean islands, whose number is estimated by international organizations to be about 5.5 thousand. Conditions in these camps defy human dignity. To date, Germany, France, Finland, Portugal, Luxembourg, Ireland and Croatia have declared their readiness to participate in this initiative.[18]

At present, there is a total of about 42,000 migrants and refugees on the Greek islands in the Aegean Sea, including 20,000 in the Moria camp on Lesbos, a center

---

[16]https://www.socialeurope.eu/what-drives-anti-migrant-attitudes.

[17]https://wyborcza.pl/7,75399,25367061,rzecznik-tsue-o-relokacji-uchodzcow-polska-zlamala-prawo.html.

[18]https://wyborcza.pl/7,75399,25839447,tsue-polska-zlamala-prawo-unijne-uchylajac-sie-od-prz yjecia.html.

that under normal conditions should house no more than 3 thousand people. The situation is becoming increasingly dangerous due to the coronavirus epidemic. On Lesbos there is no chance of self-isolation or social distancing. There are only six intensive care hospital beds. As warns Juan Fernando López Aguilar, head of the European Parliamentary Committee on Civil Liberties (LIBE), other islands possess none of the necessary medical equipment at all.[19]

4 Poland as a Country of Immigration and the Polish Government's Migration Policy

For a very long time, Poland was not perceived as an attractive place to emigrate. On the one hand, the Polish labor market did not generate strong demand for foreign workers. On the other, the relatively low wages and living standards, poor access to public services or low levels of social benefits did little to attract foreigners. The situation changed radically after 2014, after the outbreak of the armed conflict in eastern Ukraine. It is estimated that up to 2.5 million Ukrainians currently live and work in Poland. Playing an undeniable role in the influx of new arrivals to Poland was the political difficulties of Ukraine and the economic crisis in that country. Between 2013 and 2015, Ukraine's GDP fell by half, while inflation reached almost 48 percent.

Meanwhile, in Poland, unemployment has been falling every year since 2014, leaving vacancies for unskilled workers. In addition, since 2015, hundreds of thousands of well-qualified and educated Poles have left to work in other EU countries, leaving vacancies for qualified employees (e.g. in the healthcare sector). The Polish Association of Entrepreneurs and Employers estimated that by 2050 the country will need 5 million new workers if it is to maintain its recent rapid economic expansion, which is 4–5 percent annually on average (Bińkowski 2017). The mechanism for the citizens of Ukraine (as well as Armenia, Belarus, Georgia, Moldova or Russia) to start working in Poland, namely the simplified labor market access procedure that has been in place since 2008, has become a factor conducive to and enabling an increased migration movement.

"From the Polish perspective, economic immigration of Ukrainians was and still is a valuable phenomenon. Ukrainian employees filled the gaps on the Polish labor market resulting from the demographic decline, retirement and the retirement age being lowered in 2017, Poles going abroad or resigning from work after receiving benefits from the '500 Plus Family' scheme. Their employment did not generate an increase in unemployment. Geographical, cultural and linguistic proximity favored their adaptation to the Polish labor market." (Adamczyk 2018a, p. 117).

---

[19]https://www.dw.com/pl/polska-przegra%C5%82a-w-tsue-sp%C3%B3r-o-relokacj%C4%99/a-52989847.

The attitude of Poles towards Ukrainians working in Poland is generally positive (Omyła-Rudzka 2020).[20] Every third Pole surveyed (33%) declares amicable feelings for Ukrainians working in Poland. Most Poles have no problem with the presence of Ukrainians in their immediate surroundings. Almost 81% of respondents would also have no problem sharing a workplace with Ukrainians (Feliksiak 2019; Adamczyk 2018b).

The impact of Ukrainian employees on Poland's economic growth is illustrated by the following fact: the inflow of workers from Ukraine increases Polish GDP annually by 0.3–0.9 percentage points.[21] This is a large group, responsible for 11 percent of Polish GDP over the last 5 years.

According to the vast majority of Poles, the presence of Ukrainian workers is beneficial to our economic development; we rather do not harbor feelings that workers from Ukraine are taking jobs away from Poles. Unlike in other European countries, the increase in immigration in Poland has not caused major social problems, and anti-immigrant protests are few and far between. Three out of four employees from Ukraine want to continue working in Poland (Manpower Report 2019).[22]

The Work Service report "Economic migration of employees from Ukraine and Asia" (2019) shows that the most important reason for immigration (for 1/3 of respondents) continues to be salaries being higher than in Ukraine. However, this reason is gradually losing importance as the significance of other, non-financial aspects of work, such as atmosphere, relations with colleagues, development opportunities, or the attitude of Poles towards Ukrainians as foreigners, grows.

The survey also showed that employee satisfaction towards work in Poland has dropped significantly, from 80% in 2018 to almost 60% in 2019. This results from, among other things, the administrative difficulties related to staying in Poland. For example, the time a person needs to legalize their stay has more than tripled over four years, which makes it difficult for employees to continue legal employment. The decreasing pay gap in Poland and Ukraine is also important, as well as the growing expectations of Ukrainian employees regarding wages, job offers, working conditions and accommodation. In Ukraine, the economic situation has improved (GDP increased by 4.2 percent) and the government is campaigning to encourage its citizens to return to the country.

Polish employers are concerned that the opening of the German labor market will significantly reduce the supply of workers from Ukraine interested in coming to Poland. Forecasts assume that as many as 200,000 Ukrainians could leave Poland. However, the scale of this phenomenon may be slightly smaller. The Work Service report indicates that the interest in employees traveling from Ukraine to Germany

---

[20] https://www.cbos.pl/SPISKOM.POL/2020/K_031_20.PDF.

[21] Interview with Jakub Growiec, adviser in the National Bank of Poland Department of Economic Analysis for the Financial Observer. obserwatorfinansowy.pl/tematyka/makroekonomia/wskazniki-ekonomiczne/ukraincy-zmienili-polski-rynek-pracy-i-zwiekszyli-pkb/?smclient=ee5ed24c-cd33-4f08-9ad4-0bd7b4eead67&utm_source=salesmanago&utm_medium=email&utm_campaign=default.

[22] Manpower Report 2019 'Migration plans for employees from Ukraine'. https://www.manpowergroup.pl/wp-content/uploads/2019/02/Plany-migracyjne-pracownik%C3%B3w-z-Ukrainy_raport_PL_.pdf.

decreased from 60% in 2018 to less than 30 percent. In 2019, more knowledge about the requirements that the German labor market sets for candidates has forced many workers to rethink their plans to migrate to Germany at the moment. The main barrier to migration is poor knowledge of German.

The employment of workers from Ukraine will for many years to come be an important element of the functioning of the labor market in Poland. However, it cannot be overlooked that the availability of workers from Ukraine is decreasing. Burdensome restrictions associated with the relatively short duration of work permits based on a system of declarations, the long process of extending the legality of work and stay, employee turnover and rising pay expectations make employers increasingly open to employing workers from other foreign directions, including Asia. These employees receive a permit for a minimum of one year and, according to the law, can only work for one employer. They are mainly employed as industrial workers and tradesmen (37%) and employees performing simple work (31.7%); less often as machine operators and assemblers (7.1%), service and sales workers (6.3%), or specialists (6.1%).

Ukrainians very rarely take advantage of the procedure for being granted international protection, under which one cannot take up employment for half a year. They are not interested in obtaining state aid but in obtaining permission to stay and find employment in Poland.

It is different in the case of the citizens of Tajikistan, who come to Poland predominantly to submit applications for international assistance (currently several hundred people). After submitting the application almost none want to stay in Poland. Their goal is further migration to the west of the European Union; Poland is a transit country to them.

To retain foreign employees, first and foremost, an official migration strategy is needed: which employees, from which countries, do we need in our market, and in which time perspective? The strategy should be preceded by research into the labor market, verification of areas in which there is and will be a demand for qualified employees. The proposed changes should include a list of preferred professions whose members could count on faster decisions regarding permanent residence (e.g. doctors or nurses) or a number of social services.

The most desirable age group are young people, specialists below the age of 36 who would like to come to Poland for longer stints or even permanently with their families. They could stimulate our GDP, contribute to retail sales, buy real estate, etc. So far, however, there are no formal assumptions on how to attract such people.

The lack of a migration policy means that there is no system of labor migration management in Poland. Despite Article 90 Clause 10 of the Act on Employment Promotion and Labor Market Institutions, which refers to "migration policy goals" that should be followed by the minister for labor (Act, 2017),[23] there are no solutions that could keep foreign employees in the country for more than a few months. There are also no in-depth analyses regarding the impact of economic immigration on the Polish labor market. Moreover, the authorities have not yet arranged a discussion on

---

[23] https://www.lexlege.pl/ustawa-o-promocji-zatrudnienia-i-instytucjach-rynku-pracy/art-90/.

this subject, although it is a significant issue from the point of view of the Polish economy and Polish society.

5 Creating Polish Immigration Policy—Between Chaos and Calculation

At this moment, Poland is increasingly becoming an immigration destination— mostly for people from Eastern Europe. Globally, this is not a new situation, yet in Polish history it is the first such big inflow of foreigners i n such a short period of time. It has to be pointed out that it is happening without a clearly defined immigration policy. In Poland since 2016, when the PiS cabinet abandoned the document created by the PO-PSL coalition, there is no official document setting out the framework and directions for an immigration policy. The last attempt to create such a framework ultimately led to the dismissal of the vice-minister responsible for this domain. It can be claimed that in the domain of migration, chaos prevails in Poland. But this is not the case. Perhaps the lack of a document constituting the migration policy is an element of political calculation? The stubborn stance on not providing protection to refugees on the one hand and a very open approach to labor migration on the other hand may point to such a conclusion.

Over its five years in power, PiS has used the fear of immigrants for its own political purposes. Propaganda attacks and manipulation are the basic fear management tools. Fear management involves spreading negative sentiments towards an alleged enemy that threatens society and from whom society must be defended. The witch-hunt on refugees (like witch-hunts on other groups) served to make the populist party into the nation's savior from impending catastrophe.

The ruling party, warning about an invasion of refugees, at the same time opened the door widely to economic immigrants, allowing not only Ukrainians, but also Nepalese, Hindu or Bangladeshi citizens to settle in Poland.

It is worth recalling here that in 2016, when European governments were searching for responses to the increasing refugee crisis in Southern Europe, the PiS Prime Minister Beata Szydło claimed Poland could not do more to help refugees and asylum seekers because the country had already done its part by welcoming 1 million Ukrainians. Economic immigrants were presented at the EU forum as refugees, the acceptance of which justifies a violation of obligations to admit and care for legitimate refugees.

The share of labor migration in the Polish labor market is estimated at over 10 percent. Unfortunately, it is largely a gray market area, not subject to taxation and outside of the social security system, dangerous and risky for the employed Ukrainians themselves. Meanwhile, society is aging, which, combined with the high emigration of young Poles and other factors, can lead to labor shortages, a lack of stability in many industries, and, consequently, to a decrease in the competitiveness of the Polish economy. What's more, in an era of pandemics, an insufficient number of workers, especially doctors and nurses, carries with it a risk of the medical and social security systems collapsing. Therefore, it is in the interest of the Polish economic and social system as well as Polish entrepreneurs to encourage citizens of other countries to work permanently and not temporarily in Poland.

Commenting on the situation in Poland, Britain's "The Economist" writes that, paradoxically, the most illiberal government of the Union conducts the most liberal migration policy, which in practice means that the PiS government's migration policy is based on the absence of a migration policy and on pretending that there is no problem whatsoever.[24]

On the other hand, in Polish press critical of the PiS government, we read that the liberal visa issuing policy causes massive abuses and the state "tolerates" the gray area. The government is fighting for higher tax revenues from production and trade (VAT) yet it turns a blind eye to the fact that employers employ workers under the table and that employees avoid paying taxes and benefit contributions. Does the government really believe that a half-year employee contracted with one foot in Poland and one foot at home in Ukraine allows the employer employing him to plan his business sensibly? That is, if it such workers even reach Poland, because there are more and more serious signals that illegal intermediaries are exploiting loopholes in this system.[25]

In the opinion of experts from the Work Service, Poland should have developed mechanisms for connecting Ukrainian employees with Polish enterprises.[26] These solutions should be durable and long-term, controlled and supported by the state. In particular, they should apply to workers with higher professional qualifications. Meanwhile, the shortage of hands to work in an aging European Union means that other countries are also beginning to seek workers from Ukraine. In the case of Poland, the lack of a migration policy and the utter reactiveness of the state in this area hurt the advantages that Poland has in its geographic and cultural proximity to Ukraine.

The government's priorities regarding a migration policy are well reflected in the slogan "one nation, one religion", the credo guiding the authors of the PiS draft document "Polish migration policy". The government demands assimilation from foreigners but does not give them the elementary tools to put down roots in Polish society. On the issue of migration, PiS repeats the prior mistakes of Western countries—just like Germany had done in the 1960s, it tries to maintain the electorate's belief that guest workers (Gastarbeiter) came to the country only for a moment. We know by now that this was a mistake. Poland, like other European countries, needs migrants who will integrate into society but we must not expect their assimilation.

In the context described above, the answer to the question of "is the lack of naturally imposed new regulations an effect of omission or a deliberate act?" is obvious. In the perspective of PiS's current term of office, neither will immigrants

---

[24]https://www.economist.com/europe/2020/02/22/poland-is-cocking-up-migration-in-a-very-eur opean-way.

[25]https://wyborcza.pl/7,75968,25760403,imigranci-na-ratunek.html.

[26]https://www.workservice.com/pl/Dla-pracodawcow/Ekspert-HR-komentuje.

have their work permit period increased to one year, nor will the procedure for obtaining work and residence permits be simplified. There will be no clear regulations allowing for the submission of applications for temporary residence and work during a stay in Poland on a tourist/Schengen visa.

6   The Scale and Direction of Migration in Hungary

Hungary, like Poland, is an immigration and emigration country with a positive migration balance. According to the Hungarian Central Statistical Office, 350,000 Hungarians have moved abroad since 1989.[27] The phenomenon of emigration has not been as significantly influenced by Hungary joining the EU in 2004 as it has by the first waves of the international economic crisis in 2008. As a consequence of the falling employment rate, an increasing number of Hungarian nationals decided to move abroad.

The main countries of interest for Hungarians are Germany, where the number of Hungarians is estimated to be around 124,000; the United Kingdom (74,500) and Austria (36,000). The latest emigration trends show that Switzerland, the Netherlands and Belgium have also become popular destination countries for Hungarian nationals.[28]

The main motivation for emigration is the difference in earnings and greater job stability. Other reasons for this phenomenon are the opening of the labor market in Germany and Austria, as well as changes in the Hungarian social system. For example, unemployment benefits have been reduced and the early retirement system has been abolished.

The political climate is also important, having worsened since the election of Viktor Orbán's government in 2010. A wave of criticism for authoritarian governments has spread throughout Europe, and the OECD has recently warned that the economy is being blocked by excessive government intervention and insufficient investment.[29] (Graph 4).

The number of foreign workers is also growing dynamically in Hungary, despite the fact that the Fidesz government is constantly fighting immigration. In 2017, 10,000 work permits were issued to third-country nationals, though it is unofficially speculated that the actual number is six times that.

Government policy supporting Hungarian ethnic minorities in neighboring countries has led to strong—but unplanned—labor migration, especially for job seekers, and even settlement in Hungary.

According to the Hungarian Manpower Group International Organization for Migration, more than 50% of Hungarian firms have significant difficulties filling

[27] https://www.migrationpolicy.org/article/orban-reshapes-migration-policy-hungary.

[28] https://www.migrationpolicy.org/article/orban-reshapes-migration-policy-hungary.

[29] https://ec.europa.eu/info/sites/info/files/2020-european_semester_country-report-hungary_en. pdf.

Summary data of Hungarian citizens' international migration (2010–2018)

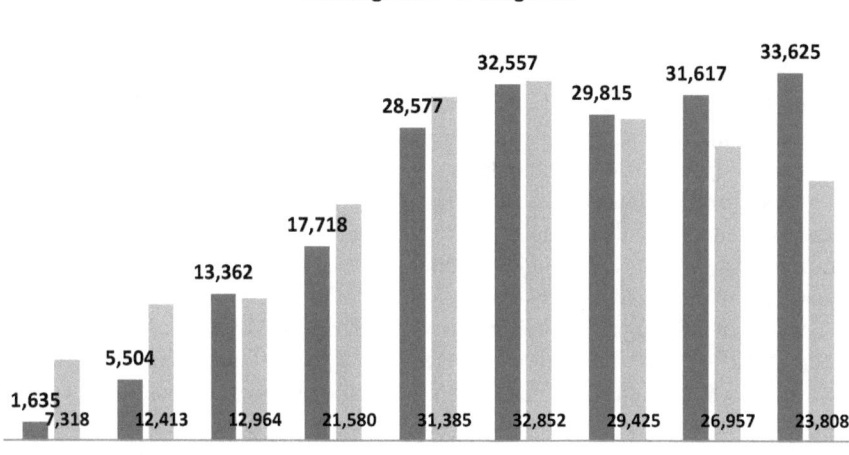

Graph 4. Summary data of Hungarian citizens' international migration (2010–2018) (*Source* KSH—Hungarian Central Statistical Office)

job vacancies, especially in the fields of information technology and health care. The country also has a serious demand for manual labor workers. (ManpowerGroup Employment Outlook Survey Hungary 2018).[30] The Hungarian Migration Strategy, adopted in October 2013, also emphasizes that although it is important to ensure the protection of the national labor market, receiving additional migrant labor is a necessity. Attracting knowledge-based immigration has been set as a goal in Hungarian migration policy but there is no developing tendency among highly qualified third-country nationals to apply for the EU Blue Card as a possible way to gain residence in Hungary. Many labor migrants with work permits are moving to richer countries in Western Europe.[31]

Hungary and Poland are demonstratively refusing to accept refugees, and at the same time, due to limited labor force resources, show tacit support for economic immigration. The two leaders of the far-right parties in Hungary and Poland, Viktor Orbán (Fidesz) and Jarosław Kaczyński (PiS), have built up asylum seekers from the Middle East to be their main enemy. By inciting and exploiting the fear of refugees, they have secured successes in domestic politics. The migration policy of both countries is subordinated to this line.

---

[30] https://www.manpowergroup.com/wcm/connect/9f7f0732-fd41-475d-b5c2-2f1cb00e2111/HU_ EN_MEOS_2Q18.pdf?MOD=AJPERES&CACHEID=ROOTWORKSPACE-9f7f0732-fd41- 475d-b5c2-2f1cb00e2111-mUxpEf1.

[31] http://www.iom.hu/migration-issues-hungary.

7 The European Migration Crisis and Hungary's "Fencing Policy"

Due to its geographic location, Hungary was one of the main transit countries in irregular land migration towards other Member States of the European Union. In summer 2015, more than 390,000 asylum seekers, mostly Muslims, crossed the Serbian-Hungarian border and descended on Keleti railway station in Budapest.[32] For Hungarian Prime Minister Viktor Orban and his Fidesz party, the arrival of these asylum seekers was not a humanitarian issue but a Muslim invasion threatening national security, social cohesion, and the Christian identity of the Hungarian nation. In the five years since this episode, the fear of the "other" has resulted in a string of anti-immigrant actions and policies. At the very beginning, barbed wire fences were constructed to deter asylum seekers from entering Hungarian territory.

The idea of building a wall was announced in June 2015 by Prime Minister Viktor Orbán. A 175-kilometer stretch of 4-meter-high wall was completed on the border with Serbia and Croatia on September 15. The completion of the wall, however, did not end the process of Hungary isolating itself from its southern neighbors. In August 2016, Prime Minister Orbán announced the reinforcement of the existing fence and the construction of a second, more technologically advanced line by spring 2017 (Kotańska 2017).

The actions taken by Viktor Orbán were strongly criticized by Western European countries and many non-governmental organizations. Hungary has been accused of adopting xenophobic and racist policies towards refugees and immigrants by closing their borders with Serbia and refusing to provide humanitarian assistance to those injured in the Middle East war. In the dispute with the EU, Prime Minister Orbán took a firm position. He ardently opposed European countries' reception of refugees and immigrants arguing that the uncontrolled influx of refugees threatens the security of Europeans by increasing the risk of terrorist attacks. Together with Poland and the Czech Republic, he stood on the side of protecting national interests in opposition to the pro-immigration policy of Germany and France.

Under the EU burden-sharing scheme, Hungary was supposed to admit 1,294 refugees. However, the prime minister said that while Hungarians have "no problems" with the local Muslim community, any EU plan to relocate asylum seekers, including many Muslims, would destroy Hungary's culture. At the end of March 2017, the Hungarian parliament adopted new legal solutions regarding the manner of managing state borders, changing the asylum act in place, the act on state borders and the act on the admission and residence of third-country nationals.

The new asylum law provides that asylum applications can only be filed individually in transit zones established at the border. Anyone applying for asylum in Hungary can only do so from a transit zone and is detained there for the duration of the asylum procedure. In addition, it was made possible to detain foreigners residing illegally throughout the country in Hungary and to escort them to the border.

---

[32]https://www.migrationpolicy.org/article/orban-reshapes-migration-policy-hungary.

Conditions inside the transit zone have been grim. The Hungarian Helsinki Committee (HHC) contends rejected asylum seekers there are denied food, to the point of starvation. Moreover, Hungary's latest anti-immigrant law criminalizes assistance to unauthorized migrants by civil-society organizations and good Samaritans.[33]

Fortifications at the border between Hungary and Serbia (*Source* Getty Images L. Balogh)

Another area of dispute in the Hungarian government's relations with the EU were the Hungarian government's financial expectations towards the EU to co-finance the costs of border protection, including wall construction. The Hungarian Prime Minister demanded the European Union's participation in these costs, estimated at 270 billion forints, fully covered by Hungarian taxpayers. He argued that he could not effectively counteract the problem of illegal immigration and protect Union citizens without building physical barriers and that financial support for the system responsible for admitting immigrants only encourages them to continue their inflow. The Hungarian government requested that half of the indicated costs of protecting the Hungarian section of the Schengen border be covered, but Hungary's expectations were met with strong opposition from Brussels (Kotańska 2017). According to Prime Minister Orbán, Hungary has proved that the uncontrolled influx of immigrants to Europe can be stopped, though it requires that difficult decisions be made, like the construction of the wall, which also hinders the functioning of Hungarian communities living in border areas.

The Government Information Center emphasized that there are still attempts to cross the border illegally and that it is therefore necessary to protect it. The crisis

---

[33] https://www.infomigrants.net/en/post/16466/starving-in-hungary-s-transit-zones.

status (emergency?) caused by the mass influx of migrants in force in Hungary has been extended from 2015 until 2020. Meanwhile, human rights defenders say that "extending the state of emergency only serves to maintain xenophobic, fear propaganda."

To sum up, the immigration policy of Prime Minister Orbán's government in recent years boils down mainly to two goals: discouraging immigrants from Africa and the Middle East from entering Hungary and reaffirming the electorate's belief that such a policy is right and that immigrants themselves pose a real threat to the security of the state and its citizens. The Court of Justice of the European Union's verdict that Poland, the Czech Republic and Hungary, by refusing to participate in the temporary refugee relocation mechanism, violated EU law failed to change Hungary's position. Victor Orbán is still convinced that no one can be forced to participate in a social experiment (as he considers the admittance and relocation of immigrants to be). Furthermore, he does not want to be associated with it and does not believe in its effectiveness.

8   Conclusion. Poland and Hungary What Do They Have in Common?

Poland and Hungary are emigration and immigration countries in which right-wing populist governments are in power. Both Poland and Hungary have seen public institutions being attacked and dismantled, judicial independence undermined, the opposition and its supporters publicly slandered, and populist and xenophobic government rhetoric practiced by the media increasingly controlled by the executive branch. "While both countries are still not dictatorships, the potential for authoritarian rule increases considerably with every new legislation expanding the power of the government." (Ekiert 2017).

Poland and Hungary have formed a hardline axis within the Visegrad group—an informal caucus of four Central and Eastern European countries—against what they see as Brussels' interference in immigration policy and constitutional issues.

In both countries, the migration crisis has been used by politicians in election campaigns by appealing to attitudes of hostility towards others. These events can be analyzed from different perspectives, e.g. via the concept of moral panic understood as "a widespread fear, most often an irrational one, that someone or something is a threat to the values and interests of a community or society at large."[34] The concept of moral panic was used by Zygmunt Bauman (2016) to analyze the migration crisis. Bauman understands this panic as reflecting a sweeping social and political trend that involves the erosion of the moral compass guiding politics in Europe and the West in general. He juxtaposed the ideals of Western culture with the attitude toward migrants adopted by a significant number of European Union citizens, and then by many European politicians. In this way, he showed the hypocrisy of those who so

---

[34] https://www.thoughtco.com/moral-panic-3026420.

willingly invoke slogans about solidarity while refusing to help all those who need it.[35]

This situation has taken place in Poland and Hungary, where there was no group on the side of the political elite that resolutely, unequivocally and effectively opposed the rhetoric of fear and threat with other rhetoric, e.g. embracing those in need in a gesture of solidarity and opposing Islam being equated with terrorism.

None of the European governments has shown as great resentment and skepticism towards immigrants as the Polish and Hungarian governments, and at the same time, no other country has accepted so many foreigners as a result of immigration policy pursued quietly. Hungary and Poland are demonstratively refusing to accept refugees, and at the same time, due to the lack of hands to work, show tacit support for economic immigration.

References

Abdelkader, E. (2017). A comparative analysis of European Islamophobia: France, UK, Germany, Netherlands, and Sweden. *Journal of Islamic and Near Eastern Law, 16*(1), 30–63. https://esc holarship.org/uc/item/870099f4.

Adamczyk, A. (2018a). Imigracja zarobkowa do Polski. Casus Ukraińców (2014–2017). Środkowoeuropejskie Studia Polityczne, 2, 115–135. https://doi.org/10.14746/ssp.2018.2.8.

Adamczyk, N. (2018b). Czy przyjmować uchodźców? Opinie i postawy Polaków wobec relokacji nielegalnych imigrantów na terytorium Rzeczypospolitej. In: B. Molo, (Ed.), Migracja i uchodźstwo wyzwaniem dla bezpieczeństwa i współpracy międzynarodowej w XXI wieku (pp. 121–140). Oficyna Wydawnicza AFM, Kraków. https://hdl.handle.net/11315/18969.

Bauman, Z. (2016). *Strangers at Our Door*. Polity. https://doi.org/10.32422/mv.1583.

Bińkowski, J. (2017). Ukraińska imigracja do Polski. Analiza zjawiska w kontekście sytuacji na rynku pracy. Kolegium Europy Wschodniej im. Jana Nowaka-Jeziorańskiego we Wrocławiu, Warszawa–Wojnowice.https://www.kew.org.pl/wp-content/uploads/2016/12/Jakub-Binkowski-Ukrai%C5%84ska-imigracja-do-Polski-Analiza-zjawiska-w-kontek%C5%9Bcie-sytuacji-na-rynku-pracy.pdf.

Ekiert, G. (2017). *How to deal with Poland and Hungary,* Occasional paper, social Europe. https://www.socialeurope.eu/wp-content/uploads/2017/08/Occ-Pap-13-PDF.pdf.

European Commission. Country Report Poland (2020). https://eur-lex.europa.eu/legal-content/PL/TXT/PDF/?uri=CELEX:52020SC0520&from=EN.

European Commission. Country Report Hungary (2020). https://eur-lex.europa.eu/legal-content/EN/TXT/PDF/?uri=CELEX:52020SC0516&from=EN.

European Islamophobia Reports. https://www.islamophobiaeurope.com/reports/2017-reports/.

Feliksiak, M. (2019). Postawy wobec Islamu i Muzułmanów. Komunikat z badań CBOS, Warszawa, Centrum Badania Opinii Społecznej https://www.cbos.pl/SPISKOM.POL/2019/K_148_19.PDF.

Goździak, E. M. (2019, October 10). *Using fear of the "other," Orbán reshapes migration policy in a Hungary built on cultural diversity.* Migration Policy Institute. https://www.migrationpolicy.org/article/orban-reshapes-migration-policy-hungary.

Goździak E. M., & Márton, P. (2018). Where the wild things are: Fear of Islam and the anti-refugee rhetoric in Hungary and in Poland. Central and Eastern European Migration Review, 7(2), 125–151.

---

[35]Bauman emphasizes that separation policy is a short-term solution and sooner or later Europe will have to find a new way for multicultural and multinational societies to coexist.

GUS—Central Statistical Office. https://stat.gov.pl/.
International Organization for Migration. Migration Issues in Hungary. http://www.iom.hu/migrat ion-issues-hungary.
Horolets, A., Lesińska, M., & Okólski, M. (Eds.). (2018). *Raport o stanie badań nad migracjami w Polsce po 1989 roku.* Warszawa: KBnM PAN.
Kotańska, A. (2017). „Fencing policy" w polityce Węgier. In M. Bodziany (Ed), Kryzysy społeczne XXI wieku, Między dezintegracją, „fencing policy" a upadkiem państwowości (pp. 105–117). Akademia Wojsk Lądowych, Wrocław. https://www.academia.edu/41767399/ KRYZYSY_SPO%C5%81ECZNE_XXI_WIEKU_Mi%C4%99dzy_dezintegracj%C4%85_fen cing_policy_a_upadkiem_pa%C5%84stwowo%C5%9Bci.
KSH—Hungarian Central Statistical Office.
Manpower Report. (2019). *Plany migracyjne pracowników z Ukrainy.* https://www.manpow ergroup.pl/wp-content/uploads/2019/02/Plany-migracyjne-pracownik%C3%B3w-z-Ukrainy_r aport_PL_.pdf.
ManpowerGroup Employment Outlook Survey Hungary. (2018). *Hungary Employment Outlook.* https://www.manpowergroup.com/wcm/connect/9f7f0732-fd41-475d-b5c2-2f1cb00e2111/HU_ EN_MEOS_2Q18.pdf?MOD=AJPERES&CACHEID=ROOTWORKSPACE-9f7f0732-fd41- 475d-b5c2-2f1cb00e2111-mUxpEf1.
Messing, V. & Ságvári, B. (2019). What drives anti-migrant attitudes? Social Europe, 28th May 2019. https://www.socialeurope.eu/what-drives-anti-migrant-attitudes.
Omyła-Rudzka, M. (2020). Stosunek Polaków do innych narodów. Komunikat z badań CBOS, Warszawa: Centrum Badania Opinii Społecznej. https://www.cbos.pl/SPISKOM.POL/2020/ K_031_20.PDF.
OECD. (2018). International Migration Outlook 2018. https://read.oecd-ilibrary.org/social-issues- migration-health/international-migration-outlook-2018_migr_outlook-2018-en#page19.
Polityka Migracyjna Polski. Projekt z dnia 10 czerwca 2019 (Polish Migration Policy. Projekt z dnia 10 czerwca 2019) Redakcja: Departament Analiz i Polityki Migracyjnej MSWiA. file:///C:/Users/user/Documents/Immigration%20policy%20of%20Eastern%20Europe.%20The%20case migracyjna-Polski-wersja-ostateczna.pdf.
Szymańska, J. (2017). Strategia Unii Europejskiej wobec kryzysu migracyjnego: priorytety, bariery, efekty. *Studia BAS, 3*(51), 159–186.
UNHCR. (2018). Desperate Journeys: Refuges and Migrants arriving in Europe and at Europe's borders. https://www.unhcr.org/desperatejourneys/.

Internet

https://www.consilium.europa.eu/pl/policies/migratory-pressures/.
https://www.consilium.europa.eu/pl/policies/migratory-pressures/history-migratory-pressures/.
https://www.consilium.europa.eu/pl/policies/migratory-pressures/ceas-reform/.
https://www.consilium.europa.eu/pl/meetings/international-summit/2016/03/07/.
http://archiwum.wspolnotapolska.org.pl/?id=pwko00.
http://info.randstad.pl/monitor-rynku-pracy-37.
https://wyborcza.pl/7,75399,25367061,rzecznik-tsue-o-relokacji-uchodzcow-polska-zlamala- prawo.html.
https://wyborcza.pl/7,75399,25839447,tsue-polska-zlamala-prawo-unijne-uchylajac-sie-od-przyje cia.html.
https://wyborcza.pl/7,75968,25760403,imigranci-na-ratunek.html.
https://www.dw.com/pl/polska-przegra%C5%82a-w-tsue-sp%C3%B3r-o-relokacj%C4%99/a-529 89847.

https://www.economist.com/europe/2020/02/22/poland-is-cocking-up-migration-in-a-very-europe
    an-way.
https://www.lexlege.pl/ustawa-o-promocji-zatrudnienia-i-instytucjach-rynku-pracy/art-90/.
https://www.workservice.com/pl/Dla-pracodawcow/Ekspert-HR-komentuje.
https://www.infomigrants.net/en/post/16466/starving-in-hungary-s-transit-zones.
https://www.thoughtco.com/moral-panic-3026420.
https://www.obserwatorfinansowy.pl/tematyka/makroekonomia/wskazniki-ekonomiczne/ukr
    aincy-zmienili-polski-rynek-pracy-i-zwiekszyli-pkb/?smclient=ee5ed24c-cd33-4f08-9ad4-0bd
    7b4eead67&utm_source=salesmanago&utm_medium=email&utm_campaign=default.

Immigration Policy Formation in New EU Member States: The Case of Estonia

Mariliis Trei

Abstract Although immigration policy formation on the European level has been researched extensively, less emphasis has been on analysing the asylum policy field of EU member states from the Central and Eastern European countries that joined the EU in 2004. This chapter looks at the formation of immigration policy in Estonia from 1991 to 2019. The establishment of the immigration policy framework and the debates around migration are analysed. The qualitative case study shows that there have been three key topics in the Estonian immigration politics that have framed political debates and legislation. The topic of sovereignty, preservation of the Estonian culture and the ethnic composition of the demographic continue guide the narrative in the Estonian immigration policy.

Keywords Immigration policy · Asylum policy · Policy making · Central and Eastern Europe · European Union

1 Introduction

Immigration policy can be regarded as one of the most challenging, ambivalent and relevant policy fields that governments in all regions of the world are faced with today. It is estimated that during the past two decades the total number of international migrants has grown faster than the global population (UN DESA 2017) and today migrants amount to almost 3.5% (272 million) of the world's population (UN DESA 2019). In addition, global processes, including climate change and various conflicts in the Middle-East and sub-Saharan African countries continue to force people to leave their homes and seek new places to stay. Currently, there are approximately 79.5 million forcibly displaced people worldwide (UNHCR 2020). These large-scale movements of people have created a plethora of issues and challenges that are multidimensional, cross-sectoral and uncertain (Meyers 2000; Alink et al. 2001;

M. Trei (✉)
Ragnar Nurkse Department of Innovation and Governance, Tallinn University of Technology, Tallinn, Estonia
e-mail: mariliis.trei@taltech.ee

© The Author(s), under exclusive license to Springer Nature Singapore Pte Ltd. 2021　　209
C.-P. Chu and S.-C. Park (eds.), *Immigration Policy and Crisis in the Regional Context*,
https://doi.org/10.1007/978-981-33-6823-1_12

Givens and Luedtke 2004; Bjerre et al. 2018), influencing the economy, demography, culture, and politics of countries or even entire regions. Concurrently, in the European Union (EU), the topic of immigration has been one of the most salient issues already since the early 1980s (Lavenex 2001; Stalker 2002; Zaun 2018) and remains an area of policy where huge discrepancies of policy integration, implementation and monitoring occur (Pastore and Henry 2016; Scipioni 2017).

Immigration policy in the European Union has been widely researched (Stalker 2002; Givens and Luedtke 2004; Plender 2008; Schain 2009; Roos and Zaun 2014; Dahlvik 2018). Bjerre et al. (2018, p. 559) define immigration policy as "government's statements of what it intends to do or not to do (including laws, regulations, decisions or orders) in regards to the selection, settlement and deportation of foreign citizens residing in the country". As the definition indicates, immigration policy is multidimensional and affects different target groups. Based on the type of "migration flow", the immigration policy in the EU is divided into subfields—legal labour migration (including seasonal workers), family reunification, students and researchers, asylum seekers and illegal migrants (European Council 2020). Policies related to these subfields can further be divided into their external (immigrant control related activities) and internal dimensions (immigrant integration related activities) (Meyers 2000) on both the supranational and national level. Despite decades long effort in communitarizing immigration policy in the EU (see e.g. Plender 2008), the sensitivity and salience of immigration issues continues to challenge cooperation between the EU Member States. This became especially evident during the events and aftermath of the European refugee crisis in 2015–2016. The inability to reach an agreement on how to tackle the sudden inflow of asylum seekers from the EU's Southern border created tensions between the Member States and has even been seen as a "shock wave for the European Union in the 21st century", posing an "existential threat for the integrity of the Union" (Dagi 2017, p. 7). Taking into account the aging population in Europe and the socio-economic differences between neighboring countries, the migration pressure towards the EU will only increase (Bagdonas 2015; Bordignon and Moriconi 2017). In this context, finding common solutions and ways of cooperation is vital in order to reduce the unequal burden between member states (Bordignon and Moriconi 2017) and, therefore, avoid "repetitive crises" situations in the EU (Bagdonas 2015, p. 7; Boswell 2000).

Many have claimed (Bagdonas 2015; Valdaru et al. 2017; Zaun 2018), that one of the most distinct divisions unveiled during the 2015 refugee crisis was that between the "old" Western European member states and the "new" Central and Eastern European (CEE) member states, which acceded to the EU in 2004. Calls for solidarity from the European Commission were met with open and strong opposition from Hungary, Poland, Czech Republic and Slovakia (Dagi 2017), but also the Baltic States (Zaun 2018). Stark differences in values, interests, attitudes towards immigrants and the framing of immigration politics became evident and "the trend towards national solutions intensified" (Lavenex 2018, p. 1203). As put by Scipioni (2017, p. 9) "The combination of low harmonization, weak monitoring, low solidarity and lack of strong institutions in EU migration policy became increasingly unsustainable during the 2015 crisis." Although, the reasons and causes of discrepancies of immigration policy and policy implementation, for example, of the Common European Asylum System (CEAS), in different member states have been analysed before (Dahlvik 2018; Lavenex 2018; Bonjour et al. 2017; Helbling and Kalkum 2018), less attention has been devoted to analysing immigration politics and its formation on the national level. This is especially the case for the CEE countries that share several similarities deriving from their Soviet past and similar historic experience with immigration (Gorny and Kaczmarczyk 2019). Although the development of post-soviet Central and Eastern European states has taken different paths (see e.g. Meyer-Sahling 2011), these states shared the "burden" of having to either build up a functioning state apparatus or conduct thorough state reforms. In addition, as immigration and asylum policy in the Soviet Union was based on closed borders and restrictions (Barnickel and Beichelt 2013), several new EU member states had to establish their immigration policy from the ground up together with the necessary regulations and administrative capacity to accept, proceed, monitor and integrate arriving foreigners. Finally, all of these developments took place at a time when the Western-European countries had already well-developed immigration and asylum policies that were rooted in the "liberal post-World War II tradition" and were continuously introducing more restrictive measures into their immigration policy framework (Lavenex 2002, p. 703). This created a different basis for new member states to formulate their immigration policy.

It is widely agreed, that despite the EU level policy and regulations, immigration policy, but also immigration politics, is very much dependant on the national context—immigration history, framing of immigration policy and the salience of immigration issues in the public discourse (Freeman 1995; Alink et al. 2001). Analysing the development of these dynamics helps to explain the institutionalization process of immigration policy and politics on the national level. Understanding these dynamics at the national level, however, is crucial to understanding immigration policy-making on the EU level (Zaun 2018, p. 45). This chapter aims to analyse how immigration policy has developed in a "new" EU member state to explain the more restrictive views towards immigration in CEE countries and the cleavage of values that have recently become evident. On the one hand, it can help explain the emerged differences and very critical opposition of some Eastern European member states and at the same time provide insight into how to find common ground and understand the different positions of member states better. The chapter takes Estonia as an example of a "new" EU member state. Estonia regained independence from the Soviet Union in 1991 and started formulating its immigration policy already in 1990. Since then, Estonia has had to integrate and try to adapt its immigration policy inside the framework of the EU, while at the same time protecting Estonia's national interests and sovereignty (Alink et al. 2001).

The chapter is organized as follows. First, an overview of immigration policy development in Estonia during 1990–2019 is given. Special focus will be on establishing the asylum policy framework in Estonia, because asylum policy is often looked at separately from other subdivisions of migration policy due to the high level of conflict and salience in asylum policy (Freeman 2006). Second, the politics of immigration in Estonia is analysed in the wider context, focusing on how the narrative and framework of Estonian immigration policy has changed and how this fits into the wider context inside the European Union. The case study uses a qualitative approach and data has been gathered through secondary sources. Documents analysed for this research include legal documents, national strategies, scientific reports, analyses, media coverage and the written transcripts of the Estonian Parliament recordings from 1990 to 2019.[1] The conducted research shows that immigration policy in Estonia has been mainly characterised as being "conservative" throughout the analysed period and the policy area has been mainly framed from the perspective of security and national sovereignty. It is interesting, that the conservative stance of Estonian immigration policy has been long accepted across the political parties in Estonia, with differences in values emerging visibly only during the 2015 refugee crisis, when the populist right-wing party in Estonia emerged as a political force. At the same time, the conservativeness has also been a result of a being mainly an emigration country since regaining independence. However, as Estonia is facing similar problems as other European countries, that is population aging and lack of workforce, Estonia is currently transitioning from an emigration to an immigration state (Tammur et al. 2018). This migration transformation is also visible in other CEE countries, where the increased level of welfare is turning the net migration rate positive (King and Okolski 2019). It is necessary, to take these processes and how they affect national immigration politics into account, in order to understand member states' stances on the EU level.

2   Immigration Policy Formation in Estonia 1990–2019

2.1   Background

Estonia is a small member state on the Eastern border of the EU with a population of 1.3 million people and an area covering 43,465.38 m^2. Estonia became an independent state already in 1918, but after enjoying independent statehood for almost two decades, the Soviet Union occupied Estonia during the Second World War in 1940. Estonia regained its independence in 1991 and virtually had to build up a functioning democratic state together with an administrative system from scratch (Sarapuu 2012). Immigration policy was one of the first important policy areas for Estonia that needed to be established (Estonian Parliament verbatim record, 11.06.1990). The important reasons behind this were the migration wave and the concurrent population changes that took place during the Soviet occupation. The events of the Second World War

---

[1] In order to follow the political discussions on the topic of immigration policy, a keyword search was conducted using the Estonian Parliament verbatim records database. Keywords included *immigration, immigration policy and migration policy*. All together 91 transcripts were analysed from 1990 to 2019. These included legislation proceedings, information sessions with government representatives, discussions of nationally important questions and other presentations.

and the repressive Soviet occupation that followed decreased the Estonian population heavily. It is estimated that in total 17.5% of the Estonian population was lost—around 80,000 people fled to the West from war and the Soviet occupation, many soldiers and civilians were killed in the war and around 30,000 Estonians were deported by the Soviet Union (Rahi-Tamm 2005). As a result, by 1945 the share of Estonians on the Estonian territory increased to around 97% (Tammur et al. 2018). During the Soviet occupation, especially in the 1960s and 70s, Estonia experienced an intensive flow of immigration from mainly Russia, but also other Republics of the Soviet Union. On the one had, the immigration was related to the period of large-scale industrialization (Lagerspetz 2007, p. 87) and quick population growth of the Slavic population, but on the other hand, it was also a political decision to "tie the new territories more firmly to the Soviet Union with the help of the immigrants" (Tammur et al. 2018). Between 1945 and 1989, the share of Estonians in the total population decreased from 97 to 62% (Tammur et al. 2018).

With the end of the Soviet occupation and opening of the borders, Estonia's migration turned from immigration to emigration—in 1989–2000 the population of Estonia decreased by 12.3%. People leaving Estonia re-migrated to their home countries (e.g. Soviet military personnel and their family members, workers) or left towards the West (Tammur et al. 2018). Emigration was further intensified when Estonia joined the EU and the Schengen area. There was no significant immigration to Estonia during the 1990s and 2000s. Instead in combination with the age structure and the decreasing fertility rate, the population of Estonia slowly started to decline since the 1990s (Lagerspetz 2007). The number of working-age persons has decreased continuously. In 2012–2013 the average decline was 9000 people a year, but since then it has slowed down and even decreased to 4000 persons per year in 2015–2017 (Tammur 2018). The latter process can be explained by the change in the net migration rate in Estonia, which has turned positive since 2015 and continues to increase (Fig. 1). But also as the socio-economic situation in Estonia has improved

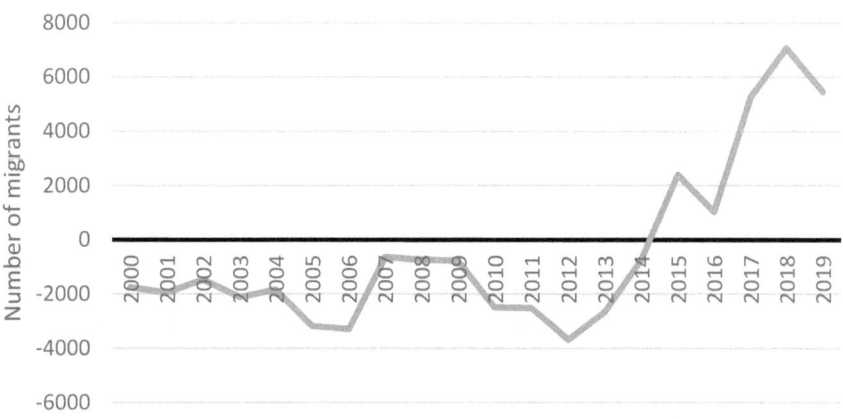

Fig. 1 Net migration rate in Estonia 2000–2019 (Source *Statistics Estonia* 2020c)

tremendously during the past 30 years, Estonia is becoming an attractive destination country (King and Okolski 2019). In addition, Estonia has become more open to immigrants, introducing several measures to attract high skilled specialists to the Estonian labour market (see e.g. OECD 2019, p. 52). It has been argued that these processes might indicate a "migration turnaround" taking place in Estonia (Tammur et al. 2018). Less Estonians emigrate and since 2017, more Estonians return than leave. Compared to the other CEE countries, that have experienced a certain level of "brain drain" during post-Soviet times, Estonians who emigrate are among the less-educated and less-skilled seeking for higher income (Tammur et al. 2018), indicating a level of welfare reached that is also attractive to young Estonian professionals.

People arriving to Estonia are mainly family migrants, labour migrants and students (National Audit Office of Estonia 2015; Luik 2019). Migrants travel to Estonia from neighboring EU member states (Finland, Latvia), but also from less-developed former Soviet Union countries (e.g. Russia, Ukraine, Belarus) (Tammur et al. 2018; Luik 2019). For the past few years, the number of short-term employment registrations among immigrants has quickly increased. In 2018 almost 80% of the overall immigration were short-term labour migrants among whom 80% were from Ukraine, Belarus or Russia (Luik 2019, p. 7). These people are usually employed in sectors with lower added value. At the same time, compared to the rest of Europe, the migration volumes in Estonia are still small—in 2019, the immigration rate was 18,259 persons and 12,801 persons emigrated (Statistics Estonia 2020c). In terms of illegal migrants, Estonia has one of the highest return rates in the European Union. In 2018, around 85% of illegal migrants were returned to their home country (Luik 2019, p. 7).

Although the positive net migration rate has slightly increased Estonian population during the past few years, the demographic predictions of Estonia are still rather bleak. The calculations of Statistics Estonia estimate that according to the baseline scenario, by 2080 the population of Estonia will decrease by 150,000 people and reach 1.17 million (Fig. 2). Because of low fertility rate and aging population, the need for labour force, and especially highly skilled experts is likely to increase in the future (National Audit Office of Estonia 2015). The top human geography researchers in Estonia have also voiced the need for more immigration, claiming that the further development of Estonia has become "migration-dependent" (Estonian Parliament verbatim record, 01.06.2017).

In 2020, other nationalities still form around 32% of the Estonian population (Statistics Estonia 2020a). Ethnic Russians account for 24% of the total population and form the largest minority in Estonia, followed by Ukranians, Belarussians and Finnish. Hence, Soviet-era immigration still "affects the present as well as the future" (Tammur et al. 2018). The immigrant population in Estonia is unevenly distributed and is concentrated to the North and North-East of Estonia (Valk 2013, p. 47). Integration of foreigners into the Estonian society has been very much dependent on citizenship (Kaldur et al. 2018, p. 5). People living in Estonia without an Estonian citizenship and insufficient Estonian language skill are on average less educated and work on lower-income jobs (Kaldur et al. 2018). Integration policies have also focused more on culture and language than on economic matters (Valk 2013). Because of the historic experience and the perceived security threat from

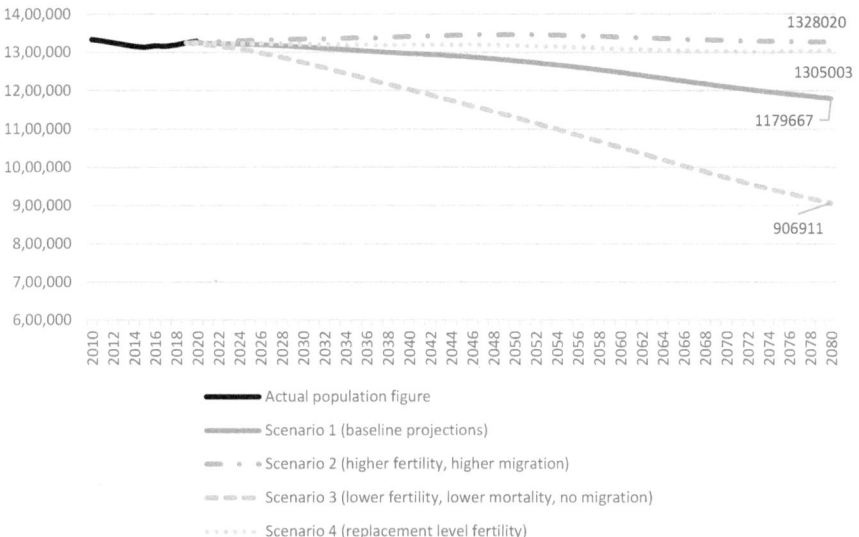

Fig. 2 Estonian population projection 2080 (Source *Statistics Estonia* 2020b)

Russia, Estonians feel threatened by possible large-scale inflow of foreigners and the topic of immigration remains highly conflictual and sensitive in public discussions.

2.2 Establishing an Immigration Policy Framework

The first legal document regulating immigration in the post-Soviet Estonia—the Immigration Act—was adopted in 1990 by the Supreme Soviet of the Estonian Soviet Socialist Republic (Parliament verbatim record, 26.06.1990). Although Estonia did not officially reclaim independence until 20 August 1991, the 1990 Supreme Soviet of the Estonian SSR was formed as a result of semi-free elections and the process of transitioning into an independent state was already underway. The Immigration Act regulated who were allowed to enter and stay in Estonia. It was stipulated in the Act that:

> (2) The aim of this Act is to promote the preservation and development of the permanent population of the Republic of Estonia, protection of its economic and social rights, organization of settlement in Estonia of persons closely connected with Estonian culture, and the rational employment and decent living conditions for persons settling in Estonia under the current act, without harming the interests of Estonian permanent residents.[2]

Concurrently, the underlying idea guiding the Act was to stop the inflow of (Russian) immigrants and create legal mechanisms to regulate who and how many

---

[2] *Immigratsiooniseadus*, RT 1990, 2, 25.

were allowed to enter Estonia. During the parliamentary debates, the Minister of Social Affairs presenting the draft added that regulating the inflow of immigrants was important in order to tackle "problems linked with migration" and avoid the already visible "ethnic tensions" and "serious adaptation problems of arriving immigrants" (Parliament verbatim record, 11.06.1991: 7). The Act laid down the categories of people who were not allowed to enter (including people who had been diagnosed with alcoholism, drug addiction, mental illness or were otherwise not able to take care of themselves), detailed the basis for issuing living, working and studying permits, and even created instruments to support outmigration. An example of the latter was the creation of a Resettlement Fond to provide one-time financial allowance for people (mainly former Soviet military personnel and labour force) wanting to remigrate back to their home country. In addition, the Immigration Act of 1990 introduced an important immigration control instrument that is an important part of Estonian immigration policy even today. Namely, a yearly immigration quota of maximum 0.1% (around 1300 people) of the Estonian permanent population was stipulated. This meant that if the immigration quota was filled, any additional applications for entering Estonia were denied for that year. It is interesting to note, that the size of the quota was a result of public discussions and that there were "no clear arguments for this concrete number" (Parliament verbatim record, 20.06.1990). Rather it was based on a perception of how many people a year would the Estonian society be able to accept without it posing a threat to the Estonian nation state. The Immigration Act also established The National Migration Agency that had the responsibility to control the issuing of permits and collect migration related information.

While the first piece of immigration legislation created the groundwork, the bulk of the framework on which Estonian immigration policy is founded on, was established in 1993 with the adoption of the Aliens Act.[3] With the Aliens Act, the legislators aimed to fill in the blanks left by the Immigration Act, and follow how other European states had regulated the area of migration and foreign residents (Parliament verbatim record, 08.06.1993). Compared to the Immigration Act, the Aliens Act defined the status of a foreigner and constituted their obligations, but also their rights, which were not previously specified. Discussions over the act were quite intense and coincided with the debate over citizenship. The main question concerned which status should immigrants who arrived during the Soviet Union hold. This was a sensitive issue in all of the Baltic States, with foreign observers and consultants from the OSCE being a part of the discussions (Galbreath 2003). Despite suggestions from international organizations, Estonia defined the citizenship status of its inhabitants according to whether the person or their parents or grandparents had gained Estonian citizenship during 1918–1940, that is, before Estonia was occupied. With this decision, all inhabitants and their descendants who had arrived during the Soviet time were determined as non-citizens or illegal migrants (Parliament verbatim record, 15.06.1993, 21.06.1993). With the Aliens Act, all people who held Soviet passports were given an opportunity to apply for citizenship (knowledge of Estonian language needed) or permanent residency in the timeframe of two years. People who did not

---

[3] *Välismaalaste seadus*, RT I 1993, 44, 637.

apply for citizenship or did not register as non-citizens were considered eligible for deportation. People who did register for residency right, received a temporary living permit and an Alien's passport which stripped these people from the rights enjoyed by citizens, e.g. the right to vote. The problem of people with undetermined citizenship or "statelessness" continues to be a controversial issue raised by human rights organizations and the Russian government as discrimination against the ethnic Russian minority. Since 1992, the population of undetermined citizens in Estonia has decreased from 32 to 5.7% in 2018 (Luik 2019) and several alleviations have been introduced for the descendants of non-citizens to claim Estonian citizenship.

The next phase in the Estonian immigration policy formulation came with the process of joining the European Union. The road towards becoming a member of the EU began shortly after regaining independence. Becoming a member of the Western part of the world was considered crucial in order to protect and secure the independence of the young democratic state. In 1997 Estonia began negotiations to join the European Union (Galbreath 2003, p. 12) and during the same year an exception into the immigration quote was introduced, removing citizens of EU member states, Iceland, Norway and Switzerland from under the immigration quota (Annus 2009, p. 4). The accession process brought additional changes into the Estonian immigration policy in terms of legislation and need to increase administrative capacity. Structural changes were also in order. The Migration and Citizenship Agency (MCA), which had merged in 1993, was reorganized due to low service quality and lack of control by the Ministry. It was mentioned, that until 2000, the MCA had existed in "a closed system, in which the drafts, regulations and laws that concerned the Agency were not developed in the Ministry, but in the MCA itself" and the Agency "interpreted every law in its operations with maximum severity, harmfully or suspiciously towards the client" (Parliament verbatim record, 19.01.2000: 6). The leader of the Agency was replaced and the organization moved more firmly under the control of the Ministry of the Interior.

During the first half of the 2000s, additional groups of people were removed from under the immigration quote. For example, citizens of the United States and Japan in 1999, foreign family members of Estonian citizens in 2002 (Piirits et al. 2018). In 2003, further restrictions were removed for high-skilled workers, professors and students wanting to stay in Estonia and the bureaucratic burden for applying for a short-term migrant status was reduced. These changes to legislation mostly derived from the EU *acquis* and were considered as further specifications rather than conceptual changes (Annus 2009). Bigger changes were related to joining the Schengen area in 2007, which allowed free movement of people inside the EU, but also made Estonia a border country for the European Union and brought with it additional responsibilities to ensure a well-protected border (Barnickel and Beichelt 2013). Older EU member states assisted new member states with the export of high standards of border control technology, communication systems and training of police and border guards (Lavenex 1998). Many researchers have claimed that the accession process of new member states proceeded in parallel with Western Europe introducing more restrictive immigration and asylum policies (Lavenex 2002; Givens and Luedtke 2004; Czaika and Hobolth 2016; Helbling and Kalkum 2018). For the Western European member states, joining of the Eastern bloc brought with it a potential threat of large-scale immigration from the East (Lavenex 1998) and, therefore, more focus was turned towards increasing the capacity to control migration flows (Helbling and Kalkum 2018).

To date, the Aliens Act has been extensively modified and complemented since 1993, turning it into what has been called a "mammoth law" in the Estonian legislation (Parliament verbatim record, 15.06.2016: 56). Most recent changes into the Estonian immigration policy have dealt with mainly labour migration. The economic development of Estonia has continuously increased the need for labour force and high-skilled specialists for the ICT field. During 2013–2018 the pressure from the employers intensified to alleviate labour migration restrictions and ease the administrative burden related to applying for visas and residence-permits. In addition, EU level developments also aimed to introduce more open measures to support labour migration and mobility (European Commission 2010). Therefore, in 2016 and 2017, additional restrictions were removed to allow short-term workers to work without a residence-permit (Anniste 2018), and to support and even attract highly qualified ICT specialists into Estonia. For example, in 2013 a welcoming programme was developed to support the integration of foreigners and in 2018, top specialists were included into the list in the Aliens Act exempt from the immigration quota (Luik 2019). However, even with the introduction of a less restrictive immigration regulation, the core of the Estonian immigration policy framework has remained the same since 1993. Even though immigration and the need for labour mobility has been voiced more frequently (National Audit Office of Estonia 2015), Estonia currently lacks a coherent migration strategy. The need for high-skilled specialists has been mentioned in strategic documents, e.g. Estonia 2020, but at the same time migration related topics remain under the Ministry of the Interior, which frames migration mainly from the perspective of security.

2.3   Organizing the Asylum System in Estonia

During the first years of independence, a formal asylum regime was not a priority for the new Estonian government. Estonia lacked an institutional and a legal basis for accepting asylum seekers who were considered as illegal immigrants and, therefore, usually detained (Parliament verbatim record, 02.05.1994). However, as the prospect of new CEE countries joining the European Union and the Schengen area became more real, neighbouring member states swiftly stepped into offer aid to new member states. As mentioned above, the Western European member states perceived the fall of the iron curtain as a potential threat for large-scale flow of immigration from the East. Therefore, establishing a well-functioning asylum system was in the interest of the neighbouring Scandinavian countries, namely Finland and Sweden who became the "agents of [EU asylum] policy transfer in the Baltics" (Lavenex 2002, p. 714). Through aid programmes like Phare Horizontal Programme on Asylum and other smaller regional cooperation projects in the Baltic Sea region (Lavenex

2002), Finland, Sweden and Denmark assisted Estonia in creating the needed infrastructure and administrative capacity to join the international asylum system. The aid provided to Estonia was seen as a "preventive strategy" (Lavenex 1998, p. 227) in order to create a buffer zone on the migration route from the East towards the Scandinavian countries. In fact, the ratification of the international refugee treaties became a precondition to conclude visa-free travel agreements with Sweden and Finland (Potisepp 2002). From the Estonian perspective, asylum was not a priority and rather it was seen as an obligation. As put by the presenter of the first draft version of the Refugee Act in the Parliament "If Estonia wants to have a say in international life, it inevitably has to join these documents which means that we can prolong acceding them but we cannot exclude them" (Parliament verbatim record, 20.01.1997).

Estonia established a formal asylum system in 1997 when the Parliament ratified the United Nations' 1951 Convention relating to the Status of Refugees and its New York Protocol of 1967,[4] and simultaneously adopted the Act on Refugees.[5] The responsibility for forming and implementing asylum policy mainly fell under the Estonian Ministry of the Interior that was made responsible for accepting and processing asylum applications. The Ministry of Social Affairs was responsible for the reception and integration of refugees. This division of functions has remained in effect today. In the process of joining the European Union, asylum policy formed one of the most important parts of the *acquis communautaire*. Estonia had to harmonize its legislation with the first phase of CEAS that had been agreed between the older member states between 1999 and 2005 (Ripoll Servent and Trauner 2014). In 2006, Estonia replaced the Act on Refugees with the Act of Granting International Protection to Aliens[6] (AGIPA), which has remained the most important legal document in the Estonian asylum policy. After Estonia adopted the Dublin regulations and joined the Schengen area in 2007, the number of asylum applications slowly increased (Kallas 2011), but Estonia has remained merely a transit country for people trying to reach Scandinavian countries. During 1997–2019, a total of 1,275 asylum applications have been presented to Estonia and international protection has been granted to 531 applicants.[7]

In late 2000s, the topic of asylum seekers and refugees started to spark public discussions when the number of asylum applications increased from 14 in 2008 to 40 in 2009. As the number of asylum seekers and refugees grew, shortcomings of the asylum system began to show. Based on a number of studies procured by the Ministry of the Interior during 2010–2013 (Roots and Kallas 2011; Kaldur and Kallas 2011), it became evident that Estonia often failed to comply with the EU asylum standards and regulations due to either faulty adoption of the EU legislation, strict interpretation of the regulations or poor quality of the support services available to the asylum seekers. For example, NGOs provided examples from cases where asylum seekers were sent

---

[4] *Pagulasseisundi konventsioon*, RT II 1997, 6, 26.

[5] *Pagulaste seadus*, RT I 1997, 19, 306.

[6] *Välismaalasele rahvusvahelise kaitse andmise seadus*, RT I 2006, 2, 3.

[7] Data received from the Estonian Police and Border Guard Board in June 2020. This figure does not include refugees that were received through the European migration scheme in 2016.

back from the border without proper application processing or placed in detention centres without valid reason (Säär 2014). During 2009–2015, several institutional changes were made in the Estonian asylum system. First, in 2010 the Citizenship and Migration Agency was merged with the Police and the Border Guard Board, creating a new joint agency under the Ministry of the Interior—The Police and Border Guard Board (PBGB) (Sarapuu 2012). This structural change meant that migration related proceedings moved from a separate organization into the jurisdiction of the Police, making the proceeding of an asylum application into an investigative task from the perspective of guaranteeing internal security.

In 2013, Estonia began the process of amending the existing AGIPA as the CEAS directives were recast. Similarly to the immigration regulations, Estonia's stance in transferring directives into national legislation has been to "do what is needed, but not more". The core idea framing Estonian asylum policy has been to "prevent the entrance of foreigners to Estonia who threaten public order, internal safety or social and cultural activities" (The Ministry of the Interior 2014). Evidence of a very strict asylum policy can be noted by looking at the refugee recognition rate (i.e. the share of positive decisions from all applications), where Estonia has stayed below the EU average. In 2018, the refugee recognition rate for Estonia was 25% compared to the EU's average of 37% (Eurostat 2019). Humanitarian and human rights NGOs have criticised Estonian asylum policy of being too strict and not in accordance with international regulations (MTÜ Eesti Pagulasabi 2015). Policy-making in this field has been criticized as being guided by "decisions made in Brussels" (Kallas 2011) and made on an ad hoc basis without a clear strategy (National Audit Office of Estonia 2016). However, the war in Ukraine and the inflow of refugees into the EU in 2015, forced Estonia to react more constructively. In September 2015, Estonia agreed to voluntarily accept 570 refugees through the resettlement and relocation scheme of the European Agenda on Migration framework (Estonian Government 2015). Taking into account that during 1997–2015 Estonia had granted international protection to less than 94 people, the capacity to accept 550 refugees needed to be established and administrative resources to process applications needed to be increased (Trei and Sarapuu 2021). Despite the very low number of refugees reaching Estonia compared to the EU member states on the Southern border, the issue of refugees became extremely salient and was high on the agenda in public debates. According to the Eurobarometer survey, the perceived salience of immigration as one of the most important issue facing the country increased from 2.4% in 2007 to 24.3% in 2016 (Hatton 2017, p. 469). In fact, a survey conducted in early 2016 showed that two thirds of the Estonian citizens saw the refugee crisis as a bigger threat to Estonia than possible aggression by the Russia Federation (Postimees 2016). Negative sentiments towards asylum seekers and refugees gained ground and similarly to other European countries, anti-migration demonstrations took place and racist social media pages emerged (Säär 2017). This was further intensified by a highly opposing political debate that contributed in creating drift not only in the society, but also in the government (Parliament verbatim record, 26.11.2018). By 2019, less than half of the accepted limit of 550 had arrived to Estonia and the number of new asylum applications decreased back to the pre-crisis level.

3   The Politics of Immigration in Estonia

There have been three key topics in the Estonian immigration politics. First, the Soviet-era mass immigration of people into Estonia and its influence on the ethnic composition of the Estonian population was the leading theme during the initial phases of immigration policy development. The efforts to gain full control over migration and stop any further immigration from other parts of the Soviet Union were met with a great sense of urgency. It was said at the time by outside observers that for Estonia "independence was more than regaining sovereignty; it was a matter of cultural survival" (Barrington 1995, p. 136). This understanding was also evident in the parliamentary debates surrounding the adoption of the first immigration regulations. Debates around the Immigration Act and the Alien's Act were filled with calls for caution and need to limit the possible inflow of "disloyal" people (Parliament verbatim record, 15.06.1993) as much as possible. Some members of the parliament called for "decolonization" of Estonia (ibid.) and did not think that strict restrictions for non-citizens could be considered discriminating, as it would be impossible for a "small nation" like Estonia to "discriminate against colonizing immigrants of a large nation" (Parliament verbatim record, 21.06.1993). The historic experience of mass immigration has also been highlighted during more recent discussions as a precaution to be remembered when talking about decisions that could bring about increased immigration. For example, during the 2015 European refugee crisis, the history of immigration to Estonia was brought out by the conservative political wing as a warning of what might happen if Estonia agrees to voluntarily accept refugees (e.g. Parliament verbatim record, 06.06.2015; 13.10.2015; 03.04.2017).

The second key topic has been the threat immigration poses for the preservation of Estonian people and their culture. Political arguments against allowing more immigrants to live and work in Estonia have often included examples of the difficulties the integration of the large minority of ethnic Russians in Estonia has faced and the necessity to protect the Estonian language. Therefore, when the need for additional workforce started to increase during the late 2000s, rather than to open up the Estonian immigration policy, efforts were turned towards reforming family policy and introducing, e.g. paid maternity leave and subsidies for young families, in order to support the fertility rate (Parliament verbatim record, 10.02.2011). Allowing increased immigration to alleviate the problems on the workforce was seen as a possible strain for the welfare system and an internal security risk, as the increase of ethnical minorities in Estonia could lead to tensions and extremism (Parliament verbatim record, 06.04.2006). The securitization of immigration is also a characteristic of Estonian immigration politics. As the topic of migration has institutionally been under the Ministry of the Interior and moved under the Police and the Border Guard Board in 2010, this has definitely contributed to framing the narrative of immigration from an internal security perspective. This is most evident in questions related to granting international protection to asylum seekers. Overwhelmingly the debate over refugees has evolved around how to "ensure solidarity and humanity as important European values while making no discounts for internal security of our people" (Parliament verbatim record, 17.11.2015). For the conservative parties, the question of security has been the key argument against accepting refugees, claiming even that "Europe is faced with an ideology that wishes to destroy the open, caring and humane Europe" and joining the European Commission's relocation scheme indicated that Estonia was no longer in control of its own internal security (ibid.).

This leads to the third key theme in the Estonian immigration policy—sovereignty and the ability to decide independently on migration related issues. Central and Eastern European countries established their immigration and asylum policy under the auspice of the European Union and neighbouring countries. Although in the early 2000s, the European asylum system was going through a reform (Ripoll Servent and Trauner 2014), the new member states were not included in these discussions (Lavenex 2002). From the perspective of Estonia, joining the EU was essential in order to guarantee the survival of a small state like Estonia. As famously said by the first president of Estonia, Lennart Meri, in 2004 on the day Estonia was accepted to NATO—"Estonia will never be alone again". Therefore, even though immigration was a sensitive topic for Estonia and caused debates about the integrity of Estonia as a free nation state, adopting the EU's *acquis* was considered a necessity in order to enter the "Western club" and avoid falling under an already familiar undemocratic regime from the East. However, this meant that while immigration policy touches the core of state's sovereign discretion to decide who and on what terms is allowed to enter the state, "the exercise of such sovereignty by the countries undergoing transition, however, was significantly constrained by their dependency on western neighbours" (Byrne et al. 2002, p. 424). The political debates show that there was a constant tug-of-war between adhering to the joint rules of the European Union, while at the same time ensuring that it would not conceptually change the conservative stance of Estonian immigration policy. For example, during the proceeding of the Alien's Act, there was a discussion if the restrictions implemented for non-citizens complied with European and international human rights regulations. Therefore, it was proposed in the Parliament that before voting on the draft, it should be sent to the European Council for commentary (Parliament verbatim record, 21.06.1993). Another example was during the 2015 refugee crisis, when the government emphasised the necessity to show solidarity with other EU member states, as this would mean member states would reciprocate Estonia when necessary in the future (Parliament verbatim record, 06.06.2015). The opposition, at the same time, perceived solidarity as a forced upon stance from the European Commission, that threatened the integrity of Estonian independence. In addition, while the political rhetoric on exemplary EU member states has traditionally highlighted either Scandinavian countries or Germany, for the conservative parties, the shift has moved more towards other CEE countries like Hungary and Poland. This indicates that the development stage of CEE countries combined with right-wing political parties being represented in the governments of these countries has given a stronger voice for CEE governments on the EU level, especially in matters related to migration.

An interesting characteristic of the Estonian immigration policy has been that until the early 2010s, all political parties across the spectre supported a conservative immigration policy and any diversions of reducing restrictions for entry always required thorough analysis and debate. The importance of a conservative stance in immigration policy has been expressed in strategic documents and political debates, even without the conservative or nation-state supporting political parties belonging to the government (Parliament verbatim record, 13.10.2015; 05.04.2016). It was only until the events surrounding the refugee crisis, when a rift on immigration between the political forces emerged and widened and the populist style of argumentation eventually led to direct confrontations between the government and the opposition. The diametrical differences between political parties on the question of refugees, continues to influence the discussions on labour immigration. In the context of an aging society and labour market shortages, the opposition between political parties has made it difficult to introduce less restrictive measures to attract highly-skilled specialists. At the same time, the pressure from employers continues to increase and demand for labour immigration is present.

4   Conclusion

Since regaining independence, Estonian immigration policy has been guided by the historical experience of occupation era mass immigration and the desire to build a system that would protect the preservation of a small independent nation state. Due to migration processes that shaped the Estonian demographics during the twentieth century, Estonia has followed a rather restrictive and conservative line in immigration policy that would enable a firm control over migration. At the same time, the economic and social development have begun to turn the migration processes around in the region and attract people from less-developed countries. This has placed Estonia "on a path that European countries have walked on already since the Second World War" (Tammaru and Eamets 2017). A somewhat schizophrenic situation has emerged where, on the one hand, there is a need for high-skilled specialists and additional labour force, but on the other hand, the institutional setting of migration does not support these developments and immigration is seen by many as potentially harmful for the Estonian society.

Estonia and all the other CEE countries established their immigration and asylum policy frameworks during the period of transitioning from post-communist states into democratic states, while the EU level immigration system was based on their historic experience of the Second World War. This has created a discrepancy in the Estonian immigration politics, as immigration is considered an extremely sensitive issue and restrictive measures are preferred, while the EU's policy derives from the ideological traditions that emphasize more the humanitarian side of the immigration coin. As said by Alink et al. (2001, p. 295), immigration and especially asylum policy in Europe has "many characteristics of a tragedy of the common situation: for at least some states /…/the incentives to maintain national sovereignty are greater than those to share the burden of the problem and develop a joint and mutually binding policy." This summarization has been very characteristic to the Central and Eastern European states during the events surrounding the 2015 European refugee crisis. With right-wing political parties gaining traction across Europe, this tendency has become even more visible. But the lack of adhering to common rules across the EU in order to find a common solution, can become harmful for the integrity of the EU.

Acknowledgements Writing of this chapter has been supported by the Estonian Research Council grant PUT1461.

References

Alink, F., Boin, A., & T'Hart, P. (2001). Institutional crises and reforms in policy sectors: The case of asylum policy in Europe. *Journal of European Public Policy, 8*(2), 286–306. https://doi.org/10.1080/13501760151146487.

Anniste, K. (2018). *Rändetrendid maailmas, Euroopas ja Eestis.* PRAXIS.

Annus, R. (2009). Eesti võimalused ja valikud immigratsioonipoliitika kujundamisel. *Riigikogu toimetised, 20,* 101–107.

Bagdonas, A. (2015). The EU migration crisis and the Baltic security. *Journal on Baltic Security, 1*(2), 7–27. https://doi.org/10.1515/jobs-2016-0019.

Barnickel, C., & Beichelt, T. (2013, August). Shifting patterns and reactions—migration policy in the new EU member states. *East European Politics and Societies, 27*(3), 466–492. https://doi.org/10.1177/0888325412474461.

Barrington, L. W. (1995). Nation, states, and citizens: An explanation of the citizenship policies in Estonia and Lithuania. *Review of Central and East European Law, 21*(2), 103–148.

Bjerre, L., Helbling, M., Römer, F., & Zobel, M. (2018). Conceptualizing and measuring immigration policies: A comparative perspective. *International Migration Review, 49*(3), 555–600. https://doi.org/10.1111/imre.12100.

Bonjour, S., Ripoll Servent, A., & Thielemann, E. (2017). Beyond venue shopping and liberal constraint: A new research agenda for EU migration policies and politics. *Journal of European Public Policy, 25*(3), 409–421. https://doi.org/10.1080/13501763.2016.1268640.

Bordignon, M., & Moriconi, S. (2017). *The case for a common European refugee policy* (Bruegel Policy Contribution, 2017/8). Bruegel, Brussels.

Boswell, C. (2000, July). European values and the asylum crisis. *International Affairs, 76*(3), 537–557. https://doi.org/10.1111/1468-2346.00150.

Byrne, R., Noll, G., & Vedsted-Hansen, J. (Eds.). (2002). *New asylum countries? Migration control and refugee protection in an enlarged European Union.* Kluwer Law International.

Czaika, M., & Hobolth, M. (2016). Do restrictive asylum and visa policies increase irregular migration into Europe? *European Union Politics, 17*(3), 345–365.

Dagi, D. (2017). Refugee crisis in Europe (2015–2016): The clash of intergovernmental and supranational perspectives. *International Journal of Social Sciences, 6*(1), 1–8. https://doi.org/10.20472/SS.2017.6.1.001.

Dahlvik, J. (2018). Inside asylum bureaucracy: Organizing refugee status determination in Austria. *Springer Open.* https://doi.org/10.1007/978-3-319-63306-0.

Estonian Government. (2015, October). *Täpsustatud tegevuskava Euroopa Liidu ümberasustamise ja ümberpaigutamise tegevuste elluviimiseks.*

European Commission. (2010). *Europe 2020: A strategy for smart, sustainable and inclusive growth,* COM(2010) 2020. https://ec.europa.eu/eu2020/pdf/COMPLET%20EN%20BARROSO%20%20%20007%20-%20Europe%202020%20-%20EN%20version.pdf.

European Council. (2020, October 7). *How the EU manages migration flows.* https://www.consilium.europa.eu/en/policies/migratory-pressures/managing-migration-flows/.

Eurostat. (2019, April). Asylum decisions in the EU. *Eurostat newsrelease,* 71/2019. https://ec.eur opa.eu/eurostat/documents/2995521/9747530/3-25042019-BP-EN.pdf/22635b8a-4b9c-4ba9-a5c8-934ca02de496.

Freeman, G. P. (1995, Winter). Modes of immigration politics in liberal democratic states. *The International Migration Review,* 29(4), 881–902. https://www.ncbi.nlm.nih.gov/pubmed/122 91223.

Freeman, G. P. (2006). National models, policy types, and the politics of immigration in liberal democracies. *West European Politics,* 29(2), 227–247. https://doi.org/10.1080/014023805005 12585.

Galbreath, D. (2003). The politics of European integration and minority rights in Estonia and Latvia. *Perspectives on European Politics and Society,* 4(1), 35–53. https://doi.org/10.1080/157058503 08438852.

Givens, T., & Luedtke, A. (2004). The Politics of European union immigration policy: Institutions, salience, and harmonization. *The Policy Studies Journal,* 32(2), 145–165.

Gorny, A., & Kaczmarczyk, P. (2019). Introduction: Migration and mobility in the context of post-communist transition in Central and Eastern Europe. *Central and Eastern European Migration Review,* 8(1), 5–8. https://doi.org/10.17467/ceemr.2019.06.

Hatton, T. J. (2017). Refugees and asylum seekers, the crisis in Europe and the future of policy. *Economic Policy,* 32(91), 447–496. https://doi.org/10.1093/epolic/eix009.

Helbling, M., & Kalkum, D. (2018). Migration policy trends in OECD countries. *Journal of European Public Policy,* 25(12), 1779–1797. https://doi.org/10.1080/13501763.2017.1361466.

Kaldur, K., & Kallas, K. (2011). *Varjupaigataotlejate sihtrühma rahulolu ja ootuste hindamine neile pakutavate teenuste ja tingimuste osas.* Tartu: Institute of Baltic Studies.

Kaldur, K., Vetik, R., Kirss, L., Kivistik, K., Seppel, K., Kallas, K., et al. (2018). *Eesti Ühiskonna Integratsiooni Monitooring 2017.* Tartu: Balti Uuringute Instituut.

Kallas, K. (2011). Eesti varjupaigapoliitika Euroopa perspektiivis. *Riigikogu toimetised, 24.*

King, R., & Okolski, M. (2019). Diverse, fragile and fragmented: The new map of European migration. *Central and Eastern European Migration Review,* 8(1), 9–32. https://doi.org/10.17467/ceemr.2018.18.

Lagerspetz, M. (2007). Estonia. In A. Triandafyllidou & R. Gropas (Eds.), *European immigration: A sourcebook* (pp. 87–98). Routledge.

Lavenex, S. (1998). Asylum, immigration and Central-Eastern Europe: Challenges to EU enlarge-ment. *European Foreign Affairs Review,* 3(2), 275–294.

Lavenex, S. (2001). The Europeanization of refugee policies: Normative challenges and institutional legazies. *Journal of Common Market Studies,* 39(5), 851–874.

Lavenex, S. (2002). EU enlargement and the challenge of policy transfer: The case of refugee policy. *Journal of Ethnic and Migration Studies,* 28(4), 701–721. https://doi.org/10.1080/136918302100 003227.

Lavenex, S. (2018). 'Failing forward' towards which Europe? Organized hypocrisy in the Common European Asylum System. *JCMS: Journal of Common Market Studies,* 56(5), 1195–1212. https://doi.org/10.1111/jcms.12739.

Luik, E. (2019). *EMN annual report on migration and asylum: Estonia 2018.* Tallinn University: European National Contact Point for the European Migration Network.

Meyers, E. (2000). Theories of international immigration policy—A comparative analysis. *International Migration Review,* 34(4), 1245–1282.

Meyer-Sahling, J.-H. (2011). The durability of EU civil service policy in Central and Eastern Europe after ACCESSION. *Governance,* 24(2), 231–260.

MTÜ Eesti Pagulasabi. (2015, March). *Varjupaiga aastaraamat 2014.* http://aastaraamat.pagulasab i.ee/.

National Audit Office of Estonia. (2015). *Overview of the state's migration policy choices: What is the role of migration in alleviating labour shortage?* Tallinn.

National Audit Office of Estonia. (2016). *Riigi ja kohalike omavalitsuste valmisolek võtta vastu rahvusvahelise kaitse taotlejaid ja saanuid.* Tallinn.

OECD. (2019). *International migration outlook 2019*. OECD Publishing.

Pastore, F., & Henry, G. (2016). Explaining the crisis of the European migration and asylum regime. *The International Spectator, 51*(1), 44–57. https://doi.org/10.1080/03932729.2016.1118609.

Piirits, M., Anniste, K., Masso, M., Melesk, K., Osila, L., & Michelson, A. (2018). *Eesti tööturg: hetkeolukord ja tulevikuväljavaated*. PRAXIS: Tallinn.

Plender, R. (2008). EU immigration and asylum policy—The Hague programme and the way forward. *ERA Forum, 9*(2), 301–325. https://doi.org/10.1007/s12027-008-0052-9.

Postimees. (2016, March 30). *Survey: 2/3 of Estonian citizens see refugee crisis as bigger threat than Russia*. https://news.postimees.ee/3637277/survey-2-3-of-estonian-citizens-see-refugee-cri sis-as-bigger-threat-than-russia.

Potisepp, A. (2002). Estonia. In R. Byrne, G. Noll, & J. Vedsted-Hansen (Eds.), *New asylum countries? Migration control and refugee protection in an enlarged European Union*. Kluwer Law International.

Rahi-Tamm, A. (2005). Human Losses. In V. Salo, Ü. Ennuste, E. Parmasto, E. Tarvel, & P. Varju. (Eds.), *The white book: Losses inflicted on the Estonian nation by occupation regimes 1940–1991* (pp. 25–46). Tallinn. Estonian Encyclopaedia Puhlishers.

Ripoll Servent, A., & Trauner, F. (2014, September 14). Do supranational EU institutions make a difference? EU asylum law before and after 'communitarization'. *Journal of European Public Policy, 21*(8), 1142–1162. https://doi.org/10.1080/13501763.2014.906905.

Roos, C., & Zaun, N. (2014). Norms matter! The role of international norms in EU policies on asylum and immigration. *European Journal of Migration and Law, 16,* 45–68.

Roots, L., & Kallas, K. (2011). *Välismaalasele rahvusvahelise kaitse andmise seaduse ja Euroopa Nõukogu direktiivi 2003/9/EÜ, 27. jaanuar 2003 võrdlev analüüs erivajadustega isikute vastuvõtutingimuste osas*. Tallinn: Institute of Baltic Studies.

Säär, A. (2014). Pagulaste ja varjupaigataotlejate õigused. In Estonian Human Right Centre (Ed.), *Inimõigused Eestis 2013*. http://humanrights.ee/inimoiguste-aruanne-2/inimoigused-eestis-2013/pagulaste-ja-varjupaigataotlejate-olukord/. Accessed 2 Apr 2016.

Säär, A. (2017) *Racism, racial discrimination and migration in Estonia 2015–2016*. Estonian Human Rights Centre. https://humanrights.ee/en/2017/07/rassism-rassiline-diskrimineerimine-ja-migratsioon-eestis-2015-2016/.

Sarapuu, K. (2012). Administrative structure in times of changes: The development of Estonian ministries and government agencies 1990–2010. *International Journal of Public Administration, 35*(12), 808–819. https://doi.org/10.1080/01900692.2012.715561.

Schain, M. A. (2009). The state strikes back: Immigration policy in the European Union. *European Journal of International Law, 20*(1), 93–109. https://doi.org/10.1093/ejil/chp001.

Scipioni, M. (2017). Failing forward in EU migration policy? EU integration after the 2015 asylum and migration crisis. *Journal of European Public Policy, 25*(9), 1357–1375. https://doi.org/10.1080/13501763.2017.1325920.

Stalker, P. (2002). Migration trends and migration policy in Europe. *International Migration, 50*(5), 151–179.

Statistics Estonia. (2020a). *Population*. https://www.stat.ee/en/find-statistics/statistics-theme/pop ulation.

Statistics Estonia. (2020b). *Population projection*. https://www.stat.ee/en/find-statistics/statistics-theme/population/population-projection.

Statistics Estonia. (2020c). *RVR03: Migration by sex, age group and type of migration [Data set]*.

Tammaru, T., & Eamets, R. (2017, March). Eesti rändepoliitika uued alused – punktisüsteem ja õpiränne? *Postimees*. https://www.kogu.ee/tiit-tammaru-raul-eamets-eesti-randepoliitika-uued-alused-punktisusteem-ja-opiranne/.

Tammur, A. (2018). Positive immigration in Estonia for the third consecutive year. *Quarterly Bulletin of Statistics Estonis, 2,* 12–13.

Tammur, A., Tammaru, T., & Puur, A. (2018). Is there a migration turnaround taking place in Estonia? Migration trends 2000–2015. In T. Tammaru (Ed.), *Estonian human development report 2016/2017: Estonia at the age of migration*. Eesti Koostöö Kogu.

The Ministry of the Interior. (2014). Konservatiivne kodakondsus ja rändepoliitika. In R. Annus, R. Raudne, L. Lugna, P. Laanist, & P. Heinsoo (Eds.), *Turvalisuspoliitika 2013* (pp. 38–42). Siseministeerium.

Trei, M., & Sarapuu, K. (2021). A Small Administration Facing a Complex Policy Challenge: Estonia and the 2015 Refugee Crisis. In T. Joensen & I. Taylor (Eds.), *Small States and the European Migrant Crisis: Politics and Governance* (pp. xx–xx). New York: Palgrave Macmillan. (Forthcoming).

UNHCR. (2020, June 18). *Figures at a glance.* https://www.unhcr.org/figures-at-a-glance.html.

United Nations, Department of Economic and Social Affairs Population Division. (2017, June 1). *Trends in international migrant stock: The 2017 revision* (United Nations database, POP/DB/MIG/Stock/Rev.2017). https://www.un.org/en/development/desa/population/publicati ons/pdf/popfacts/PopFacts_2017-5.pdf.

United Nations, Department of Economic and Social Affairs Population Division. (2019). *International migrant stock 2019.* https://migrationdataportal.org/?i=stock_abs_&t=2019&m=1.

Valdaru, K., Asari, E.-M., & Mälksoo, L. (2017). The impact of the refugee crisis on Europe and Estonia. In T. Tammaru (Ed.), *Estonian human development report 2016/2017: Estonia at the age of migration.* Eesti Koostöö Kogu.

Valk, A. (2013). Integration policies and acculturation in Estonian society in the last two decades. In A. Horgby & V. Nordlund (Eds.), *Immigration in times of emigration: Challenges and opportunities of migration and mobility in the Baltic Sea Region.* Global Utmaning.

Zaun, N. (2018, January). States as gatekeepers in EU asylum politics: Explaining the non-adoption of a refugee quota system. *JCMS: Journal of Common Market Studies, 56*(1), 44–62. https://doi. org/10.1111/jcms.12663.